Policing and Prosecuting Sexual Assault

Policing and Prosecuting Sexual Assault

Inside the Criminal Justice System

Cassia Spohn
Katharine Tellis

LYNNE
RIENNER
PUBLISHERS

BOULDER
LONDON

Published in the United States of America in 2014 by
Lynne Rienner Publishers, Inc.
1800 30th Street, Boulder, Colorado 80301
www.rienner.com

and in the United Kingdom by
Lynne Rienner Publishers, Inc.
3 Henrietta Street, Covent Garden, London WC2E 8LU

Library of Congress Cataloging-in-Publication Data
Spohn, Cassia.
  Policing and prosecuting sexual assault : inside the criminal justice
system / Cassia Spohn and Katharine Tellis.
  Includes bibliographical references and index.
  ISBN 978-1-62637-024-1 (hc : alk. paper)
  1. Sex crimes—United States. 2. Law enforcement—United States. 3. Criminal justice,
Administration of—United States. I. Tellis, Katharine, 1979– II. Title.
  HV6556.S66 2013
  345.73'0253—dc23   2013013659

British Cataloguing in Publication Data
A Cataloguing in Publication record for this book
is available from the British Library.

Printed and bound in the United States of America

The paper used in this publication meets the requirements
of the American National Standard for Permanence of
Paper for Printed Library Materials Z39.48-1992.

5 4 3 2 1

Contents

Tables and Figures

Tables

Figures

Acknowledgments

We are tremendously grateful to the National Institute of Justice for sponsoring this study, to Arizona State University and California State University, Los Angeles, for their support of our scholarship, and to the numerous law enforcement officials whose participation made this study possible. Their partnership and collegiality fostered an environment that was open and safe for sharing ideas, solving problems, and translating research into policy and practice. We owe special thanks to Chief Charlie Beck of the Los Angeles Police Department (LAPD), who was the deputy chief over the Detective Bureau at the time of this study's conception. His support for sexual assault research paved the way to include both the Los Angeles County Sheriff's Department (LASD) and the Los Angeles County District Attorney's office. We are also very grateful to LAPD Assistant Chief Michel Moore, Assistant Chief Sandy Jo MacArthur, and Sergeant Marie Fellhauer. We owe special appreciation to Los Angeles County Sheriff Leroy Baca. His support for our work was genuine, immediate, and ongoing.

This book would not have been completed without the assistance of the Los Angeles County District Attorney's Office, which at the time of the study was led by Steve Cooley. We are also grateful to Pam Booth, Michele Daniels, and Chris Longe at the District Attorney's office for their assistance with data retrieval and interview logistics. We would also like to extend our gratitude to Gail Abarbanel and the Rape Treatment Center at the Santa Monica–University of California, Los Angeles, Medical Center; Gail Pincus and the Domestic Abuse Center; Kim Roth and the Valley Trauma Center; and all of their staff. Through their support we were able to interview sexual assault survivors, who shared their stories with us in hopes that the criminal justice system will improve its response to rape. Our thanks also go to Eryn O'Neal, Clair White, and Danielle Romain for their excellent research assistance.

We wish to offer special thanks to all of the LAPD and LASD detectives, sex crimes prosecutors, and advocates who work tirelessly in the pursuit of justice for sexual assault victims in Los Angeles City and County.

* * *

This project was supported by Award No. 2009-WG-BX-009 of the National Institute of Justice, Office of Justice Programs, US Department of Justice. The opinions, findings, conclusions, and recommendations expressed in this publication are those of the authors and do not necessarily reflect those of the Department of Justice.

1

Sexual Assault and the Criminal Justice System

In 2008, the Los Angeles Police Department (LAPD) received a sexual assault report from a 13-year-old girl who was a runaway and who stayed with various friends, all of whom, including the alleged suspect, were gang members. One night the complainant and a female friend were invited to a party at the residence of one of the gang members. The complainant, who admitted to drinking more than 10 beers and smoking marijuana while at the party, told the investigating officer that one of the males at the party offered to let her sleep on the fold-out couch in his living room. She stated that she fell asleep and awoke to find the suspect on top of her. She said that the suspect touched her breasts, rubbed her buttocks, and penetrated her rectum. She stated that she told the suspect that it hurt and that she told him to stop.

The complainant's forensic medical exam revealed evidence of acute anal trauma, and the suspect, who lied about his gang affiliation and who had a criminal record, was identified by the victim through a photo lineup. When the suspect was interviewed by the police, he denied assaulting the teenager, saying that he went straight to bed after the party and that he shared a room with his father, who would confirm this. The suspect further alleged that the complainant had snuck into his house and slept in his living room without his knowledge. The suspect's father stated that the suspect returned home alone and that the complainant was not in the house when he (the suspect's father) went to bed. Moreover, the complainant told the investigating officer that her friend, a fresh complaint witness who also was a gang member, would not cooperate with law enforcement (a fresh complaint is one made voluntarily and reasonably promptly). Moreover, the detective told the district attorney that the complainant stayed with the suspect for two days after the alleged assault.

The LAPD did not arrest the suspect. Rather, the investigating officer presented the case file to the Los Angeles County District Attorney's (DA's) Office for a prearrest charge evaluation. Despite evidence that the victim had been sexually assaulted (in fact, the nurse who conducted the examination noted in her report that "sexual abuse [was] highly suspected"), the district attorney screening the case refused to file charges, citing insufficient evidence. The investigating officer then cleared the case by exceptional means. On the charge evaluation worksheet, the district attorney noted: "Victim is a runaway who gives inconsistent and unlikely versions of *her adventures. No evidence* of any assault taking place. Defendant has a witness that corroborates his version" (emphasis added).

The fact that the prosecutor used the phrase "her adventures" to describe the complainant's behavior on the night of the alleged sexual assault and stated that the complainant's testimony was both inconsistent and unlikely indicates that the prosecutor was concerned about the complainant's credibility. The prosecutor's statement that there was "no evidence of any assault taking place" is clearly incorrect, as the forensic medical exam cited anal trauma, anal bleeding, and anal lacerations, all of which would be consistent with the complainant's allegation that she was sodomized. Finally, the prosecutor failed to note that the so-called witness who could corroborate the defendant's version of event was the defendant's father.

This case illustrates both the problematic nature of some sexual assault cases reported to the police and the problematic response of the criminal justice system to these cases. Although it is not the classic "she said/he said" scenario, in which the victim claims that she was sexually assaulted and the suspect claims that the sexual contact was consensual, the case nonetheless does not match the stereotype of a "real rape" (Estrich, 1987), in which the victim is assaulted by a stranger wielding a gun, knife, or other type of weapon. The complainant and the suspect know one another, no weapons were involved, there are no witnesses who can (or are willing to) corroborate the complainant's testimony, and the suspect denies any sexual contact with the complainant. In addition, the complainant does not match the stereotype of a "genuine victim" (LaFree, 1989); she is a runaway, she drank and used illegal drugs at the time of the alleged incident, and she associates with known gang members. On the other hand, the forensic medical examination revealed injuries to the complainant consistent with her allegation of forcible sodomy, and the suspect's "alibi witness" was his father. Clearly, this is a case that would have been difficult—but not impossible—to prosecute successfully. The fact that the district attorney (DA) who reviewed the case file determined that there was insufficient evidence to file charges against the suspect, and that this determination was made before the results of the analysis of DNA evidence collected from the complainant during the medical exam were known, suggests not that the DA did not believe the complainant, but rather that the DA believed a jury would not believe the complainant and that therefore a conviction would be unlikely.

As we illustrate in the sections that follow, the decisions made by the police and prosecutor in this case are not atypical. In fact, there is compelling evidence that sexual assault remains a crime characterized by high rates of case attrition, and that the locus of case attrition lies with the gate-keepers of the criminal justice system: police and prosecutors. Despite the rape-law reform movement, which attempted to shift the focus of a sexual assault case from the behavior of the victim to the behavior of the suspect, sexual assault remains a crime in which the credibility of the victim—especially, but not exclusively, in crimes involving nonstrangers—affects case outcomes. It remains a crime in which stereotypes of real rapes and genuine victims play a key role in determining whether the suspect will be arrested, charged, prosecuted, and convicted.

We explore these issues in this book, which details the findings of our mixed-methods study of police and prosecutorial decisionmaking in sexual assault cases reported to the LAPD and the Los Angeles County Sheriff's Department (LASD). The objectives of the book are to provide a comprehensive assessment of the extent of case attrition in sexual assault cases, to identify the factors that increase the likelihood of case attrition, and to highlight the decision rules that guide the handling of these cases. Our focus is on decisions made by the police and the prosecutor: the decision to unfound the report, the decision to make an arrest or to clear the case by exceptional means, and the decision to file charges.

Throughout the book we use the terms "sexual assault" and "rape" interchangeably to refer to sexual penetration by force and against the will of one person by another person. We define sexual penetration broadly: it includes not only penile-vaginal penetration, but also oral copulation, sodomy, and penetration with an object. By contrast, we use the term "sexual battery" to refer to touching the breasts or genitals of another person without that person's consent. (See Chapter 4 for a discussion of recent changes to the Federal Bureau of Investigation's definition of "forcible rape.")

In this chapter, we present a broad overview of prior research on processing decisions concerning sexual assault cases. A more detailed discussion of past research is presented in subsequent chapters on unfounding (Chapter 5), the use of the exceptional clearance (Chapter 6), and intimate partner sexual assault (Chapter 7). We also present an overview of our study and a brief summary of each chapter.

Review of Prior Research

Victim's Decision to Report and to Cooperate

There is compelling evidence that sexual assault is a seriously underreported crime.

Tjaden and Thoennes (2006: 33), who analyzed the results of the National Violence Against Women Survey, found that only 19.1 percent of women who were raped since their 18th birthday reported the crime; a similar survey in Canada found that only 6 percent of sexual assaults were reported to the police (Du Mont, Miller, and Myhr, 2003). Studies using data from the National Crime Victimization Survey (NCVS) also found that reporting rates for sexual assault were lower than those for other violent crimes and that offenses involving nonstrangers had especially low reporting rates (Hindelang and Gottfredson, 1976; Lizotte, 1985; for a more recent review see Fisher, Daigle, and Cullen, 2000). Reasons that victims gave for not reporting included: fear of retaliation from the rapist; feelings of shame and embarrassment; a belief that the rape was a minor incident and not a police matter; and a concern that police and prosecutors would question their veracity and credibility (Bachman, 1998).

Victims who report the crime to the police may nonetheless decide later that they do not want to cooperate in the investigation of the crime or the prosecution of the suspect. They may withdraw their allegations against the suspect, fail to show up for a precharging interview, or ask that the case be discontinued. The extent to which this happens is largely unknown; moreover, there is very little research on the factors that influence the victim's decision to "decline prosecution." A study of outcomes of sexual assault cases in San Diego (Tellis and Spohn, 2008) found that victims refused to cooperate with the police in 36 percent of the cases; the rate was even higher (42.7 percent) for victims who reported a felony sexual assault to the police in Tucson, Arizona (Spohn, Rodriguez, and Koss, 2008). Holmstrom and Burgess (1978: 58–59) found that a fourth of the victims in their study changed their minds about cooperating with police and prosecutors, with most of them becoming "less willing to press charges because of their increasing concern about what court would entail" or because they were worried about retaliation from the suspect or his family and friends if they pursued the case.

Regarding the factors that influence the victim's decision, research has shown that cooperation is more likely if the crime is more serious (Kerstetter, 1990) or the victim suffered collateral injuries (Spohn, Rodriguez, and Koss, 2008), if the victim was assaulted by a stranger rather than an acquaintance or dating partner (Tellis and Spohn, 2008), or if there were witnesses or forensic evidence that could corroborate the victim's testimony (Kerstetter, 1990; Spohn, Rodriguez, and Koss, 2008); cooperation was less likely if the victim was under the influence of alcohol or drugs or had a history of drug use (Spohn, Rodriguez, and Koss, 2008; Tellis and Spohn, 2008).

These findings suggest that victims of sexual assaults that do not conform to stereotypes of real rapes involving genuine victims may receive either overt or subtle messages from police regarding the difficulties that will be encountered in prosecuting the case (Kerstetter and Van Winkle, 1990). As Kerstetter (1990: 309) noted, a police officer who believes that a case is unlikely to be solved may attempt to convince the victim that it is not in her interest to pursue the case; the officer "may vividly portray to the complainant the personal costs involved by emphasizing such things as the repeated trips to court, the inevitable delays at court, and the humiliating cross-examination by defense counsel." Given the importance of victim co-operation for subsequent case-processing decisions (discussed later), these findings are an obvious cause of concern.

Victims of sexual assault who report the crime to the police and are willing to cooperate with police and prosecutors as the case moves forward may confront criminal justice officials who are skeptical of their allegations and who question their credibility (see Estrich, 1987). The process begins with the police, who decide whether a crime has occurred, the amount of investigative resources to devote to identifying the suspect, whether to make an arrest of an identified suspect and, if so, the charges to file, and whether to refer the case to the prosecutor. These "gatekeeping" (Kerstetter, 1990) decisions, which largely determine the fate of the case, do not nec-essarily produce the outcome—arrest and successful prosecution—that the victim expected. As Taylor (1987: 89) pointed out:

> Police determine how rape victims and cases are treated by the criminal justice system. . . . After giving a valid rape report and fully cooperating with the police, a woman may find herself in the unexpected and bewil-dering predicament of having come to the police for aid . . . only to have the door slammed firmly in her face.

Police Unfounding Decision

One of the most important, and highly criticized, decisions made by the police is the decision to "unfound" the charges. If the police officer inves-tigating the crime believes the victim's account of what happened and determines that the incident constitutes a crime, the case becomes one of the "crimes known to the police" that will be included in the jurisdiction's crime statistics. If, on the other hand, the officer does not believe the vic-tim's story and therefore concludes that a crime did not occur, the case is unfounded.

Technically, cases can be unfounded only if the police determine that a crime did not occur. In reality, however, police may use the unfounding decision to clear—or "erase" (Konradi, 2007)—cases in which they are convinced that a crime occurred but also believe that the likelihood of arrest and prosecution is low. According to Martin (2006: 53), police departments are evaluated in terms of clearance rates, which "encourages officers to unfound ambiguous or difficult cases, including those where a victim is reluctant, emotional, uncooperative, or compromised in some way (e.g., had smoked marijuana, was a prostitute, had a former sexual relationship with the rapist)." Other scholars (see McCahill, Meyer, and Fischman, 1979) similarly argued that police may label a case unfounded for illegitimate reasons, including the fact that they do not like the woman (e.g., if she is poor, African American or Hispanic, a prostitute, or has a criminal record), they believe that the victim in some way precipitated the attack, or they believe that her case will not stand up at trial.

There is very limited research on police unfounding decisions in sexual assault cases and most of the research that does exist is dated (Kerstetter, 1990; LaFree, 1989; McCahill, Meyer, and Fischman, 1979; for more recent research see Bouffard, 2000; Tellis and Spohn, 2008). An early study by the Law Enforcement Assistance Administration (1977), in which police officers were asked to identify the factors that affected their decisions, found that the two most important predictors of whether cases would be founded or unfounded were proof of penetration and the suspect's use of physical force. A later study (Kerstetter, 1990) examined sexual assaults reported to the police in Chicago in 1981. Kerstetter differentiated between cases in which the identity of the suspect was not known and those in which the victim and the suspect were acquainted in some way. In the "identity" cases, the most important predictors of the police founding decision were the complainant's willingness to prosecute, whether the victim physically resisted the attack, whether a weapon was used, and whether the suspect was in custody. In contrast, in cases in which the victim and suspect were acquainted, the police were more likely to label the case a crime if the suspect was in custody, if the victim suffered collateral injury, and if there was no discrediting information, such as a pattern of alcohol or drug use, a history of mental illness, or a record of false complaints, about the victim. These findings led Kerstetter (1990) to conclude that the police unfounding decision was affected by a combination of legally relevant instrumental factors and legally irrelevant victim characteristics.

Decision to Arrest and Other Decisions Made by the Police

Studies examining the police decision to make an arrest (Alderden and Ullman, 2012a, 2012b; Bachman, 1998; Bouffard, 2000; Du Mont and Myhr, 2000; Feder, 1998; Horney and Spohn, 1996; LaFree, 1981; Robinson and Chandek, 2000) also highlight the importance of both evidentiary factors and victim characteristics. Legal factors that have been found to increase the likelihood of arrest in sexual assault cases include the presence of a witness, the suspect's use of a weapon, and the victim's willingness to cooperate (Alderden and Ullman, 2012b; Bouffard, 2000; Kernstetter, 1990; LaFree, 1981). LaFree's (1981) analysis of sexual assaults reported to the police in a large metropolitan jurisdiction in the Midwest revealed that the arrest decision was influenced by a combination of legal and extralegal factors: the victim's ability to identify the suspect, the victim's willingness to prosecute, whether the victim had engaged in any type of misconduct at the time of the incident, the promptness of the victim's report, whether the victim was assaulted by an acquaintance rather than a stranger, and the suspect's use of a weapon. On the other hand, the arrest decision was not affected by the victim's race, whether the victim resisted, the location of the incident, whether there was a witness who could corroborate the victim's allegations, or whether the victim was injured. These findings led LaFree (1981: 592) to conclude that, at least in this jurisdiction, the emphasis on the role played by "the victim's attributes and the interpersonal context of the crime" was "greatly overstated."

Several more recent studies call this conclusion into question. For example, Alderden and Ullman (2012b) found that the likelihood of arrest decreased by 57 percent in cases where victims refused to undergo a forensic medical exam, that male officers were more likely than female officers to make an arrest, and that the odds of arrest increased in cases involving acquaintances, relatives, and intimate partners. Although Bouffard (2000) found that crimes involving African American suspects and white victims were not more likely than other crimes to result in arrest, he did find that arrest was more likely if the victim and suspect had a prior relationship, if the victim agreed to undergo a sexual assault exam, and if the credibility/ seriousness score of the crime (which measured whether other crimes were committed during the sexual offense, whether a weapon was used, and whether the crime occurred outdoors) was high. He concluded that the "positive effect of the credibility scale might indicate increased police effort devoted to investigating the offense, because they believed the claim was true or was otherwise 'worthy' of investigation" (Bouffard, 2000: 537). Evidence of the role played by victim characteristics also surfaced in a study where police officers evaluated vignettes in which the beverage consumption (beer or cola) of the victim and suspect was systematically varied (Schuller and Stewart, 2000). The authors of this study found that whereas officers' perceptions of the suspect's level of intoxication had no effect on their evaluation of the suspect's credibility, blame, or guilt, perceptions of the victim's intoxication did affect their assessment of the case. In fact, "the more intoxicated the respondents perceived the victim to be, the less blame they attributed to the alleged perpetrator and the more likely they were to believe that the perpetrator honestly believed that the complainant was willing to engage in intercourse" (Schuller and Stewart, 2000: 547).

A somewhat different approach was taken by Frazier and Haney (1996), who examined case attrition in 569 sexual assaults reported during 1991 to a Midwestern metropolitan police department. They focused on whether a suspect was identified by the police, whether an identified suspect was questioned by the police, and whether the suspect was referred to the prosecuting attorney for charging. They found that suspects were identified in 273 (48 percent) of the cases, that the police questioned suspects in 187 (68 percent) of these cases, and that 68 percent of the suspects who were questioned were referred to the prosecutor (p. 617). Their analysis of the factors that affected these outcomes revealed that identified suspects were more likely to be questioned by the police if they were strangers to the victim, if there was evidence of penetration, if the victim was injured, and if there was a witness to the crime. The only variables that affected whether the case would be referred to the prosecutor for charging were whether the victim was injured and whether the suspect verbally threatened the victim. Similar to Kerstetter, they concluded that "evidentiary and credibility factors as well as offense severity are associated with cases proceeding to the prosecuting attorney's office" (Frazier and Haney, 1996: 624).

Prosecutors' Charging Decisions

All of the decisionmakers in the American criminal justice system have a significant amount of unchecked discretionary power, but the one who stands apart from the rest is the prosecutor. The prosecutor decides who will be charged, what charge will be filed, who will be offered a plea bargain, and the type of bargain that will be offered. The prosecutor also may recommend the sentence the offender should receive. As Supreme Court Justice Robert H. Jackson noted in 1940, "the prosecutor has more control over life, liberty, and reputation than any other person in America" (Davis, 1969: 190).

None of the discretionary decisions made by the prosecutor is more critical than the initial decision to prosecute or not, which has been characterized as "the gateway to justice" (Kerstetter, 1990: 182). Prosecutors have wide discretion at this stage in the process; there are no legislative or judicial guidelines on charging, and a decision not to file charges ordinarily is immune from review. As the Supreme Court noted in *Bordenkircher v. Hayes* (434 U.S. 357, 364), "So long as the prosecutor has probable cause to believe that the accused committed an offense defined by statute, the decision whether or not to prosecute, and what charge to file or bring before a grand jury, generally rests entirely in his discretion."

Research on prosecutors' charging decisions in sexual assault cases reveals that these decisions are strongly influenced by legally relevant factors such as the seriousness of the crime, the offender's prior criminal record, and the strength of the evidence in the case (Alderden and Ullman, 2012b; Kingsnorth, MacIntosh, and Wentworth, 1999; Spohn and Holleran, 2001; Spohn and Spears, 1996). A number of studies, however, also document the influence of victim characteristics, including the victim's age, occupation, and education (McCahill, Meyer, and Fischman, 1979), "risk-taking" behavior such as hitchhiking, drinking, or using drugs (LaFree, 1981; Mc-Cahill, Meyer, and Fischman, 1979; Spohn, Beichner, and Davis-Frenzel, 2001; Spohn and Holleran, 2001; Spohn and Spears, 1996), and the character or reputation of the victim (Feldman-Summers and Lindner, 1976; Field and Bienen, 1980; McCahill, Meyer, and Fischman, 1979; Reskin and Visher, 1986; Spohn, Beichner, and Davis-Frenzel, 2001).

Relationship, Race, and Stereotypes of Rape

A consistent theme found in research on sexual assault case outcomes is the role played by legally irrelevant factors, especially the relationship between the victim and offender, the racial composition of the suspect-victim dyad, and stereotypes regarding "real rapes" and "genuine victims." Consistent with Black's (1976) relational distance theory, a number of studies conclude that reports of sexual assaults by strangers are more likely than reports of sexual assaults by acquaintances or intimate partners to be investigated thoroughly (McCahill, Meyer, and Fischman, 1979). Stranger assaults also are less likely to be unfounded by the police (Kerstetter, 1990) or rejected by the prosecutor (Battelle Memorial Institute, 1977; Loh, 1980; Spohn, Beichner, and Davis-Frenzel, 2001); they are more likely to result in police and prosecutor agreement on the severity of charges to be filed (Holleran, Beichner, and Spohn, 2008). Some research, on the other hand, concludes that prosecutors' charging decisions in sexual assault cases are not directly affected by the victim-suspect relationship. Rather, different predictors affect charging decisions in stranger and acquaintance cases (Kingsnorth, MacIntosh, and Wentworth, 1999; Spohn and Holleran, 2001).

Adding to the already complicated dynamics particular to the suspect-victim relationship is the role played by the race of the victim and the race of the suspect. The sexual stratification hypothesis (LaFree, 1989) posits that reactions to crimes will vary depending upon the race of the suspect and the race of the victim. More to the point, the hypothesis is that sexual assaults involving white women assaulted by African American men will be treated more harshly—and thus will be more likely to result in the filing of charges by prosecutors—than those involving other racial combinations. Some scholars argue that the effect of race is unambiguous and omnipresent (Brownmiller, 1975; Kennedy, 1997; Spohn, 1994), whereas others conceive of it in context-specific circumstances that emerge both directly and indirectly (Bouffard, 2000; LaFree, 1980, 1989; Kingsnorth, MacIntosh, and Wentworth, 1998). In other words, extant research indicates that the effect of race on charging decisions is mitigated by both the relationship between the victim and offender and by victim characteristics such as "blame and believability" and "moral character" (Holleran, Beichner, and Spohn, 2008; Horney and Spohn, 1996; Kalven and Zeisel, 1966; Kerstetter, 1990; Spears and Spohn, 1997; Spohn and Holleran, 2001; Spohn and Spears, 1996; Stanko, 1988; Whately, 1996).

A number of scholars contend that the response of the criminal justice system to the crime of rape is predicated on stereotypes about rape and rape victims (Estrich, 1987). LaFree (1989), for example, asserts that nontraditional women and women who engage in some type of "risk-taking" behavior are less likely to be viewed as genuine victims who are deserving of protection under the law. Frohmann (1991) similarly maintains that the victim's allegations will be discredited if they conflict with decisionmakers' "repertoire of knowledge" about the characteristics of sexual assault incidents and the behavior of sexual assault victims, and Estrich (1987) contends that aggravated rapes are taken more seriously and are treated more harshly than are simple rapes.[1] The authors of a comprehensive review of research on the treatment of acquaintance rape in the criminal justice system (Bryden and Lengnick 1997: 1326) reached a similar conclusion, noting that "the prosecution's heavy burden of proof has played an important role in the justice system's treatment of acquaintance rape cases, but so have public biases against *certain classes* of alleged rape victims" (emphasis added).

Unanswered Questions

The research reviewed here suggests that definitive answers to questions concerning the outcomes of sexual assault cases and case-processing decisions remain elusive. We know very little about the patterns and causes of case attrition in sexual assault cases, and studies of police and prosecutorial decisionmaking in these types of cases reach somewhat different conclusions. These studies indicate that while legal factors—particularly the seriousness of the crime and the strength of evidence in the case—play an important role in processing decisions concerning sexual assault cases, victim characteristics—especially the relationship between the victim and the offender—may also influence these decisions. Some studies conclude that the effect of stereotypes concerning real rapes and genuine victims may not be as pronounced as previous research has suggested, and others state that the influence of victim characteristics may be conditioned by the nature of the case. Considered together, the results of these studies suggest that we need additional research designed to untangle the effects of evidence factors and victim characteristics on processing decisions concerning sexual assault cases.

Although research on all stages of case processing is required, there is a particular need for research on police decisionmaking, especially the decision to unfound the charges and, in cases in which a suspect has been identified, the decision to clear a case with an arrest or by exceptional means (e.g., Addington and Rennison, 2008). Despite its importance, we know very little about either the prevalence of unfounding or the factors that affect unfounding in sexual assault cases; similarly, there is little research investigating whether unfounded reports are in reality false or baseless, as required by the *Uniform Crime Reporting Handbook* (Federal Bureau of Investigation, 2004). Understanding and evaluating the response of the criminal justice system to sexual violence is critically important, as is identifying system-generated barriers to reporting and to cooperating with police and prosecutors.

Sexual Assault Case Processing in Los Angeles

This mixed-methods study, which was funded by the National Institute of Justice, entailed the collection of quantitative and qualitative data on sex crimes reported to the Los Angeles Police Department (LAPD) and the Los Angeles County Sheriff's Department (LASD). From each agency, we obtained data on all sex crimes[2] involving female victims over the age of 12 that were reported from January 2005 through December 2009. For those cases that resulted in the arrest of an adult suspect, we obtained data on the outcome of the case from the Los Angeles County District Attorney's Office. We used these longitudinal data to document the broad patterns of case attrition for sexual assaults reported during this time period.

From each agency we also obtained the complete case files for sexual assaults that were reported in 2008; the LAPD and the LASD redacted all information that could be used to identify the victims, suspects, witnesses, or law enforcement officials assigned to investigate the case and then provided us with a copy of the redacted file. From the LASD we obtained case files for all reports that met our selection criteria (N = 543). Due to the large number of cases reported to the LAPD in 2008, we selected a stratified random sample of cases (N = 401). Because we wanted to ensure an adequate number of cases from each of the LAPD's 19 divisions,[3] as well as an adequate number of cases from each case clearance category (cleared by arrest, cleared by exceptional means, investigation continuing, and unfounded), the sample was stratified by LAPD division and, within each division, by the type of case clearance.[4] We then created a weighted sample that divided the percentage of each stratum (that is, each case closure type for each division) in the population of cases by the percentage of each stratum in the sample.[5] We used the unweighted data when focusing on a particular type of case closure (e.g., unfounded cases or cases that were cleared by exceptional means). We used the weighted data when discussing 2008 case outcomes and when providing descriptive statistics for these cases.

Because we were provided with the complete case file for each of the 2008 cases, we were able to extract very detailed information (quantitative and qualitative data) on each case. The case file included the crime report prepared by the patrol officer who responded to the crime and took the initial report from the complainant, all follow-up reports prepared by the detective to whom the case was assigned for investigation, and the detective's reasons for unfounding the report or for clearing the case by arrest or by exceptional means. The case files also included either verbatim accounts or summaries of statements made by the complainant, by witnesses (if any), and by the suspect (if the suspect was interviewed); a description of physical evidence recovered from the alleged crime scene; and the results of the physical exam (forensic medical sexual assault exam) of the victim (if the victim reported the crime within 72 hours of the alleged assault). Members of the research team (the two coprincipal investigators and a graduate student at California State University, Los Angeles) read through each case file and recorded data in an SPSS data file. Coding protocols were developed by the coprincipal investigators; the coprincipal investigators reviewed a sample of the files coded by the graduate student to ensure that there was consistency and intercoder reliability.

Our third source of data comes from interviews with (1) LAPD and LASD detectives who had experience investigating sexual assaults, (2) deputy district attorneys from the Victim Impact Program, and (3) sexual assault survivors. We interviewed 52 detectives from the LAPD, 24 detectives from the LASD, and 30 attorneys from the Los Angeles County DA's Office. We also partnered with three Los Angeles agencies—the Domestic Abuse Center, the Valley Trauma Center, and the UCLA Rape Treatment Center—and interviewed 17 sexual assault survivors about their experiences with the criminal justice system. The authors of this book conducted all of the interviews and recorded responses in a text file.

Overview of the Book

In the chapters that follow, we present the findings of our study and discuss the policy implications of our findings. Chapter 2 discusses the policies and practices that guide police and prosecutorial decisionmaking in sexual assault cases in Los Angeles. The chapter includes qualitative data from our interviews with detectives and with deputy district attorneys, who were asked to discuss these policies and practices. Chapter 3 provides a detailed discussion of the qualitative data from our interviews with sexual assault detectives, district attorneys who reviewed sexual assault cases, and sexual assault survivors. We explore the themes that emerged from these interviews and explain how the perceptions and attitudes of police and prosecutors shape the response of the criminal justice system to the crime of sexual assault.

In Chapter 4 our focus shifts to case outcomes and the predictors of case outcomes in sexual assault cases. This chapter provides descriptive data on the outcomes of cases reported to the LAPD and the LASD from 2005 to 2009. We demonstrate that the locus of case attrition is the decision to arrest or not and that each agency uses (or misuses) the exceptional clearance to "solve" a substantial number of sexual assault cases. We also present more detailed descriptive data on the cases reported to each law enforcement agency in 2008. Finally, we use the data from 2008 to analyze decisions to arrest and prosecute, with a focus on identifying the factors that predict these outcomes.

The next three chapters focus on unfounding sexual assault reports (Chapter 5), the overuse (misuse) of the exceptional clearance by both law enforcement agencies (Chapter 6), and the nature and outcomes of intimate partner sexual assault (Chapter 7). In Chapter 5 we use data from the LAPD to analyze the decision to unfound the report, and we identify the predictors of unfounding. We also address the question of whether the cases that were unfounded were actually false reports and the factors that motivated victims to file false reports.

The focus of Chapter 6 is the exceptional clearance, which is one of two methods for solving, or clearing, cases, according to the Federal Bureau of Investigations (FBI's) Uniform Crime Reporting (UCR) guidelines. We discuss historical evidence regarding the use of the exceptional clearance, as well as the limited research on this issue. We use the LAPD and LASD data to demonstrate that each agency clears a substantial number of cases by exceptional means, and we argue that in many of these cases, the agencies are using the exceptional clearance inappropriately. We provide qualitative data on cases cleared by exceptional means and on officials' use of this case clearance category. We conclude the chapter with a discussion of the implications (for victims, for suspects, and for the criminal justice system) of the overuse of the exceptional clearance.

In Chapter 7 we examine intimate partner sexual assault. We analyze detailed quantitative and qualitative data on intimate partner sexual assault, as well as data from our interviews that focus on this topic. We provide a description of the victims and suspects in these cases, as well as the contexts and circumstances under which these assaults occur. We also discuss case attrition in these types of cases and compare and contrast outcomes in nonintimate and intimate sexual assaults.

In Chapter 8, we summarize our findings and their implications and we present a series of policy recommendations designed to reduce attrition in sexual assault cases and improve the treatment of sexual assault victims. We identify the policies and practices that contribute to high rates of case attrition and we discuss policy implications for (1) the LA County District Attorney's Office, (2) the LAPD and LASD (and other law enforcement agencies), and (3) the FBI and the Uniform Crime Reporting Program.

Notes

1. According to Estrich (1987; see also Kalven and Zeisel, 1966), an aggravated rape is one involving multiple suspects, a suspect who is a stranger to the victim, a suspect who used a weapon, or collateral injury to the victim. A simple rape is a rape with none of these aggravating circumstances.

2. We obtained outcome data on the following sex crimes: rape, attempted rape, sexual penetration with a foreign object, oral copulation, sodomy, unlawful sex, and sexual battery.

3. Although the LAPD currently has 21 divisions in four bureaus, in 2008 there were only 19 divisions.

4. Our goal was to select 6 cases from each case closure type from each of the 19 divisions that existed in 2008. This would have produced a sample of 456 cases. Because each division did not necessarily have 6 cases from each case closure type in 2008, the final sample included only 401 cases.

5. To illustrate, in 2008 there were 15 cases from the Central Division that were cleared by arrest (0.7 percent of all of the 2008 cases); our sample contained 5 cases from the Central Division that were cleared by arrest (1.2 percent of all of the cases in the sample). Thus, Central Division cases that were cleared by arrest were overrepresented in the sample of cases. Dividing the proportion of cases in the population (0.7 percent) by the proportion of cases in the sample (1.2 percent) yielded a weight of .58 for the cases in this stratum. In contrast, Rampart Division cases that were cleared by arrest were underrepresented in our sample. There were 35 cases (1.7 percent) in the population but only 5 cases (1.2 percent) in the sample. Dividing the proportion of cases in the population (1.7 percent) by the proportion of cases in the sample (1.2 percent) produced a weight of 1.42 for the cases in this stratum.

2

Policies and Practices

In 2008, a case involving a complainant and suspect who had known each other for three years was reported to the Los Angeles Police Department (LAPD). According to the complainant, she encountered the suspect at a bus stop and the suspect asked her if she wanted to be his girlfriend; she said that she did. She stated that the suspect then took her to a hotel, where he told her that they were going to have sex and that he wanted her to have his baby. The complainant stated that she told the suspect that she was a virgin and that she did not want to have sex until she was married. She said that the suspect then told her to sit on the bed, pulled down his pants and hers, orally copulated with her, and vaginally penetrated her. The complainant suffered from schizophrenia and made inconsistent statements during the course of the investigation. The complainant also said that she initially agreed to have sexual relations with the suspect but that she changed her mind when they arrived at the hotel.

The investigating officer interviewed the suspect, who stated that the incident was a "loving act" and that no force was used. He said that the complainant asked him if he had a condom and that when he said he did not, the complainant still "allowed" him to have sex with her. When the officer asked him why he had sex with the complainant even though he knew she was mentally ill and could not rationally make the decision to have sex with him, he replied that he "forgot that she was mentally ill."

This was one of only a few cases in the 2008 database in which the complainant made pretext phone calls to the suspect (a pretext phone call is a call that is recorded by the police; during the call the complainant asks the suspect about the alleged rape and attempts to get the suspect to incriminate himself). In the first call, the suspect told the complainant that he would not have sexual relations with her again unless she wanted to; he said that he would not force her to have sex with him. In the second call, the suspect stated that on the day of alleged incident she "looked so pretty that he went crazy and just had to be with her," and in the third call the suspect swore a number of times that he would not force her to have sex with him if she would see him again. In this call the suspect also admitted that he forced

15

the complainant to have sex with him on the day of the incident that was reported to the police.

Despite the incriminating evidence from the pretext phone calls, including the suspect's admission that he forced the complainant to have sex, the suspect was not arrested. Instead, the case was presented to the DA for a prearrest charging decision. The DA who reviewed the case rejected it for insufficient evidence, noting on the charge evaluation form that it "cannot be proved that the incident was not consensual."

This is an interesting case, which effectively illustrates the policies and practices of policing and prosecuting sexual assault in Los Angeles. The investigating detective for the LAPD did a thorough investigation. He interviewed the complainant twice, interviewed the suspect, and arranged for the complainant to make a series of audio-recorded pretext phone calls to the suspect. Although the detective had probable cause to make an arrest— the suspect admitted that he forced the complainant to have sex with him— he instead presented the case to the DA for a prearrest charging decision. Using a standard of proof beyond a reasonable doubt, the DA reviewing the case declined to file charges. As a result, the suspect was not arrested and the case was not prosecuted. Instead, the investigating officer cleared the case by exceptional means.

In this chapter, we examine the policies and practices that shape the handling and determine the outcome of sexual assaults reported to the LAPD and the Los Angeles County Sheriff's Department (LASD). We begin with a discussion of the policies and practices of the two law enforcement agencies and of the Los Angeles County District Attorney's (DA's) Office. We then use qualitative data from our interviews with detectives and DAs to illustrate the ways in which official policies and practices are interpreted and applied.

Policies and Practices in the Investigation and Prosecution of Sexual Assault Cases

Policies and Practices of Law Enforcement

Reports of sexual assault are handled differently by the LAPD and the LASD. Crimes reported to the LAPD are initially handled by a uniformed patrol officer in one of the LAPD's 21 divisions. The responding officer (whether called to the crime scene or to a medical facility or taking a report from a victim who makes a report at the division's station house) will prepare the initial report of the crime based on the statements of the victim and witnesses (if any); included will be a description of the suspect and, if known, identifying information about the suspect. If the crime was reported promptly, the responding officer also will collect evidence from the scene of the crime and from the victim and, if she agrees, transport the victim to a rape treatment center or other medical facility for a forensic medical exam. The case is then investigated by one of the detectives in that division who is assigned to the "sex table."[1] The investigating detective will reinterview the victim, interview witnesses, attempt to locate and interview the suspect (if a suspect is identified), and prepare follow-up reports that detail the results of the investigation. There are, however, two variations to this scenario. West Bureau, one of the LAPD's four bureaus, currently has a centralized response to sex crimes. Consequently, sexual assault detectives who would otherwise be distributed throughout the five divisions that comprise West Bureau are housed together and work cases from the bureau's headquarters. The second variation occurs when the Robbery-Homicide Division assumes investigative responsibility for a sexual assault from division detectives, which tends to occur in serial stranger-rape cases and in cases involving "high-profile" suspects or victims.

The LASD has a bifurcated approach to the investigation of sexual assault that is based on the age of the victim. Crimes involving victims who are age 18 or older are handled in much the same way as are all sexual assaults reported to the LAPD; the initial report is taken by a sheriff's deputy in the jurisdiction where the crime occurred and the case is then assigned to a detective from the station house in that jurisdiction. Whereas LAPD has a sex table staffed by detectives who investigate only sex crimes, LASD detectives investigate all types of crimes, from theft to robbery and sexual assault; the only exception to this is that homicides are investigated by a centralized Homicide Bureau. Crimes involving victims under the age of 18 are referred to the Special Victims Bureau; detectives assigned to this unit will take the initial report from the victim and investigate the crime.

As already noted, the follow-up investigation of a sexual assault is handled by the detective assigned to the case, who will pursue leads, interview the victim and any witnesses, and attempt to identify, locate, and interview the suspect. If the detective believes that the complaint is false or baseless, he or she can unfound the report (see Chapter 5 for a detailed discussion of unfounding). If there is an identified suspect and probable cause to make an arrest, the detective can clear, or solve, the case by arrest or, under specified circumstances, by exceptional means. If a suspect has not been identified or if there is not probable cause to make an arrest, the case can be kept open or, in the vernacular of the LAPD, "IC'd" (investigation continued).

The process of case clearance. According to the *Uniform Crime Reporting Handbook* (*UCR Handbook;* Federal Bureau of Investigation, 2004), offenses are cleared either by arrest or by exceptional means (known in the LAPD as "cleared other"). The handbook states that "an offense is cleared by arrest, or solved for crime reporting purposes, when at least one person is (1) arrested, (2) charged with the commission of the offense, and (3) turned over to the court for prosecution (whether following arrest, court summons, or police notice)" (p. 79). Regarding exceptional clearances (see Chapter 6 for a detailed discussion of the use of the exceptional clearance), the handbook notes that there may be occasions where law enforcement has conducted an investigation, exhausted all leads, and identified a suspect but is nonetheless unable to clear an offense by arrest. In this situation, the agency can clear the offense by exceptional means, provided that each of the following questions can be answered in the affirmative (pp. 80–81):

- Has the investigation definitely established the identity of the offender?
- Is the exact location of the offender known so that the subject could be taken into custody now?
- Is there enough information to support an arrest, charge, and turning over to the court for prosecution?
- Is there some reason outside law enforcement control that precludes arresting, charging, and prosecuting the offender?

To illustrate the types of cases that might be cleared by exceptional means, the handbook provides a list of examples, many of which involve the death of the offender or an offender who is unable to be arrested because she or he is being prosecuted in another jurisdiction for a different crime or because extradition has been denied. One of the examples provided is that in which the "victim refuses to cooperate in the prosecution," but there is an added proviso, which states that this alone does not justify an exceptional clearance and that the answer to the first three questions in the list must also be yes (Federal Bureau of Investigation, 2004, p. 81).

Analysis of case outcomes and interviews with detectives revealed that both the LAPD and the LASD have complicated rules for clearing cases and misinterpret Uniform Crime Reporting (UCR) guidelines regarding the two types of case clearances (cleared by arrest and cleared by exceptional means). If the detective investigating the crime has identified a suspect and has probable cause to arrest the suspect, the detective will either arrest the individual and present the case to a deputy DA from the Victim Impact Program (VIP) of the Los Angeles County DA's Office for a filing decision, or delay making an arrest and present the case to a deputy DA for a prearrest charge evaluation.

The deputy district attorney (DDA) reviewing the case following the arrest of the suspect can either accept the case for prosecution, send the case back to the investigating officer for further investigation (although this is complicated by the fact that charges must be filed within 48 hours of the suspect's arrest), send the case to the city attorney for prosecution as a misdemeanor, or decline the case for prosecution. Because LAPD policy states that cases can be cleared by arrest only if the DA files charges, if charges are declined, the LAPD detective changes the case clearance category from "cleared by arrest" to "cleared by exceptional means." The LASD does not have a similar policy, but, depending on the preferences of the detective's supervisor or the detective's own interpretation of UCR policies on exceptional clearances, an LASD detective may also recategorize the case from "cleared by arrest" to "cleared by exceptional means" if the DA declines to file charges against the suspect. Because the *UCR Handbook* clearly states that cases can be cleared by exceptional means only if there is something beyond the control of law enforcement that prevents them from making an arrest, this is a misuse of the exceptional clearance. Cases in which a suspect is arrested should be cleared by arrest, regardless of whether charges are filed by the DA.

Similar procedures are followed if the case is evaluated by the DA prior to the arrest of the suspect. As is the situation with cases assessed following the arrest of the suspect, the deputy DA reviewing the case before the suspect has been arrested can accept the case for prosecution, send the case back to the investigating officer for further investigation, send the case to the city attorney for prosecution as a misdemeanor, or decline to file charges. If the evidence in the case meets the DA's standard for filing, the suspect will be arrested and the case will be cleared by arrest. If the case is sent back for further investigation or if the evidence is deemed insufficient to justify charging, the investigating officer will either continue the investigation and, once additional evidence is obtained, resubmit the case for a second review by the DA, or—and this is what more typically happens— end the investigation and clear the case by exceptional means. As is explained in more detail in Chapter 6, this, too, may be a misuse of the exceptional clearance. If the detective has probable cause to make an arrest but the victim tells the DA that she does not want the suspect arrested or is unwilling to cooperate in the prosecution of the case, the case can be cleared by exceptional means. Although one might argue that the suspect should be arrested if there is probable cause to make an arrest, the victim's unwillingness to cooperate is something that is beyond the control of law enforcement. On the other hand, the case should not be cleared by exceptional means if the DA declines to file charges because the evidence in the case does not meet the filing standard of proof beyond a reasonable doubt. If there is probable cause to arrest the suspect and the victim is cooperative, the suspect should be arrested and the case cleared by arrest, as there is nothing beyond the control of law enforcement that prevents them from making an arrest. Alternatively, the detective may continue the investigation and, once additional evidence is obtained, resubmit the case to the DA.

(However, as we discuss in Chapter 6, this rarely happens; the typical outcome if the DA declines prosecution is for the detective to clear the case exceptionally.)

Policies and Practices of the DA's Office

Since 2001, the Los Angeles County DA's Office has had a specialized sex crimes unit, the Victim Impact Program (VIP), that vertically prosecutes sexual assault, meaning that a single DA handles the case from start to finish. The DA's office describes[2] VIP as a program that is

> designed to specifically address the needs of victims with unique vulnerability. These crimes include those committed against the elderly and children, hate crimes, and crimes of sexual abuse, stalking and domestic violence. The goal of the program is to obtain justice and support for these victims throughout Los Angeles County and to hold offenders accountable for their crimes. To accomplish this goal, the District Attorney's Office has doubled the number of highly trained and qualified prosecutors in Branch and Area offices across the county who will vertically prosecute the targeted crimes. Law enforcement officers investigating and filing these cases deal directly with local VIP coordinators and work with deputy district attorneys who will handle each case from start to finish.

Each of the 11 branches of the DA's Office utilizes a VIP team approach, with an experienced deputy designated as the VIP deputy in charge (DIC). The VIP DIC works closely with the DDAs assigned to the VIP team to ensure that sexual assault cases are appropriately prepared and prosecuted. All deputies assigned to a VIP team receive enhanced, ongoing training focusing on legal issues, potential defenses, and trial tactics.

Although all of the prosecutors interviewed for this project affirmed that the VIP is philosophically committed to the notion of vertical prosecution, many noted that the case screening process varies by branch and by the VIP DIC. In some branches case-screening and -filing decisions are handled by the DIC, in others there is a designated case screener, and in still others all members of the VIP team participate in case screening and make filing decisions. In branches where "everyone screens cases," if the DDA screening the case decides to file charges, he or she is assigned to prosecute the case. As one respondent noted, "After filing, we own the case so we take the filing decision very seriously." Another respondent expressed a more cynical attitude, noting that "if you file the dog, you walk the dog." In some branches, the VIP DIC screens cases initially and decides whether the case should be rejected; cases that are not rejected outright are assigned to a member of the VIP team, who will conduct the prefiling interview with the victim and decide whether charges should be filed and, if so, what the charges should be. In other branches, the VIP DIC conducts the interview with the victim and makes the filing decision; cases that are filed are assigned to a member of the VIP team for prosecution.

It is important to point out that the standard used by the Los Angeles County DA's Office in screening cases (either before or after arrest) is a trial sufficiency standard (Jacoby, 1980). That is, the DDA will file charges only if there is sufficient evidence to prove the case beyond a reasonable doubt at a jury trial. Moreover, the policy in sexual assault cases is that charges will not be filed without some type of corroboration[3] of the victim's testimony—DNA evidence that establishes the identity of the perpetrator, injuries to the victim, witnesses who can corroborate the victim's testimony, or physical or medical evidence that is consistent with the victim's account of the incident. Although there are some exceptions, a prefiling interview designed to assess the victim's credibility and willingness to cooperate in the prosecution of the case also is required. Many of the respondents interviewed for this project emphasized that rejection is likely if the incident is a "she said/he said" situation in which the victim is claiming that she was forced to engage in sexual relations but the suspect contends that the sexual acts were consensual and there is no corroboration of the victim's testimony. In fact, when asked whether there were any types of "she said/he said" cases that would be filed without corroboration of the victim's allegations, most admitted that there were not. As one DDA replied: "No. That would be a violation of office policy. There are cases where I would like to, but no."

In the sections that follow, we focus on the perceptions and attitudes of the detectives and DDAs who were interviewed for this project. We use the qualitative data from our interviews to illustrate the ways in which the formal policies and procedures of the two law enforcement agencies and the DA's office are interpreted and applied.

Perceptions and Attitudes of Law Enforcement

We interviewed 52 detectives with the LAPD and 24 detectives with the LASD. The LAPD detectives, who ranged in rank from Detective I to Detective III,[4] reflect a wide range of time on the job generally as well as time investigating sex crimes. Length of time on the LAPD ranged from 10 to 33 years, and length of time investigating sex crimes ranged from 2 months to 25 years. The LASD detectives either were assigned to the Special Victim's Bureau, which handles sexual assault cases involving victims younger than 18, or to one of the stations that handles all types of crimes, including sexual assaults involving victims age 18 and older. Our interviewees' tenure at the LASD ranged from 5 to 29 years, and length of time investigating sex crimes ranged from 1 to 18 years.

Specialized Training in Investigation of Sexual Assault

The LAPD and LASD detectives interviewed for this study all emphasized the need for specialized training in the investigation of sexual assault cases, which involve highly sensitive issues and victims who may be severely traumatized or reluctant to speak about what happened to them and which may involve delayed reporting, victims and suspects who are nonstrangers, and a lack of corroborating evidence. However, only 60 percent of the LAPD detectives reported that they received training specific to the investigation of sexual assault. Although most of those reporting specialized training stated that they received training at the LAPD's major assault crimes (MAC) school there was inconsistency in the extent to which detectives reported that issues specific to sexual assault were covered during the training. Those with longer tenure with the agency noted that during the 1990s there was a department-run, three-day sexual assault school, which was ultimately merged with the MAC school with the intention of covering both domestic violence and sexual assault. Other LAPD detectives noted that the MAC school focused more on family violence, with less time devoted to sexual assault. The detectives who reported that they did not receive any specialized training emphasized that the LAPD primarily relies on "on-the-job training," which, one detective stated, "hasn't changed over time."

Of the 24 sheriff's department deputies interviewed for the project, all but 3 reported that they had some type of sexual assault–specific training, ranging from the 8 hours for which sexual assault is covered in the LASD Academy to LASD's detective school. The most comprehensive training experiences they described were the LASD's 40-hour sexual assault investigation course and the somewhat less comprehensive, 1-week course taught by the Federal Bureau of Investigation (FBI).

Respondents unanimously agreed that specialized training should be required for all detectives who handle sexual assault. For example, two detectives, one from LAPD and one from LASD, stated that specialized training was more essential for sexual assault than for homicide:

> Sex work is so totally different than any other type of detective work, more so than homicide. Homicide in this area is typically one gang member shooting another gang member; to me there is not much to it. [Working] sex crimes is totally different. You have the complexity of delayed reporting, the psychology of delayed reporting. Often they feel—especially teen and adult victims—that they put themselves in compromising situations and so they are embarrassed and delay the report thinking, "I was stupid and I deserved it." So you have to deal with that psychology, and let them know that everyone makes

mistakes but that doesn't give the person the right to harm you. It doesn't mean that you're not a victim [just] because you made a dumb decision.

Yes, not only specialized training but specialized units are needed to work in sex crimes. Sex crimes are as unique—if not more unique—than any other investigation unit, including homicide. You need the training because of all of the changes with DNA and cyber-communication that all [have] to be understood and learned, but mainly it's the dynamics of victimization. With homicide your victim isn't going to be interviewed; their trauma is over. In most property crimes the trauma is there; your car was stolen, but nothing can compare to sexual assault. But we don't get enough training in trauma, and dealing with the trauma of victims, interviewing victims, and when to interview them.

Other respondents emphasized that the investigation of sexual assault is complicated by evidentiary issues and the need to establish rapport with victims. Typical of their comments are the following:

There is so much that goes on with sex crimes—DNA and preservation of evidence and dealing with victims—that it takes specific investigative skill to do a thorough investigation and have the level of sensitivity needed.

Yes [specialized training is needed], because everything they teach you in detective school in terms of investigations, interrogations, etc., does not apply to sex crimes. [They require] different interrogations and styles with victims. [Detective school] does not cover it [sex crimes] enough.

[Specialized training is] absolutely [necessary] because it is a very set, specific type of crime and you must have training on what questions to ask, what is needed for the DA's office for filing and prosecution, and sensitivity training for [dealing with] the victim, because obviously we have to handle sex crimes differently than you do robberies or burglaries. There are specific elements and points that we have to ensure we understand.

In summary, although the sample of detectives interviewed reflects a wide range of time on the job and experience in sex crimes, respondents from both the LAPD and the LASD agreed that specialized training is needed for all sexual assault detectives due to the sensitive nature of the crime, the skills required to interview victims and interrogate suspects, and the intricacies of investigating and gathering evidence in these cases.

Investigating and Clearing Sexual Assaults

We asked the detectives interviewed for this project a series of questions about their case clearance policies and practices. We asked them how they decide whether a report should be unfounded and whether the victim was required to recant the allegations in order to unfound the report. We also asked them about the types of cases likely to be cleared by arrest and by exceptional means, and we asked them several questions about the "prearrest screening process."

The decision to unfound. FBI guidelines on clearing cases for Uniform Crime Reporting purposes state that a case can be unfounded only if it is "determined through investigation to be false or baseless" (FBI, 2004, p. 77). The handbook also stresses that police are not to unfound a case simply because the complainant refuses to prosecute or they are unable to make an arrest. Similarly, the International Association of Chiefs of Police policy on investigating sexual assault cases (IACP, 2005) states that "the determination that a report of sexual assault is false can be made only if the evidence establishes that no crime was committed or attempted" and that "this determination can be made only after a thorough investigation" (p. 12). Both sources, in other words, emphasize that the police must conduct an investigation and that their investigation must lead them to a conclusion that a crime did not occur. It is important to note that victim recantation cannot be the sole basis for unfounding the report, because, as some detectives noted, the fact that the victim recants does not necessarily mean that a crime did not occur. Moreover, the victim may insist that a crime did occur, despite evidence that the allegation is false. Victim recantation, therefore, is neither a necessary nor a sufficient condition for unfounding the report.

Interviews with detectives from both law enforcement agencies revealed that there was confusion regarding when cases could be unfounded and whether victim recantation was required. Some detectives clearly understood and accurately interpreted the guidelines. For instance, a LAPD detective stated that a case will be unfounded "if the victim recants and there is clear evidence that the crime did not occur. It is unlikely that the case will be unfounded if the victim recants and the evidence indicates that a crime did occur." Another LAPD detective emphasized that unfounding was rare and that victim recantation was not required. According to this respondent: "A very small percentage of cases are unfounded because there is some kind of evidence that nothing happened. It is very rare that we unfound a case. It is not mandatory but probable that the victim will recant." A third detective said that recantation does not necessarily lead to the case being unfounded, stating that "if the victim recants but it is clear that something happened, it would not be unfounded. A case like that would not meet the criteria for unfounding. However, it is probably another case that would end up in the DA's office and they would reject it."

Other detectives appeared to not understand what unfounding is or what is required to unfound a report. Consider this comment from an LASD detective:

> Unfounded would be where there is no way of finding out who the suspect is, and there is no DNA or no sexual assault kit done on the victim. I have a case now involving a woman who claims that she was assaulted by a taxi driver. She was very drunk and her friends put her in cab but they don't even know what taxi company it was. If there is no DNA or no DNA hit, that case will be unfounded because most likely we will never know who committed the crime. Unfounded means that we cannot confirm or deny that it happened.

What is troubling about this comment is the detective's assumption that cases can be unfounded if there is no way to identify a suspect and if they "cannot confirm or deny" that a crime occurred. Cases without an identified suspect can either be kept open or, if all leads have been exhausted, closed or inactivated, and cases cannot be unfounded unless the investigation proves that a crime did not occur. A number of detectives, primarily those from the LASD, also mistakenly stated that cases involving false allegations could be exceptionally cleared. According to one respondent: "Even if we feel that it should be unfounded, we still submit it to the DA. We make sure that we inform the DA of the inconsistencies and of our concerns that a crime did not occur. This would be cleared exceptionally because of insufficient evidence. I have never used unfounded." A similar misperception is found in this detective's comments:

> Unfounding meaning that no crime occurred? Usually the victim will recant and there won't be evidence to support her allegations, no findings of any type of abuse. If it is a recanted story where the victim said that she made it up to get attention or for some other reason, it would be cleared as no crime. Unfounded is used very rarely. Instead we clear exceptionally, meaning that no crime occurred.

When asked whether reports would be unfounded simply based on the victim recanting the allegations, one LAPD detective said: "Oh hell no. Victims recant all the time." Another emphasized that

> many victims recant because of the attitude [by the police] that is being perceived [by the victim] in dealing with the investigation.

They are tired of dealing with it, and they want to go back to normal.
[Victims often] feel responsible for stresses that have emerged. A
victim recant can be used but should be corroborated and followed
up by a detective. The next question should be, "Where were you
then?" and seek that corroboration and clarification to make sure
the recantation is valid and not being driven by another alternative.

Along similar lines, two detectives (the first from the LASD and the second
from the LAPD) stated:

If the victim in the case recants, the case will be closed as unfounded.
I would not present it to the DA. But if there is evidence that the
victim is being threatened or intimidated I would definitely present
the case to the DA. If there are injuries and if the victim made a fresh
complaint, if we have all of that kind of evidence, we will go forward
with it.

In [this division] we get a lot of girls coming in who ditch
school, hang with a boyfriend, get in trouble for being late, but say
they were raped because they do not want to get in trouble. If [in]
speaking to witnesses, we corroborate the victim's story that it did
not happen, then we will unfound. If she says it didn't but I think
that it did you have to follow the evidence.

Although some respondents acknowledged that recanting is not a
requirement to unfound the case, others insisted that "the case will not be
unfounded unless the victim denies that it occurred" or that "the only time
I unfound is when I can prove that it did not happen and the victim recants." Other detectives stated that if the victim "sticks to her story" the
case will not be unfounded, but will remain as an open, investigation-
continuing, case:

The only way we can unfound is if the victim tells us it did not
happen; there is no other way. The victim has to recant to unfound
the case. She has to tell us that she made it up, she lied. If we have
enough evidence to substantiate that in fact she did make it up. If we
think differently, we would keep the case open as I/C [investigation
continuing].

Here we are very strict. A case is not unfounded unless the victim
says it didn't happen. For example, a teenage girl who ran away from
home and left school and didn't want to get in trouble. Once we get
her here and start doing the interview the stories don't match and
[the] story doesn't make sense. Sometimes they will come forward
and say, "I completely made it up." But if she sticks with the story
those will be I/C.

Another theme that emerged from the interview data was that many detectives would present cases to the DA in which they either suspected the victim was not telling the truth or the victim recanted but there was evidence that a crime did occur, with the expectation that the DA would decline to file charges, under the erroneous impression that this would allow them to clear the case by exceptional means. This attitude is reflected in comments from two LAPD officers. One said: "I believe all my victims until I can prove that they are not telling the truth. If the victim says that it did not happen, I still present it to the DA and he or she will decide. They will reject it, of course." The second detective made an almost identical comment, noting that "I would not unfound if the victim recanted and the evidence suggested that the crime did occur. But the DA would reject it, absolutely." Similarly, when asked whether a case would be unfounded if the victim recanted, one LASD detective explained that

> it depends on where the case is in the investigation. If it has not yet been presented to the DA's office, I would investigate to find out why the victim is saying something different now than what . . . she [or he] said from before. I would present it to the DA's office, putting in details about the recantation, and ultimately it would be a DA reject because the DA will not go forward with a victim who is recanting.

Overall, interviewees demonstrated two general perspectives about unfounding. Some detectives emphasized that they would unfound if that was where the evidence led, regardless of whether the victim recanted the allegations, but the rest stated that detectives should unfound only if the victim recants. It is important to note that many detectives emphasized that unfounding seldom occurs, and some had no experience with it and only spoke of it in the abstract. It also became evident that some detectives were reluctant to unfound because of uncertainty as to the criteria and concerns about political correctness related to the implication that a victim is lying. Consequently, they present the case to the DA, knowing that the lack of evidence or the victim's unwillingness to cooperate will lead the DA to decline to file charges. Although some detectives correctly stated that a case rejected for prosecution under these circumstances cannot be cleared by exceptional means but rather should remain as an open, investigation-continuing case, the majority stated unequivocally that these cases are cleared exceptionally.

The decision to arrest and the prearrest screening process. We asked detectives from the two law enforcement agencies to describe the criteria they use in deciding whether to arrest the suspect. Generally, their explanations fell into three, somewhat overlapping, categories: arrest if there is probable cause to make the arrest; arrest if there is probable cause and the suspect is a threat to the victim or public safety; and arrest only if there is a good likelihood of prosecution and conviction. Although not by any means their typical response, LASD detectives were more likely than those from the LAPD to report that they would arrest based on probable cause alone. One detective was adamant that the suspect should be arrested if there was probable cause:

> If you have a victim that does not have any motive [to lie]—and most don't—and there are no extenuating circumstances and you have a victim saying she was sexually assaulted and this guy doesn't have an alibi—for example, saying he was out of the country—then you should arrest. It is as simple as that. He should be going to jail. You should not take into consideration what the DA is going to do. Why are sex crimes different than any other crime? Why is there a higher standard in these cases? Victims are put on . . . trial from the beginning. Why should we look at it differently and make the victim jump through hoops when we wouldn't on any other crime? We have probable cause if the victim says it, he was in proximity, and he doesn't have an alibi. He should go to jail.

Two other LASD detectives stated that they would arrest using a probable cause standard, but added that arresting the suspect was a means to an end—it allowed them to obtain enough evidence to present a solid case to the DA.

> Every case is different. If a situation arises where the suspect is in a location and we can go arrest him, we will. The faster the arrest, the more likely we will gather more evidence. If the victim claims she fought the suspect, the suspect will have defensive wounds. And once he is arrested you can take photos and evidence needed to support an assault rather than waiting several months or [a] year when injuries have healed.
>
> If I have a feeling that the victim is consistent with the statements they gave me relative to what they said to patrol and I feel this suspect really committed this crime then I like to immediately arrest him and then interview him. If I coordinate a meeting with the suspect at his house or another place that he is familiar with he is less likely to admit the crime as alleged. But when I arrest someone and take them in our environment I find that suspects are more likely to talk because they think that if they [the police] have enough to arrest me they might have enough to file criminal charges.

Three other detectives—all from the LAPD—cited other benefits that resulted from arresting the suspect. The first explained that DAs were more likely to file if the suspect was in custody, noting that "it's the time element—he is right there, so it's easier to go ahead and file." The second LAPD detective provided a more complex explanation, stating that arresting a suspect based on probable cause produced a criminal history for the suspect and got the suspect into the state's DNA database:

> My practice is that I don't present it to the DA prior to making an arrest. If I have probable cause to make an arrest, I will make an arrest. Even if he is going to be out in forty-eight hours, I think that it is important to send a message to the suspect and to ensure that the suspect has a criminal history. Also, by arresting him I get him in the DNA database so that if he does it again we can link him to earlier cases. But this does not mean that I will arrest just anyone. I have to have probable cause, strong probable cause to believe that he is the guy who committed the crime.

These comments were echoed by a third LAPD detective, who explained that if the DA rejected the case for filing before the suspect was arrested, the suspect could not be arrested. As this respondent noted: "If the DA files charges, then good, but if not then it [the arrest] still is on his record. A lot of times that is the avenue we have to take because a lot of times you know the DA will not file so if we don't arrest then he is getting off scot free."

A number of interviewees explained that they would arrest if there was probable cause to do so only if the suspect posed a threat to public safety or was likely to flee if not arrested. Typical are these comments from LASD detectives:

> It depends on whether the suspect is a flight risk or if the suspect is in the home and is a danger to the victim. If the suspect is a business-person and you know that he or she will show up you can present the case to the DA and get a warrant for that.
> It depends on the time frame and the fact that we only have 48 hours to develop the case. If the suspect is a danger to the victim or to anyone else we will make the arrest.
> If I have DNA or physical evidence I will probably arrest him before something bad happens like he flees the country, kills himself, [or] hurts the victim.

A respondent from the LAPD gave a very similar explanation. He stated that he looks "at the type of guy who is being investigated," adding that he asks: "Is he going to come up in the future? Is he going to harm others? Is there anything predatory about his nature? Does he have a paper trail?" As this detective put it, "If he has a history, he needs to be booked [but] we don't do that in every case."

In contrast to the first two justifications for arresting the suspect, both of which emphasize probable cause or public safety, the third explanation given by detectives focuses on whether there is sufficient evidence to convince the DA to file charges against the suspect. A number of detectives stated that they would not arrest unless they were confident that the DA would file charges and that a conviction was likely. One LAPD detective, in fact, went so far as to aver that "the *rule* is if you know the DA is not going to file, then you don't arrest," adding that "if I know the DA won't file, then we *can't* arrest" (emphasis added). Another respondent explained that they could not make an arrest based solely on the crime report, but had "to weigh the totality of the circumstances." The respondent added:

> Especially if it is a one-on-one situation and there are credibility issues, I would be reluctant to make an arrest. I would probably seek a filing first and build a stronger case before we simply put handcuffs on someone knowing the DA will reject it and the guy is right back out. When I arrest someone it is at the point where the case is strong enough to go through the criminal justice system and we are pretty confident we will get a conviction.

Although some respondents noted that using a "filing standard" was a reflection of scarce resources, others stated that it reflected concerns about false allegations and the potential for labeling an innocent person a rapist. According to one LAPD detective:

> If it's a one-on-one consensual we leave it up to the DA's office because I'm not going to arrest someone if he's saying it was consensual and she says it wasn't. And if I don't have bruising, etc., then I am apprehensive to make an arrest in those cases. I would rather leave it up to the DA's office and say, "It is your call, you tell me what you want to do." Unless I have some sort of evidence: bite marks, scratches, something to indicate a struggle, then I am reluctant to just arrest someone based on someone's word, even if she is a righteous victim.

An LASD detective, who asserted that the arrest should be based not on "whether the DA can win it, [but on] whether he did it," stated that "for some reason we have this taboo about ruining someone's reputation on sexual assault." This respondent went on to say:

We'll arrest them for burglary, for robbery, but not sexual assault. That term raises people's awareness. Sometimes detectives are afraid to make that call so they will go to the DA and let the DA make that decision for them. I'm not saying you make the arrest in every case, but I'm saying you don't treat it any differently than you do other felonies. I think it is fear of labeling this guy a rapist.

The following comments, which were made by an LAPD detective, illustrate how the "fear of labeling this guy a rapist," can distort detectives' reasoning about when an arrest is appropriate:

You have the ones that report rape and they're with this person and they get together, hang out, go to dinner, and spend the night. But at some point they're not sure, change their minds, or the person doesn't call them back or something where it's like, ok, there's not enough to book this guy and put this on his rap sheet when she just didn't know how to say no or changed her mind. I've had this where she'll say, "I was thinking no," or he didn't have a condom and she told him no, that she would have if he had a condom but she said no and he did anyway. So we don't book them and get that on their rap sheet.

The assertion that "we" do not book suspects in cases where the victim says no because the suspect does not have a condom yet he has sex with her anyway suggests that some detectives do not have sufficient understanding of the legal definition of sexual assault or their discretion is inappropriately influenced by rape myths (Page, 2008; Temkin, 2010).

Making sense of detectives' comments about the circumstances that lead them to arrest (or not to arrest) suspects in sexual assault cases requires an understanding of what we refer to as the "prearrest screening process." Many detectives present the case (that is, the case file) to the DA for a filing decision prior to making an arrest. Most of these are "problematic" cases where the officer believes that the odds of prosecution are low: cases involving intimate partners or acquaintances and a consent defense, cases involving victims who were under the influence of alcohol or illegal drugs at the time of the incident, cases where the victim delayed reporting, and cases with little, if any, corroboration of the victim's allegations. If the DA reviewing the case declines to file charges because of insufficient evidence or lack of victim cooperation—and this is the outcome in almost all of these cases (see Chapter 4)—the case typically is cleared by exceptional means. As explained in more detail in Chapter 6, this would be an appropriate use of the exceptional clearance only if the officer had probable cause to make an arrest and there was something beyond the officer's control that prevented him or her from making an arrest. Cases in which the officer either did not have probable cause to make an arrest or had probable cause to make an arrest but the case was rejected by the DA because it did not meet the standard of proof beyond a reasonable doubt should not be cleared exceptionally.

Although some of the detectives interviewed for this project reported that cases were not presented to the DA prior to arrest and emphasized that the appropriate way to handle these cases was to arrest the suspect if there was probable cause to do so, most stated that screening by the DA prior to arrest was common practice. Many noted that prearrest screening either was unique to sexual assault cases or occurred much more frequently in these types of cases due to "the consent issue" and to the fact that sexual assault "is a very sensitive type of crime and raises a whole host of issues that other crimes don't raise." As one LASD detective, who emphasized that prearrest screening "depends on the case," explained: "Typically my cases are the party rapes and the victim does not remember what happened. In these cases we present it to the DA. If it's rejected then we won't arrest." Similarly, an LAPD detective commented that prearrest charge evaluation was "unique to sexual assault because usually there is no evidence," adding that "it makes it more difficult [to arrest] because there is most likely a relationship between the suspect and victim."

Many of the detectives from both agencies acknowledged that they presented cases to the DA prior to making an arrest with an expectation that the case would be rejected for prosecution. For example, one LAPD detective said, "If I've investigated a case and I think that all things being equal the suspect should not have an arrest jacket put on him and I know that the case will be rejected anyway, *I am going to take it to the DA's office and get it rejected*" (emphasis added). Another LAPD detective, who said that the DA evaluated the case similarly regardless of whether the suspect had been arrested, justified presenting the case to the DA prior to making an arrest on the grounds that doing so saved time and avoided unnecessary paperwork:

> It makes it easier for everyone if there is not a body [a suspect who has been arrested] involved given the time constraints. . . . They [the DA] can read the case file at their leisure and *write a reject* at their leisure without worrying about the clock. A lot of it just comes down to a time issue and recognizing that every time you go out and arrest someone you are creating more paperwork . . . if you ultimately know what the end result will be why would you go through that process? (Emphasis added)

An LASD detective made a very similar comment, noting, "I'm not going to waste my time and arrest the suspect if I don't think I'll get the case filed." Other detectives reported that they presented cases to the DA prior to making an arrest in order to get his or her assessment of whether the evidence was sufficient to file charges. As one LASD respondent noted, "If you are unsure whether the DA will reject or not, you present it first so that you cross all your t's and dot all of your i's." This comment was echoed by a second LASD detective, who said that "if you go to a DA and present the case they can give you advice as to how to strengthen the case."

As noted, some detectives stated that they personally did not submit their sexual assault cases to the DA for a prearrest charge evaluation if they had probable cause to make an arrest. One LAPD detective went so far as to say that "for a detective to go to a DA for booking advice is a sign of weakness," and an LASD detective stated that "I know the law just as well as the DA—perhaps better—so I don't feel that I need to check with someone on this; I have been doing this a long time and feel pretty confident that I know what to do." Another LAPD detective expressed surprise when asked about the prearrest charge evaluation and stated, "I am hoping that is not being practiced."

We asked detectives what happens to a sexual assault case if, as a result of the prearrest charge evaluation, the DA determines that the evidence does not meet the standard for filing and therefore rejects the case for prosecution. Most respondents stated that they would notify the victim of the DA's decision and that the case would then be cleared by exceptional means. Respondents also stated that they had little recourse if the DA did reject the case. According to one LASD detective:

> Some detectives will come screaming to me and say this is a bunch of crap and we will take it to their bosses. Rarely, if ever, does it get overturned. If the first DA rejects it, the second and third will also. They pick only slam-dunk cases and sexual assault cases are always a lot of work. And, to be fair, some of it is law enforcement's fault. Detectives take shortcuts. They get overworked and get too many cases. All of this can lead the DA to say, "Screw it, this is too difficult." But you can't say it's too much work when this person's life is on the line and their quality of life. There have got to be cases where you file because you know he did it.

Another detective, who noted that "generally a DA reject is where the path ends," added that "if the DA doesn't file there are few options. If new information comes out we can present the case again with the new evidence and try to get a filing then." Only two detectives, both of whom were with the LAPD, stated that a case rejected by the DA prior to arrest of the suspect should remain open as an investigation-continuing case. As one of them noted: "If we get a reject, it should be IC'd. They write 'lack of evidence' a lot but that poses a problem for us in clearing the case other [by exceptional means]. The detective manual says you have to have sufficient evidence."

Detectives' assessments of likelihood of prosecution. We asked detectives from the two law enforcement agencies to describe the characteristics of cases that were most and least likely to be prosecuted. They generally agreed that the cases with the best odds of prosecution were cases involving strangers, timely reporting by the victim, a victim who is willing to cooperate as the case moves forward, and evidence that could corroborate the victim's allegations. One LASD detective referred to these cases as "legitimate rapes," adding that none of the cases she had handled thus far fell into this category.

The type of case deemed least likely to be prosecuted is, to use one detective's characterization, the "infamous he said/she said" case, in which the suspect and the victim are nonstrangers, there are no witnesses, and the victim alleges rape but the suspect says it was consensual. As one detective noted, "Acquaintance rapes are the most difficult because there are rarely any witnesses, corroboration, or evidence because even if you have evidence of sexual activity, proving non-consent is the hard part." Another made a similar comment:

> The most difficult rapes are those that involve acquaintances. It's very hard to get them to file on the suspects because the suspect will say that the two of them were drinking and that sex was consensual. It's one person's word against another's and these cases don't get filed.

A number of respondents stated that the problems associated with cases involving nonstrangers are exacerbated by the fact that they also typically involve delayed reporting, which makes it difficult, if not impossible, to collect physical evidence from the crime scene or from the victim. According to one detective, "The hardest sexual assaults are the ones where the victim waits to disclose so we have lost all of our DNA, we have lost the crime scene, and potential witnesses that we could have contacted if she had reported sooner."

Another common theme was that cases involving "party rapes" or "party sexual assaults" (to use the detectives' terminology) were unlikely to be prosecuted. According to one respondent: "The majority of house party sexual assaults result in a DA reject. Those are difficult cases to prosecute. Although I approach each case impartially and believe everybody until there is a reason not to, typically the DA does not like them. Drunk people make horrible witnesses and victims." The detectives who mentioned these types of cases had a very cynical view of the victims who reported them. One stated that the motivation for reporting in these cases was "buyer's remorse"; that is, they involved "girls who have been partying and drinking and have sex with a man willingly." Another respondent, who claimed to have never yet handled a "good case," stated that "all of them that I have had involved rapes where the victims were extremely intoxicated or under the influence of drugs and woke up the next day and did not know what happened." Similar comments were made by a second detective, who said that the type of case most likely to be prosecuted "would be one involving a stranger where we have good evidence, possible witnesses, and timely reporting." This detective went on to say: "But where I work, these cases don't occur very often. I can't remember the last stranger assault that I had. The stuff I handle are the big parties where a girl gets drunk and wakes up in someone's bed the next day." Another respondent had an even more jaundiced view of the victims in these cases. This detective stated that many of his cases involved victims who went to bars, had too much to drink, and "made bad choices." He added, "We see a lot of self-victimization in these types of cases." An LAPD detective's comments offer a counterpoint to these views. This detective stated that in nonstranger cases where the suspect claims that the victim consented or cites alcohol use by the victim, "the next step is not DNA, it is evaluating injury, the condition of clothing, fresh complaint witnesses, and doing those other things to figure out who is telling a lie because someone is; there are other avenues that an investigator can take to establish who is lying."

Detectives from the LAPD also noted that the likelihood that the DA would file charges varied depending on the individual who was evaluating the case. One noted, for example, that some DAs "do everything they can to not file a case," adding that "some are afraid of trial, some fear losing." A second detective stated that there is one DA who "as soon as . . . he [or she] hears 'alcohol,' . . . is quick to reject it," and another noted that "some DAs will not go forward" once they find out that the victim is a prostitute. Two other detectives offered even harsher criticism of the DA's office:

> Certain district attorneys are horrible. Unless there is a signed confession and the assault is caught on video camera, these DAs will not file. And that is not fair to the victim because 90 percent of the victims we get are not perfect, pristine citizens. Sure, I had one 60-year-old woman sleeping with her husband when the suspect broke in. But God forbid if you are young and in college and drinking. You are fair game. Prostitutes as well.
>
> Often we have enough evidence to go to a preliminary hearing, but they may not want to take the case, they want more, a slam-dunk case. I often wonder why. Rumor is they get rated based on convictions, so they hesitate unless it's a sure win. . . . The problem is that there are career serial rapists who go unnoticed because the DA isn't filing.

These comments suggest that at least some LAPD detectives are frustrated by the DA's failure to file charges in sexual assault cases involving non-strangers that are not "slam-dunk" cases.

The law enforcement policies and practices that shape the handling and determine the outcome of sexual assault cases in Los Angeles are multifaceted and complex. Although the LAPD and the LASD use somewhat different procedures for investigating and clearing these types of cases, there are more similarities than differences. Moreover, detectives from the two agencies expressed remarkably similar views about issues such as the need for specialized training in the investigation of sexual assault reports, the criteria they use in deciding whether to make an arrest or clear a case by exceptional means, the prearrest screening process, and the types of cases most and least likely to be prosecuted. There were, on the other hand, more differences in detectives' understanding of the process of unfounding sexual assault reports; some respondents clearly understood and accurately interpreted the UCR guidelines but others were confused about the circumstances under which reports could be unfounded.

Detectives' explanations regarding the criteria they used in deciding whether to make an arrest generally fell into three overlapping categories: arrest if there is probable cause to do so; arrest if there is probable cause and the suspect is a threat to the victim or public safety; and arrest only if there is a good likelihood of prosecution and conviction. Detectives from both agencies also acknowledged the existence of a prearrest screening process in which problematic cases are presented to the DA for evaluation prior to arrest and, if the DA rejects the case for prosecution, the case is then cleared by exceptional means. Detectives also agreed that the cases most likely to be prosecuted were those involving strangers, a victim willing to cooperate as the case proceeds, and substantial evidence to corroborate the victim's allegations; by contrast, the cases least likely to be prosecuted were cases involving nonstrangers, a consent defense, and some type of risky behavior (e.g., drinking, using illegal drugs) on the part of the victim. In other words, the types of sexual assault cases that detectives are most likely to encounter are the cases that are least likely to be prosecuted.

In the next section, we discuss the perceptions and attitudes of the DDAs who were interviewed for this project.

Perceptions and Attitudes of DDAs

We interviewed 30 DDAs at 12 courthouses and office locations. We also spoke with several DDAs from the Family Violence Division of the DA's Office because they prosecute intimate partner sexual assault, and it was not uncommon for more senior DDAs to have experience working in both the Family Violence Division and the Victim Impact Program. The attorneys we interviewed had anywhere from 3 to 23 years of experience as prosecutors; the range of experience prosecuting sex crimes in particular ranged from 1 to 23 years. Like the detectives cited earlier, all of the interviewees stated that specialized training is fundamental to working sex crimes. They most frequently cited in-house trainings given by the DA's Office as well as seminars offered by the National DA's Association as the basis of their training to work sex crimes. The majority of respondents stated that whereas most DAs do not want to prosecute sex crimes or domestic violence, they requested the assignment because they wanted to make a difference. Although a number of respondents noted that working sex crimes is an important prerequisite for promotion, some stated that they reluctantly accepted a request from a supervisor to join a VIP unit, but that sex crimes are now the only cases they want to work.

> I was asked by the Head Deputy to join the VIP team. I didn't
> want to at the time and he [or she] said it was a minimum two-year
> commitment. The reason I didn't want to at that time was because
> I really didn't like the domestic violence [DV] cases. You have
> reluctant victims; the victim hates you, the defendant hates you, all
> are against you, and you're fighting for someone who doesn't want
> to be fought for. Almost all of my cases now are sex crimes. The only
> DV-related one I have [is one in which] the suspect beat up his
> wife—he was sleeping with her 12-year-old daughter.

The following sections describe the findings from interviews with DDAs specific to working with law enforcement and the factors that affect filing, charging, and plea-bargaining decisions.

Working with Law Enforcement

With few exceptions, DAs reported that they had good working relationships with detectives from both law enforcement agencies. Many respondents used terms such as "collaboration," "teamwork," and "good rapport" to describe these relationships. As one noted: "we deal with the same detectives . . . and they really care about what they're doing and everyone works so hard and is out to seek justice. We have a good bond with the detectives. They do great investigations." Other respondents stated that most, but not all, detectives are "smart and thorough" but that there are some who clearly are "burned out," "disinterested," and "don't want to do the work." One DA put it this way:

> I think that I have a fantastic relationship with most of my detectives.
> Most do a fabulous job with their investigations, but like anything

else there are some who are better than others. Right now, LAPD has serious budget restrictions and detectives are limited in terms of overtime. Things will start falling through the cracks if you have detectives who can only work 9 to 5. This is not a 9-to-5 job.

Another DA made a very similar comment, stating that

Ninety percent of detectives are good and care about victims and want to file a case. . . . They like the victims and believe in the case; they will do whatever it takes to get it filed. There are a few detectives that don't care about their cases and won't do extra work even when you ask, but those are few and far between.

Respondents also emphasized the importance of the first contact with victims and the potential damage to an investigation if the criminal justice system personnel who work sex crimes do not have effective interviewing skills and do not produce written documentation that is unbiased and professional.

Although some DAs mentioned specific LAPD divisions as exemplary, those who worked with detectives from the LASD's Special Victims Bureau consistently described them as the most professional and comprehensively trained detectives. Typical of these comments is the following: "I love LASD's Special Victims Bureau. I wish that 100 percent of my cases would come from them. . . . I think those that don't specialize don't care or put as much into it. They don't have the passion." Another DA made a similar comment, noting that the "Special Victims Bureau is specialized and has had the same people for a long time. The Special Victims Bureau of LASD is well trained. Newer detectives are always with a supervisor until they come in on their own. I have no complaints with LASD, but others, yes."

These comments suggest that DAs believe that the majority of detectives who work sex crimes in Los Angeles are well trained and competent. Their views of the LASD's Special Victims Bureau, which are especially positive, highlight the value of using a specialized unit to investigate these sensitive and complex cases.

The Prearrest Screening Process

We discovered through analysis of data on the outcomes of sexual assaults reported to the LAPD and the LASD that a significant proportion of cases were presented to the DA prior to the arrest of the suspect, and if the DA refused to file charges based either on lack of victim cooperation or insufficient evidence, the case was cleared by exceptional means. We asked the DAs to comment on the prearrest screening process and to indicate whether it occurred in all types of cases or was unique to sexual assault. Respondents acknowledged that the police did present cases for evaluation prior to arrest and that if a case was not "fileable," an arrest would not be made. Although some stated that the types of cases likely to be presented to them prior to arrest were those where the "suspect is in the wind" or "can't be located," most indicated that these cases typically involved victims who were not willing to cooperate as the case moved forward or a victim and suspect who were acquainted in some way along with a lack of corroboration of the victim's allegations. Prosecutors stated that these types of cases were likely to be rejected during the prearrest screening process and that detectives "usually won't make an arrest because we won't be filing the case."

A number of DAs stated that detectives presented cases to them prior to arrest so that they (the DAs) could advise the detectives regarding the types of evidence needed to make the case fileable. In fact, some stated that arresting the suspect early in the investigation was not a good strategy unless the suspect posed a threat to the victim or to public safety. According to one DA: "One of the main reasons we don't want them arrested prior to us having input is that it destroys potential investigative strategies. It impacts our ability to get a pretext phone call. So typically we say, 'Why did you arrest him? You blew the investigation.'" Another made a similar comment, noting that

> We don't want to tip our hand and let the suspect know that he is under investigation. If he doesn't know that he is under investigation, he doesn't have time to come up with a story or an alibi. We need the time to put the case together because most of them are one-on-one situations.

DAs also emphasized that office policy required, with very few exceptions, an interview with the victim before charges could be filed. As a result, it made sense to wait and "gauge the strength of the case and the credibility of the victim" before making the arrest.

We also asked DAs whether prearrest screening occurred in other types of crimes or was unique to sexual assault. Although some stated that it happened in other serious crimes like homicide and robbery, most indicated that it occurred only in sexual assault and, to a lesser extent, domestic violence cases. Typical responses were that "this is unique to sex crimes because we have specific filing standards and the nature of these cases is that they are harder to prove" and that "this is unique to sex crimes as far as I know—I don't know of any other unit that does that." Another attorney, who contrasted what happens in sexual assault cases with what happens in robbery cases, explained it this way:

> With robbery, for example, you are more likely to have immediate reporting and evidence of a robbery. The person will have the

evidence of the robbery, and they will probably spend the money if we wait. It is unique to sex crimes and part of the reason for that is that there are women who will say, because they are upset, "Hey, this happened," and you don't want to run out and put someone in jail, especially with late reporting. They [the police] want to make sure they're not arresting someone just on someone's word.

In summary, prosecutors described the prearrest screening process, which most acknowledged was unique to sexual assault, as a result of their office policy requiring a prefiling interview with the victim and as helpful to build cases that require more investigation and stronger evidence to support a filing. However, some prosecutors, like detectives who stated that they would not make an arrest unless there was a strong likelihood of prosecution and conviction, said that there should not be an arrest unless the case was fileable.

Charging Decisions in Sexual Assault Cases

We asked the DDAs interviewed for this project a series of questions designed to identify the factors they take into account in making charging decisions and the evidentiary hurdles they face in prosecuting different types of sexual assault cases. When asked about the filing standard that guides charging decisions in their office, respondents unanimously agreed that their standard was a trial sufficiency standard (Jacoby, 1980) that required proof beyond a reasonable doubt and a strong likelihood of conviction at a jury trial. As numerous respondents stated, "We cannot file a case by policy unless we believe that we can prove it in court to a jury." Although many acknowledged that most cases are not tried by juries, they nonetheless insisted that they "would not be following the law" if charging decisions were based on something less than proof beyond a reasonable doubt. According to one DA:

> That doesn't mean we worry about winning or not. We are happy to go to trial because it should be filed and should be a trial. But we do have to file according to the law and if there is no chance it could be proven then that wouldn't be a proper file.

Another attorney provided a more detailed explanation of the filing standard that focused on the legal elements of the crime and the suspect's possible defense as well as proof beyond a reasonable doubt:

> Is there a valid defense? Standard operating procedure is that I need to know are the facts there—legally sufficient admissible evidence of all elements of the crime, the identity of the person who did the

crime? [And] we [must] believe he is guilty and believe a jury would find him guilty even after considering all of the foreseeable defenses.

DAs provided two additional justifications for their reliance on a trial sufficiency standard, one of which focused on fairness to the victim and the other of which focused on protection of the rights of suspects (defendants). A number of respondents noted that it was "not fair to the victim" to file charges against the defendant only to have the case dismissed later in the process or to have the jury return a not-guilty verdict. Typical of these comments was the following:

> Our ethical duty is we cannot prosecute a case we don't think we can prove beyond a reasonable doubt. In a lot of the he said/she said cases . . . I truly believe the victim but I don't think I can prove it to a jury. I tell them it's not fair to them to put them through the process if I don't think we can win. It's very stressful and emotional, and to put them through the year the case is pending and to have a jury come back "not guilty," then they're not just a victim of the rape. Then the jury is saying "We don't believe you were a victim." I don't think that's helpful to them. We want to put someone through it only if we think we can get justice for them.

Other respondents focused on their ethical obligation to defendants and the presumption of innocence. These comments were similar to those made by detectives who stated that they did not arrest based on probable cause alone because it was not "fair to put a rape charge" on the suspect unless there was compelling evidence of his guilt.

> If it ever starts to look like a he said/she said, I may have to reject it. I may believe the victim, but the jury instructions say if two people are saying different things you have to give the defendant the benefit of the doubt. If you hear him saying one thing and she's saying [another] thing and I don't have a witness or direct evidence, they [the jury] have to take his side. To put a defendant through this process is a deprivation of his life and liberty. I am not here to harass people with cases and need to know I can prove it beyond a reasonable doubt.

As these comments illustrate, DDAs emphasized that they had an ethical duty to file charges only in cases with a strong likelihood of conviction and that it was not fair to either victims or suspects to file charges if the evidence did not rise to the standard of proof beyond a reasonable doubt.

When asked what factors would lead them to reject charges, all of the DAs we interviewed emphasized that "lack of corroboration" was the primary factor and that this was particularly critical in the "he said/she said" cases, in which the victim alleges that she was sexually assaulted and the suspect admits the sexual activity but claims that it was consensual. Many respondents stated emphatically that "if it lacks corroboration, I would not file" or "I would reject if there is no corroboration." Most also emphasized that office policy requires some type of corroboration to file charges, despite the fact that California law does not require corroboration to obtain a conviction for sexual assault; these respondents noted that corroboration is a practical, rather than a legal, requirement:

> Our office policy is that sex crimes are not filed without some type of corroboration of the victim's testimony. I used to think that this was terrible—I don't need corroboration in a robbery—but I have come to believe that it is a good thing. We don't want to put victims, especially children, through the process unless there is a good chance of conviction.
>
> I can have a woman sitting in that chair and I know that she is telling me the truth but I also know that I cannot file the case because I don't have any corroboration. I know that I have rejected cases where I truly believed the victim and knew that she was a crime victim but there was nothing that we could do to prove that case in court.

The attorney who made that statement also noted that even if charges are not filed against the suspect, the fact that the allegations are documented means that if the suspect does something similar in the future, it will make the new case stronger. This respondent added:

> This is something that I tell victims if I reject the case: "You did the right thing by coming in even if the evidence is not strong enough to file the case. If he does this again, to you or to someone else, we have the documentation from this case that will make subsequent cases stronger."

DAs stated that in cases in which the victim and the suspect are acquainted or are intimate partners, they are "looking for medical evidence: bruising, tearing, defensive wounds," or, absent that, some type of admission by the suspect or eyewitness testimony that can corroborate the victim's allegations. They also noted that delayed reporting complicated such cases by making it difficult, if not impossible, to collect any type of physical evidence and that DNA evidence was not particularly helpful, because "the guy will say it was consensual and that is the classic he said/she said and it is very difficult at that point. A lot of those cases do not get filed." Another respondent referred to these types of cases as "technical rapes":

> She says no but he didn't stop and technically that is a rape, but the problem is context is everything. Jurors are not going to hear just, "I said stop but he didn't." They want to know what was going on, how well they know each other, and often those factors do not work well for the victim.

Another factor that predicted case rejection, according to DAs, was alcohol or drug use at the time of the incident. Respondents generally agreed that the victim's use of alcohol or illegal drugs increased the odds of charge rejection but the suspect's use of these substances either had no effect on charging or increased the odds of charge rejection by bolstering the suspect's assertion that he had reason to assume the victim had consented. Many DAs stressed that jurors do not like cases in which the victim drinks to excess and either passes out or does not remember what happened. They emphasized that it is not the drinking or illegal drug use per se that increases the likelihood of charge rejection, but the fact that victims who are under the influence of alcohol or illegal drugs often cannot recount with any degree of specificity what happened to them. As one respondent noted:

> It is a reality in reviewing these cases that alcohol is present. It doesn't make it a reject, but it makes the case, from an evidence standpoint, complicated because if talking about adults, it makes arguing lack of consent very hard. What if she consented, but she just doesn't remember? It doesn't affect credibility, it affects the ability to recollect.

DAs also stated that the defendant's assertion that the sexual activity was consensual carries more weight if the victim was under the influence of alcohol or illegal drugs, since the defendant "can say he thought the victim was giving him signs it was consensual." This respondent added that "if the victim was on drugs and alcohol and can't remember everything then jurors believe the defendant reasonably [could have] believed the victim was consenting, unless it was really forcible rape with injuries."

Other DAs evinced a more cynical view of victims who were drinking or using illegal drugs at the time of the incident. Echoing the comments of the detective who was quoted earlier in this chapter, these attorneys described the victim's allegations of sexual assault as stemming either from "buyer's remorse" or from "regrettable sex." According to one respondent:

"It is hard with those cases to tell the difference between being taken advantage of while drunk versus being raped. People may have done things they wouldn't do when sober but it doesn't rise to the point of rape—it's more like regrettable sex." Another attorney, who emphasized that the victim's use of alcohol and illegal drugs played a more important role in nonstranger cases, stated that it came into play even in cases involving strangers:

> Alcohol or drugs play a large role when it is an acquaintance case and we are discussing consent. Does she remember what happened and is the jury likely to believe it? Does she have buyer's remorse as a result of her behavior and how is the jury likely to view this? A woman who passes out and can't remember what happened—this will affect her credibility and how difficult it will be to prove the case. If it is a stranger rape, I am less concerned about whether drugs and alcohol are present, but even in this type of case it is going to impugn the credibility of the victim.

Postcharging Decisions: Dismissals and Plea Bargains

We asked prosecutors a number of questions about their postcharging decisions—what would lead to the dismissal of a sexual assault case after a defendant had been arraigned, what types of plea bargains were negotiated in these cases, and whether the negotiations focused on the number of counts, the severity of charges, or the sentence. Prosecutors stated that the case would be dismissed following the filing of charges if the victim refused to cooperate as the case moved forward, if the victim's story changed and became less believable, or if exculpatory evidence was discovered. Typical of their comments are the following:

> If we found out that the victim was lying, if there was exculpatory evidence, or if the victim suddenly was completely uncooperative.
>
> If we are going to straight out dismiss it, it would be because we can't find the victim. Or if evidence that exculpates the defendant is found—for example, she says it was one guy but the DNA comes back and indicates that it was someone else.
>
> A situation in which we find too many holes in the story and the victim was not honest in the initial report. If you don't even know if your victim is telling the truth, you can't go forward. If the victim doesn't want to cooperate with prosecution we don't pursue it.
>
> After the preliminary hearing you are still gathering evidence and doing the investigation. As time progresses, you may realize that the evidence you have is not as strong as you thought it was.

We sometimes use the phrase, "the case fell apart," because something comes out about the victim that pokes holes in her story and that the defense is going to use against us at trial.

Several respondents, however, noted that an uncooperative victim who was refusing to testify at trial did not necessarily mean that the case would be dismissed. These DAs explained that under California law they can present the transcript of the victim's testimony at the preliminary hearing at the trial, provided the defense attorney had an opportunity to cross-examine the victim at the preliminary hearing. These respondents emphasized that they would do this only if there was strong and credible evidence of the defendant's guilt. As one DA put it:

If the victim disappears or refuses to cooperate we don't necessarily have to dismiss the case. If we have done the prelim [preliminary hearing], we have her testimony and can go to trial without her. But we don't like to do that. If we do, we need strong corroborative evidence outside of the victim's statement. If you don't have the victim and the corroborative evidence is not strong, you may have no choice but to dismiss the case.

Another DA provided an example of a case that was dismissed even though the victim's testimony at the preliminary hearing had been preserved and could be introduced at trial. This attorney explained that there was corroborative evidence from the forensic medical exam but the evidence corroborated the victim's story only if it was true that the victim had never had sex before. During the prefiling interview the victim claimed that she had not had sexual relations with anyone prior to the sexual assault incident. When the victim recanted following the preliminary hearing, the attorney was prepared to proceed by introducing her testimony from the preliminary hearing into evidence at trial. However, the attorney decided to dismiss the case after discovering that the defense was going to introduce evidence that the victim had a prior sexual relationship with someone other than the suspect.

When asked about plea-bargaining practices in sexual assault cases, DAs were nearly unanimous in stating that negotiations focused on the type and length of sentence; they indicated that count and charge bargaining occurred infrequently. Respondents indicated that they seldom reduced the most serious charge from sexual assault to a nonsex offense. According to one DA: "Whatever we file, we try to get. We usually don't plea down to a lesser charge. We put those charges in the complaint because we believe the evidence demonstrates it." In addition, respondents emphasized the importance of securing a plea to a charge that would require the offender to register as a sex offender and that reflected the reality of the defendant's conduct.

However, some did indicate that whether the offender would be required to register was negotiable if it was a "borderline" case or a case of unlawful sex with a minor. They also stated that plea-bargaining strategies vary depending on the courthouse and the VIP supervisor, with some indicating that all plea offers must be approved by the supervisor and others indicating that they have discretion to offer pleas in certain types of cases. One DA, for example, noted that although generally "penetration equals prison," this was not "a hard and fast rule," adding that "if you go to different offices you will find significantly different dispositions because jurors and crimes differ in each jurisdiction."

Regarding the practice of sentence bargaining, a majority of respondents stated that they were "looking for prison" in sexual assault cases and that therefore the negotiations focused on the amount of time the offender would serve. They emphasized that the "offer" would vary depending on such things as whether the offender used a weapon, whether there were any aggravating circumstances, the offender's criminal history, and the strength of evidence in the case. As one DA noted, "If it is a weak case and we have an uncooperative victim there will be a better offer." Some respondents indicated that they would offer probation in certain types of cases. One, for example, stated that in cases without a significant amount of corroboration, "I may think that I would rather have a bird in the hand than in the bush and get five years of probation and registration as a sex offender rather than an acquittal at trial." Another stated that probation was an option in cases involving "party girls." A probation sentence was justified for offenders in such cases, according to this attorney, because "he wasn't seen as a predator, like the guy grabbing the girls off the streets. He was more of an opportunist. He saw the girls having sex with everyone else and so he thought, 'Why don't I?'" However, a third attorney stressed that offenders in some types of cases—for instance, penetration of a victim under the age of fourteen—would not receive an offer of probation regardless of the other factors in the case.

Another common theme from the interviews was that the timing of the defendant's plea affected the negotiations, with the "best offers" being made early in the case. According to one respondent:

> When cases are first brought before the court, we give the best offer. It's often not pleading to every single count, but [rather] some version of the counts, for the best sentence. We look at the seriousness of the crime, the defendant's rap sheet, and we will keep the offer open until prelim. The minute the victim has to testify and relive these horrors then the offer goes up.

Similarly, a second DA stated that the offer might be five years before the preliminary hearing, but eight years after it, and a third indicated that "we say if he takes it [a plea] today, then I'll give him probation. If you wait too long, all of your bargaining chips are gone."

Interviews with DDAs focused on their relationships with law enforcement and the factors that they take into account in making charging and plea-bargaining decisions in sexual assault cases. Respondents stated that they generally had a positive relationship with law enforcement, particularly with the LASD's Special Victim's Bureau, and acknowledged that many cases are rejected by their office prior to arrest. Some emphasized that the prearrest screening process was designed to improve the odds of prosecution by identifying evidentiary weaknesses that could be remedied prior to arresting the suspect, but others stated that the process was designed to identify weak cases that were not fileable and said that these cases should not lead to the arrest of the suspect.

It is clear that the filing standard used by the Los Angeles DA's Office in sexual assault cases is a trial sufficiency standard that requires proof beyond a reasonable doubt in order to file charges. DDAs stressed that they had an ethical duty to file charges only when the likelihood of conviction at trial was high and only if there was some type of corroboration of the victim's allegations. They also agreed that cases involving nonstrangers were more difficult to prosecute and that this was exacerbated if the victim was under the influence of alcohol or illegal drugs at the time of the incident. Respondents stated that case dismissal, which occurred infrequently, was likely only if the "case fell apart" or the victim refused to testify at trial and her testimony from the preliminary hearing could not be introduced at trial. They also noted that plea negotiations focused on the type and length of the sentence, and they stated that in most, but not all, sexual assaults they were looking for a prison sentence.

Conclusion

We began this chapter by describing a sexual assault case involving a victim and suspect who were acquainted. In spite of the fact that the suspect admitted, during a recorded pretext phone call, that he forced the victim to have sex with him, the investigating officer did not arrest him. Instead, he presented the case to the DA, who rejected it based on insufficient evidence. The detective then cleared the case by exceptional means.

Although we did not ask detectives and DAs to respond to this particular case, our interviews reveal that had we done so, most would not have been surprised at the outcome of the case. Both detectives and prosecutors agreed that problematic cases—especially the so-called he said/she said cases, in which the victim alleges she was sexually assaulted but the suspect claims that the sexual activity was consensual—are presented to the DA prior to arrest; they also agreed that these types of cases are likely to be rejected for prosecution based on insufficient evidence or lack of victim cooperation and, when that occurs, are cleared—or solved for UCR reporting purposes—by exceptional means.

As this scenario suggests, the decision to arrest in sexual assault cases is influenced by detectives' expectations regarding the likelihood that the DA will file charges. Most detectives stated that they would arrest based on probable cause alone if the suspect was a stranger to the victim or a threat to the victim or public safety, and a minority insisted that their arrest decisions in nonstranger cases were not affected by their assessments of whether the DA would file charges. However, most detectives agreed that problematic cases were presented to the DA prior to making an arrest, with an expectation that the DA would reject them for prosecution and that the defendant would therefore not be arrested.

The existence of this prearrest screening process reflects both the fact that many detectives believe that there is no point in making an arrest if the prosecutor is not going to file charges and the fact that the DA will only file charges if the victim is cooperative and there is proof beyond a reasonable doubt that the suspect committed the crime. Use of a trial sufficiency standard, in other words, leads to a high rate of case rejection and encourages detectives to bring cases to the DA for screening prior to arrest. It also means that in a substantial number of cases the decision to arrest is based, not on the law enforcement standard of probable cause, but on the DA's filing standard of proof beyond a reasonable doubt. We return to this issue in Chapter 6, which focuses on the misuse of the exceptional clearance.

Notes

1. LAPD divisions have designated "tables" specific to homicide, sexual assault, robbery, burglary, auto theft and so on. Detectives investigate only those types of cases specific to the table to which they currently are assigned.

2. For details see http://file.lacounty.gov/lasd/cms1_145173.pdf.

3. The persistence of corroboration requirements raises questions about the true impact of rape law reform, as was demonstrated during the US Senate hearing on rape in September 2010 (US Senate, 2010). Along with her testimony, Professor Michelle Madden Dempsey provided a copy of a letter sent to the Cook County State's Attorney's Office in Illinois alleging that

> the Cook County State's Attorney's Office is generally not authorizing felony charges for sexual assault reported by victims against nonstrangers unless there is "corroborative evidence" such as bodily injury, a third-party witness, or an offender confession. Whether or not this custom is explicitly endorsed by written policy, it appears that the Cook County State's Attorney's Office has adopted a charging standard that effectively adds extra-statutory elements to the crime of sexual assault. This practice

protects most rapists from the threat of criminal prosecution, devastates most victims who seek criminal justice assistance, and leads to the continued silence of most victims of sexual assault. (US Senate, 2010)

4. In a few instances Police Officer IIs and Police Officer IIIs who work sex cases volunteered to be interviewed.

3

Detective and Prosecutor
Perspectives

In 2008, a sexual assault was reported to the Los Angeles County
Sheriff's Department (LASD) involving a suspect and a victim who met the
night before in a West Hollywood restaurant while the victim dined with a
female friend. A detective attempted to interview the victim as she recovered from emergency surgery due to a vulvar hematoma sustained during
the incident. From a hospital bed and still groggy from anesthesia, the victim told the detective the suspect "is a nice guy" and added, "I don't want
to get him in trouble"; her desire was to get a rape kit to find out what happened and if she had been raped. The detective characterized the victim in
the police report as "uncooperative," noting her state of mind as "in shock
and denial of the event."

In subsequent interviews with the victim and the friend who accompanied her that evening, the detective learned that between 8:30 and 10:30 PM
the two women shared chili fries and the victim drank three shots of tequila
and one beer. During this time they began chatting with the suspect, who
introduced himself as the manager of a nearby nightclub. When the victim's
friend left the restaurant because she had to work the next morning, the victim decided to stay, saying she would get home on her own a little later.
The victim's friend told law enforcement that when she left the restaurant
the victim was "fine," "holding her liquor," and "not incapacitated." She
also stated that the victim "is a very conservative and religious girl and
would not engage in sex with someone she just met." The suspect and victim eventually left the restaurant together in the suspect's car. He drove her
to the club he managed—it was closed that evening but he had access to the
building—where they drank a glass of champagne. Soon thereafter the victim began to feel dizzy and asked the suspect to take her home, but he
stated he felt too inebriated to drive that far (the detective noted her house
was only two miles from the suspect's) and would prefer she came to his

house instead. The victim felt uncomfortable with this course of action and called a taxi soon after arriving at his house. Her last memory of the evening is the taxi company calling her cell phone; the next thing she remembers is waking up the following morning in the suspect's bed wearing only her underwear and a pair of the suspect's boxer shorts, with bruises on her neck, arms, and legs, and a swollen and bloody vagina.

The victim asked the suspect to drive her home and she immediately went to a free clinic due to her vaginal pain and bleeding. She was told her injuries were consistent with a sexual assault and she needed to be seen right away at a hospital. The emergency room doctor who completed the rape kit told the detective it is highly unlikely a penis caused the victim's injuries and they more likely resulted from a fist or object. Analysis of the rape kit indicated the victim's urine contained benzodiazepines and opiates, but there was no evidence to suggest the victim knowingly ingested them. The detective assigned to this case interviewed the emergency room doctor, the victim, her friend (the witness), and the suspect and his three house-guests. The detective also served a search warrant at the suspect's house and retrieved bloody clothing and secured video from the bar area at the restaurant where the victim and suspect met. When interviewed, the suspect told law enforcement the following before referring any further questions to his lawyer: he and the victim had consensual sex in two different positions; it was not rough; and he never placed any foreign objects inside her. The detective presented the case file to a deputy district attorney (DDA) for felony filing consideration and it was rejected for insufficient evidence. The suspect in this case was never arrested despite the victim's severity of injuries, immediate reporting, and the existence of probable cause.

This case demonstrates how victim characteristics—particularly in cases involving nonstrangers—affect law enforcement officials' perceptions of the feasibility of prosecution, and, as discussed in Chapter 2, subsequent decisions about whether to present the case to a DDA pre- or postarrest. In this chapter we examine how victim characteristics and credibility affect the handling and outcome of sexual assaults reported to and prosecuted by the Los Angeles Police Department (LAPD), the LASD, and the Los Angeles County District Attorney's (DA's) Office. We use qualitative data from our interviews with detectives and DDAs to describe their perceptions of the challenges faced by victims when reporting a sexual assault, strategies for building rapport with victims, and how they assess victim credibility. As the following sections demonstrate, both LAPD and LASD interviewees' responses demonstrated what we categorized as either an "innocent until proven guilty" approach toward victims, which recognized the complexities specific to these types of cases, or a "guilty until proven innocent" approach that emphasized stranger rape as the only "real" rape.

LAPD and LASD Detectives on
Working with Sexual Assault Victims

Perceptions of Challenges
Faced by Victims When Reporting

> Patrol officers, instead of treating [the rape victim] like a victim, center more on disproving her testimony. The victim is traumatized and/or she is intoxicated at the time of interview. Their interviewing techniques are not the same as ours. We do not try to disprove her. We just want her story. The patrol officer writes the report and notes all the inconsistencies.
>
> —LAPD detective

We asked detectives to describe their perceptions of the difficulties faced by victims when reporting a sexual assault. Both LAPD and LASD respondents overwhelmingly stated that the police are the biggest challenge in terms of patrol officers and detectives who routinely question victims' "righteousness," along with the overall invasiveness of this type of criminal investigation, which was described by some as "a homicide except you live with it forever." Respondents also commented on the personal challenges for victims such as blame and shame, especially for those who are acquainted with the suspect and must contend with the social, emotional, financial, and logistic sequelae of social intertwinement. Likewise, many detectives stated that the biggest challenges stem from the court process itself and overcoming the biases of jurors, judges, and society as a whole. An LAPD detective shared the following story:

> There has only been one case in all of the years that I have been investigating sex crimes where the DA filed charges in a she said/he said situation. It involved a schizophrenic victim who was off her meds and was raped by someone she met at a bus stop. She was a transient and went with this guy; they drank and hung out for five hours and he ended up forcing her to orally cop[ulate with] him. She did not want to go to court but I arrested him anyway and I about fell off my chair when [the DDA] agreed to file charges. She may regret it later, but she did file.

Conversely, other detectives reserved empathy for "real" crime victims, as demonstrated by this LASD respondent:

> The fact that so many nonvictims report crimes affects law enforcement response to the crime and to the real victims. I wish it wasn't this way, but we see so many women who aren't telling the

truth that it affects our attitudes toward victims who are telling the truth. It makes us suspicious of all victims. So, if somehow we could convince the nonvictims to not file false complaints, it would make things better for the real victims.

Similarly, an LAPD detective commented:

I have thought about this a lot. The righteous victims don't know where to turn. If they were just to notify anybody, they do not know what to do. If they are actual victims, they are traumatized and they don't know where to turn. They know to call 911 but after that they do not know what to expect. It is also their upbringing. They have to be taught to trust in law enforcement for help.

Another LAPD detective stated:

We see a lot of self-victimization. Girls who go to Hollywood clubs and drink alone. [You] don't need to drug her, as she will drink until she is drunk. Guys will be there at closing time looking for the drunkest girl in the bar. They will buy her one drink and she will end up leaving with him. As one suspect said to me, "Everyone knows that drunks are easy."

Other detectives offered reflections specific to the department bureaucracy, dynamics with the DA's Office, and the overall investigative process as being the most challenging for victims. For instance, recalling personal experience, a detective stated, "I worked seventeen years of patrol. We do not have any training for report writing. There is not enough training on report writing. The report writing and interviewing skills are not there." Another stated that it boils down to

the casual indifference of patrol officers who don't have the experience to know what they're dealing with; the bureaucratic face of the department that is not cognizant between property crime and a rape. Officers know they have to take them [victims] to the [local rape treatment center], but [they adopt a] by-the-numbers approach rather than a "What can I do to help this victim?" approach. It is a major training issue, which is something that cannot be totally changed. Victims have the most problems at that first contact with law enforcement where they feel not understood or judged. A P-II [Police Officer II] working the front desk who has a victim walk in to tell him she was raped, he should go to an interview room [with the victim for privacy]. Some issues have to do with manpower, and in the best of all possible worlds an officer would call someone from the field. The initial first contact is most problematic. Patrol doesn't ask the right questions. It's an education level. They will take a rape report and there is no [mention of] insertion of a penis into a vagina; they haven't asked what happened. Our weak, lame, and lazy are put on the front desk. You've just been raped and you have to talk to the grumpy guy who can't work the field.

Many detectives echoed this sentiment. For example, an LAPD detective stated the biggest challenge was

Us. Sometimes you [the victim] will get good people, otherwise you get people who are sure you are lying. [They might say,] "I asked her, 'If [you] didn't remember the concert, how do you know you didn't consent to sex?'" You go through hell: make the report, undergo the exam, feel disgusting. *Often I feel we victimize the victim more than the suspect does.* (Emphasis added)

An LASD detective described it as follows:

They have to relive and retell the incident over and over again; fear and embarrassment about what happened to them; fear that people will pass judgment on their choices. I do think that there are times when you get so used to hearing the same old song and dance and don't see the evidence to back up their statements and so you judge them off the bat. But things are getting better. I would say that 99 percent of our deputies will take the report even if they don't think that it happened and then allow a detective to make the decision as to whether something happened or not. An incident can be documented as "Suspicious Circumstances, Possible Rape." This is a noncriminal report, but it is referred to me and when I get enough information to show that it really happened, I can change the status to a crime.

This statement demonstrates the extent to which patrol and detectives function as gatekeepers to the criminal justice process for sexual assault victims. They decide whether and what type of documentation (a crime report, a noncrime report, or nothing at all) will result from their contact with a victim, and the quality and depth of the subsequent investigation will be an important factor in the DA's filing decision. Emphasizing the role of bias as a factor that impacts the quality of investigations, an LAPD detective supervisor stated:

I am not confident that every officer keeps their personal thoughts to themselves and remains unbiased. We've had a lot of victims say they "would have gone for medical treatment but I knew he [patrol] didn't want to take me." Then we see "Victim refused medical treatment" [in the report] and we know that's a red flag. Plus her own obstacles, how she will deal with family, adjust to counseling, and get all of that in their life. Plus, court is a scary world they don't know how to deal with. Everything they see on TV [is] of persecution of victims, but I joke they persecute the detectives because defense attorneys see that juries don't like that [persecuting victims]. But, first responding officers, plus another big obstacle is most detectives have so much work to do that the victim may not be contacted for a while. We try within two to three days but it doesn't always happen.

Often detectives supplemented their answers with a story. Consider the following, which segues into the other notable arenas of challenges for victims when reporting, including, but not limited to, their personal challenges, social support (or lack thereof), and the court process:

> I handled a case involving GHB[1] where the victim was drugged. The victim did a pretext phone call, which was successful; . . . the suspect admitted that he slipped it to her without her consent. I found GHB in his refrigerator. I asked my victim, "Have you ever done this or that before, it doesn't matter, just tell me." She denied she was a party girl, [said she had never] done GHB before. In the course of my investigation I came across a witness that was supposed to be used for corroborative purposes who said she was no stranger to GHB and did that all of the time. The DA didn't like the fact the victim had lied to me and to her and rejected the case. And this came from her own personal experience. The DA had just finished a high-profile GHB case and put herself on the line for the victim and it was like the scenario I described earlier. The defense unearthed evidence proving the victim was lying about something else and perjured herself on the stand. It left a bad taste in [the] DA's mouth and it's one of those things—you just say, "I'm not going down that road." We all bring biases. Unfortunately the timing was such the DA was coming off the heels from a distasteful scenario where the victim proved to be a liar and they said they [wouldn't] go down that road. I took the case to the City Attorney's Office and misdemeanor charges were filed. Lessons learned. Credibility is huge. The victim's credibility is huge.

This scenario alludes to an issue raised by many detectives; that is, the fear, shame, and self-blame experienced by victims in contemplation and during the process of reporting to the police. For instance, a detective noted that victims have a "fear of not being believed; an embarrassment. They're worried they will be blamed for putting themselves in a bad situation because of their judgment." Another stated:

> They have a lot [of challenges]: (1) coming forward, which is difficult to do. I'm positive there are so many others out there that don't have the courage to go through the process; (2) the court system; (3) family dynamics—we have to notify family members, the family breakups that happen, all of which the victim has to live with; (4) not being believed; (5) when they are raped by a husband, boyfriend, cousin, etc.—those are major obstacles they have to live with.

An LASD detective described the biggest challenge for victims as

> whether they are going to be believed that something did happen. The field deputy just gets the facts and may send a message that . . . [she or] he does not believe the victim. A first encounter that is kind of negative. We know how to ask the questions and get the victim to disclose. We need better training during the academy regarding how to talk to victims of sexual abuse due to their fear of retaliation and fear of getting in trouble.

Another emphasized that the primary challenges are "fear, retaliation, the court process, alienation from family, and fear of the unknown." These challenges are so great, they noted, that it sometimes prevents victims from wanting to criminally prosecute so they can focus instead on internal healing:

> They're ashamed. A lot [of victims] feel like they could have prevented it from happening. Facing the fact of what happened [is also difficult]. If they're going through rehab [rehabilitation] and doing the 12 steps [Alcoholics Anonymous], it is just closure for them. They're not interested in prosecuting the guy; it's just getting it over with.

Cultural issues are relevant as well. For instance, an LAPD detective noted: "Depending on the victim they are apprehensive, especially in the Hispanic community. They do not want to talk, want to keep it to themselves, and move on." Reflecting on the extent to which suspects benefit from these difficulties for victims, a detective emphasized that "getting over the embarrassment [is difficult]; even the kids are ashamed. They somehow feel responsible. How [are we] to convey to victims that whatever you did you didn't deserve to be a victim? There are a lot of guys who get away with it." Similarly, an LASD detective characterized it as: "They are embarrassed and ashamed because of the negative connotation of rape. They don't want anyone to know what happened to them. Some of my victims have lost friends when they report the crime and cooperate with us."

Finally, in terms of the court process, an LAPD detective stated the biggest challenges relate to "[the loss of] confidentiality and embarrassment; having to tell family. Also [their] safety, and the repercussions of talking in court." More specifically, a detective asserted:

> It is very difficult to talk about sex crimes in particular. Some people do not like saying the body parts. I had a case that went to jury trial recently, and the reason the girl did not disclose the oral copulation was because she was embarrassed. She did not want her family to know that. It is difficult to report and then see it through. [They have to] tell the story too many times.

Establishing Rapport

Consistent with the discussion in Chapter 2 of the need for specialized training to work sexual assault cases, many LAPD and LASD respondents reported that the onus is on the detective to interview victims in a way that is sensitive to the trauma of sexual assault because, as one detective who encapsulated the sentiments of many stated, "Most [victims] are cooperative based on how they are treated." This requires setting a tone of sincerity and respect on first contact with victims to facilitate cooperation and maximize the likelihood of full disclosure about the incident. For instance, an LAPD detective stated, "Initial contact is huge. A lot I have learned through trial and error. . . . As far as interviewing skills, that is something that is critical. If you don't have sincerity the victim is going to feel it." Detectives emphasized the importance of meeting victims halfway to build rapport by putting them at ease, explaining every detail of the investigative process, and "getting to know them as a person and not just a victim." Examples of this include the following:

> I try to make them feel as comfortable as possible; explain the process as candidly as possible, walk them through it, provide them with resources and let them know what's available. I also try to convey that regardless of what the circumstances are, we still are in their corner but they need to be honest with me. For the most part they are not uncooperative.
>
> First thing is putting them at ease and showing them I'm on their side. Getting them to relax, and then I tell them [an] admonition, if you will: "Sometimes people are compelled to omit things when telling a story to make themselves feel more credible/believable;

well, don't do that. Tell us the truth. We've heard it all. You're not alone with this, it has happened before, just tell us the entire story."

In interviewing the victim, you have to explain what your job is. Don't jump to conclusions and say, "Well, you were out drinking." I explain everything, I never raise my voice, never accuse them. Explain the entire process. They have been through a lot to begin with, the trauma of sexual assault; if they are not willing to talk to us then, we tell them that we will do it later.

The main thing that I do with my victims is just listen. They have just been through a traumatic experience, and I imagine, what if this was my family member, my daughter?

Initially I just listen and keep an open mind, and if there are inconsistencies in their statements I will make note of those, because ultimately my job is to seek the truth. But I think that having an approach that is more empathetic allows them to feel more comfortable with me and trust in the system, perhaps, that everything will be done to bring justice to the case. And if the DA still decides to reject the case, the victim is confident that I did everything I could. I always want to project to the victim that: (1) I take the case seriously; (2) I have an open mind; (3) every stone is turned; nothing is left undone.

We try to feel for their emotion. Convey to them that their feelings are the normal cycle: fear, remorse, anger. Offer them comfort and convey that we will work with them on the case.

Detectives' statements also highlighted the simultaneous relevance and irrelevance of gender in detective/victim interactions. For instance, a male LASD detective noted:

It is different depending on who it is: you introduce yourself and tell her that you are sorry that this happened to her. You ask if she would feel more comfortable talking to a female detective. I only had one case where this happened. I've been told after the fact by victims that they would rather talk to a male detective because they think other women will judge them and their behavior. I begin by just talking with them about their family, about what they do, and then go from there. I don't just jump into questions about the incident.

Another male LASD detective commented:

With an adult or older victim the key is sincerity. They have to know you understand what they're going through, and even though I was never raped, I have to relay that I understand the dynamics and the trauma. Even though I might be obviously checking their credibility, they believe from the get-go that I am going to believe what they say and will take them at face value until proven otherwise. I have interviewed a victim who was called a "fucking liar" [by other LASD personnel,] who was kidnapped and raped by gang members. I had to overcome this with her at an interview facility. While I interviewed her I didn't get up. I sat below her, and I told her, "I take this very seriously and I am passionate about prosecuting these crimes." If you don't do that and they think you're looking at them jaded, they will be hesitant to give you information they might be nervous about. They have to know they have your complete trust. In order to convey that you have to understand the dynamics of sexual assault.

These assertions suggest that the most effective sexual assault detectives exhibit empathy and truly understand the dynamics of sexual assault, regardless of gender. However, deep-seated cultural norms can impact some female victims' comfort level in speaking with male detectives, as was explained by an LASD detective:

I try to make them feel as comfortable as possible. We have a diverse ethnic group at my station, a huge Asian population. They're very private and don't want to be involved with police. It is very hard to build rapport with them, but I can usually develop a rapport with them. Asians want to speak with a female, and if they speak to a male they don't give full information. If a female [officer] respond[ed] from the beginning it would be better.

In summary, LAPD and LASD detectives who stated a preference for working sex crimes emphasized that the majority of victims are cooperative and their cooperation is largely influenced by the ability of the detective to set a tone that builds rapport and engages the victim as a partner in the investigation. This is consistent with the findings from our analysis of case files from 2008, which revealed that 56.3 percent of females age 12 and older who reported a sexual assault to the LAPD and 72.5 percent of females age 12 and older who reported to the LASD cooperated with the investigation. Further, a detective stated that "a lot of times they are frustrated because they had to tell the story to the hospital and to the responding officer and now they are here again and having to tell the story again." Recognition of these factors, knowing one's limitations, and responding sensitively, many asserted, is the key to overcoming the victim's frustration.

Discussion of how to build rapport with victims also raised some of the sex crimes–related challenges that detectives face, which are exacerbated if their preference is not to work these types of cases. For example, an LAPD detective who emphasized that sexual assault victims seldom cooperate with the police commented:

> Oh yeah, it happens a lot where they hang up in your face or curse in the phone, or you call back and they start avoiding you. I say: "We have a crime report and I have to do something with it. Let me know what you want me to do. I can't assume anything; I need you to tell me."

Another detective, reflecting on the dynamics of the tone set by detectives on the initial contact with victims, stated:

> A lot of cops who work the streets come off really coppish, rough, authoritative, and sound really official and do not come across as a human being and that gets magnified if they've ever had a bad experience with the police. If the detective comes off really cold they can get withdrawn. Often it's your demeanor and being able to key in on victims who are leery about prosecuting, who are scared, and being able to convince them of the importance of moving forward. Often victims do not want to prosecute because they have moved on but we tell them if this person is out of jail we can put him in jail and get him to stop doing this to others. I hate to do that and make them feel guilty but they will often take that into consideration. It is important to let them know you care about their case and not that it is just any other case.

Often the detectives who exhibited frustration associated with what many termed "victim management" also described both a discomfort with and a reluctance to incorporate rape crisis advocates into the rapport-building process. For example, a male LAPD detective described the relief he feels when female victims express a preference for speaking with a female: "I tell them they have the right to speak with a female officer and I hope that works." Another detective expressed frustration related to how rape-related trauma impacts a victim's ability to provide information for the police investigation: "I have one now where it's so traumatizing for her I can't even show her a six-pack.[2] It's been a month and she wants an advocate there and I can't even get there with her. She needs kiddy gloves." Along similar lines another detective stated,

> I don't try to be overly dramatic with compassion. Empathize and let them know you are there to try and find the person by trying to do everything possible to get this information. If a victim wants an advocate during the interview that is fine, but the trust factor is important and I like to put her at ease and speak alone.

It is important to note that rape crisis advocates are trained to address the precise issues that some detectives reported being the most draining aspect of working these kinds of cases, including but not limited to: fostering victim cooperation, crisis intervention, and providing referrals for counseling, follow-up medical care, and civil legal services. That said, many of the detectives interviewed for this study recognized the critical role that advocates can play to address victims' psychosocial needs, which, they asserted, ultimately allows them to focus on their primary role as investigator and evidence gatherer.

In summary, many LAPD and LASD detectives emphasized the importance of creating an environment in which victims feel safe and comfortable to disclose the details of their experience. Their comments indicate that the manner in which patrol deputies or detectives who are either untrained or do not want to work sex crimes interact with sexual assault victims is detrimental to the process of building rapport with law enforcement. This is particularly important because interaction with law enforcement constitutes victims' first experience with the criminal justice system; if inappropriately handled, this increases the likelihood that the case will not move forward in the system. The next section describes how detectives evaluate a victim as credible, along with their strategies for dealing with uncooperative victims.

Ascertaining Victim Credibility

I feel like I found my cup of tea; the investigation I want to do. I give 100 percent because of the satisfaction I get in being able to help these victims. I know they can be traumatic and it takes something away from women and girls and if I can put a little back by putting someone in jail and bring closure to that victim then it gives me satisfaction and makes me want to go out and keep doing it. People always ask me, "Don't you get tired of that investigation? I say no, bring it on."[3]

[A local agency's] entire focus is the victim, which is at odds with the police department's, which is the objective application of justice. Because someone comes in, male or female, and 99 percent is female, and says they were sexually assaulted does not mean we have to believe them. They complain that we are suspect sympathizers.

A commonality among LAPD and LASD interviewees' evaluations of victim credibility was a focus on the mechanics of reporting[4] and consistency[5] in retelling how the incident occurred. However, the major difference between the responses was the extent of detectives' recognition that the process through which information is obtained from victims often creates the inconsistencies that seemingly discredit them. We begin by providing examples of the first set of responses, which reflect an "innocent until proven guilty" approach toward victims and encompass the notion that sex crimes are complicated. Two themes are integral to this idea: first, victims must be taken at face value and not prejudged; second, the police (including patrol and detectives) have an important role to play in maximizing the likelihood of obtaining consistent information from victims:

> I can only think of one in 11 years that lied to me and I think she was put up to it to get her father out of a court case. I have picked up cases that were unfounded and have later got felony charges filed. We always judge everything and are taking in what they're saying. Often when they are lying it is for a legitimate reason. Listen for inconsistencies. Sometimes it is an issue of questioning. It is the same dynamics with adults and kids. You have to be sure they understand, you have asked the right question, and understand their answer if it seems inconsistent.
>
> I don't initially look at someone and say she's lying. I'm working on a case right now where the victim lives elsewhere, comes to LA once a month; she has regular clients here. She was legitimately assaulted by an individual who picked her up and wanted her to work for him. He's a pimp. He's been arrested; has numerous counts against him. I hate to say it but officers did not believe her. I said to bring both into the station and [now] he's looking at a lot of time. What is unique about this case is the guy has a prior record; he lied about his identity and prior conviction. He copped out to the fact that he smacked her around a little bit but he then said he did it. The victim is cooperative in this case.

An LASD detective emphasized the importance of interviewing the victim in person:

> Face-to-face interviews are best. One-on-one is the best. You have to judge it on the totality of the interview and take everything into consideration. You can't judge it based on conflicting statements. That is normal; trauma is going to cause that. And you can't judge it based on emotion as I've had victims talk about it as a movie they saw last week. You have to throw out your preconceived notion in which you think what you would do or what she should have done. You can't go by injury as many victims are not. Delayed reporting [is] also an issue but should be seen as normal given the crime and

not a reason to be skeptical. You have to look at whether there is a motive to make this up and that is rarely the case.

Detectives noted that while they never can be totally certain, it often boils down to a gut feeling. However, gut feelings took detectives in two different directions depending on whether their orientation toward victims was "guilty until proven innocent" or "innocent until proven guilty."

> I never really know for 100 percent sure whether she is telling the truth or not. I gauge it based on her testimony, the way that she describes certain things, certain smells, and her emotional state, to a point, as she is telling the story. Basically, it comes down to a feeling. If you work law enforcement long enough you develop a sixth sense about whether someone is telling you the truth or not. For a woman to put herself into that situation—the exam, retelling the story several times, perhaps going to court—you have to assume from the outset that she is telling the truth.
>
> Ultimately you don't know whether the victim is telling the truth or not. Even with training and experience, we all have biases and sometimes those biases affect our evaluation of the victim. Only God knows for sure unless there is a video of the incident. I'm not sure how you really do know. Even if forensic evidence is missing it does not mean it did not happen.
>
> It is hard to determine whether someone is telling the truth. I have one where a young girl came in who seemed unstable. The initial report sounded like she had consensual sex and when I interviewed her she seemed unstable, mentally off. But I still felt emotionally that something happened. As I investigated the suspect more I found that he had done something earlier, which gave more credibility to her. It was gratifying as most detectives would just stop there. I don't leave those. I finished a MySpace warrant on that suspect; my interviews with her tell me something happened plus statements made by the brother. If it turns out she didn't tell the truth I know I investigated it on my part.
>
> I never start a case by thinking "What is the jury going to think about the victim and her behavior?" If the victim is well prepared— by me and by the DA—we can take it forward. But the victim has to know that her behavior is going to come out and the fact that she is a stripper or a prostitute does not mean that something did not happen.
>
> Victims will tell us that what the patrol officers wrote is not what really happened. Some officers are coming off duty and want to get out of there so they rush the reports. Younger male officers [are] not as experienced in sex or sexual assault. They are almost scared of it

because they do not know. The officers have to take them to a local rape treatment center. Then it is easier for them to watch the interview there and take notes there. I think it has kind of streamlined in the past 10 years. Still at times the younger officers are fearsome so they do not dig as deep as they should.

Most problems I have encountered credibility-wise are when the crime scene evidence does not match or is inconsistent with her rendition. Once again, it could be perception based. One thing to do is we walk a victim through a crime scene. It is better when she walks through the house and it is cognitive and she is using more of her senses and you will get better information than if she is only doing something like answering a question in a sterile environment like this [interview room] or the hospital. But you also have to be able to deal with trauma. Always start with believing there was an event, but it will take a while to get there. I never believe intoxicated or mentally ill victims or those who have been involved in something in that first hour of an interview. That first contact is not where you are going to get all that [you need for] your interview. For example, I heard somebody talking to a victim on the phone on a cold hit case. The victim contacted the detective after getting a postcard in the mail. It was a few years back. The detective told the victim the suspect was identified and [said] "I need to know if you would be willing to go to court." They wanted a decision this moment when it was eight years ago. I cannot even tell you what I am going to make for dinner tonight let alone testify in court! We need to do better for them. Court is a big decision. Give them a week. Say "Can I come speak with you?" Give it a level of respect.

The preceding statements illustrate the complexities of sex crimes in relation to gathering consistent information from victims and the subsequent impact on detectives' perceptions of victim credibility. Their "innocent until proven guilty" approach toward victims emphasizes that trauma-sensitive interviewing skills, withholding judgment, and thorough investigations are key ways to ascertain victim credibility.

The second trend of responses about victim credibility reflect the "guilty until proven innocent" approach toward victims that reflects an emphasis on stranger rape as "real" rape (Du Mont, Miller, and Myhr, 2003; Estrich, 1987), the need to conduct criminal record checks on victims,[6] suspicion about delayed reporting, and a focus on consistency between the patrol officer's report and their first attempt at gathering information from the victim as primary methods to evaluate victim credibility. Something notable about these responses was the frequency with which detectives stated that their strategies for evaluating victim credibility were based on assumptions about how righteous victims should behave. For example, an LAPD detective establishes victim credibility "from how it was reported; if the story made sense. You need more, to probe for further explanation. It's not like you walk in there and believe someone." Another stated:

> Everyone's different. I try not to stereotype. We have a good share of 5150s,[7] people who are bipolar, schizophrenic, on drugs, etc. If they tell me up front they're on medication then I put them in a category of how to deal with them. If a teenager, I talk to their parents first. Is she attending [school], how are her grades; if they give a good report then it is usually an issue of a new boyfriend. If grades are bad and they're cutting school and smoking weed then I'll put them in another category. Then you have a righteous case, stranger rape, then we get excited about them because *then we have a real case to investigate.* (Emphasis added)

You can push some victims hard enough that they will recant because they don't want to deal with a difficult investigating officer (I/O). I don't do this but I know that there are I/Os who do. They will challenge the victim, confront the victim until she decides that she does not want to have anything more to do with the police.

A lot of factors come into play; for example, age. Young victims for the most part have not developed a personality where they can create a story and lie. I try to get as much detail as I can. If she says they went to a hotel, go there, see if I can get evidence, see if her story makes sense. Sometimes you check their background and see if they have made other reports before and it is important because it will come out in court. For instance, if they had an opportunity to get away from the suspect and didn't. How come they didn't notify the police sooner? Why didn't they get medical treatment when it was explained to them and they still refuse to go?

Obviously it has a lot to do with the victim's past. We run the victim. Has she made false reports in the past or made reports that she did not follow through on; has she been arrested for prostitution,[8] narcotics offenses, or other crimes.

You get a feeling for how open people are when talking to you. If truly a victim they are not guarded of the incident. They may be afraid or emotional, but they won't try to hide or watch what they say or things of that matter. If there is a feel of them not telling the truth then we express the seriousness of the allegation and make them see that once you make this allegation and it moves forward it affects them for the rest of their lives. That kind of helps, unless they have a motive. If I really think they're not being honest I'll run them in the system to see how many complaints they've made before.

I have a lady in my area who has made two or three allegations of rape against different men. She does take medication for mental issues, so it does play a big part in terms of whether she will make what we call a "good" victim on the stand in terms of whether she will be able to testify and remember what occurred. It's not necessarily just mental issues but dementia and age. I had a 75-year-old victim, a wonderful lady. We got her right in the hospital right after it happened. She hadn't had sex in 10 years. There was great evidence. She was cooperative and she had all her wits—no meds. He ended up pleading at prelim [the preliminary hearing]. When he saw her at court he took a deal for 25 to life.

If their story changes; if they come in and are laughing and joking and not taking it seriously. It is their demeanor. You try to figure out if laughing is their way of attacking it. By interviewing people; giving them a cell phone to call and see who they call when we leave the room. Most sex victims, if they are actual victims, they take it very seriously. They sit in here and shake and cry. You can see it by body reactions.

I may have my opinion that she is not telling the truth; however, their burden is low. I will take what you tell me. I don't get to be the devil's advocate and say you're lying. I may try to go around and see if I can catch them in a misstatement but it's pretty hairy on calling a victim that's claiming to be raped a liar. In all my years in law enforcement 98 percent of victims have said at least a little lie.

I take the victim's story and then review the case. I will try to clarify any conflicting stories. If the victim is telling me what is happening I have no choice but to present the case to the DA's office as long as the elements have been filled and the victim insists it has occurred. I will not sit and call a victim a liar, nor will I ever. A very small percentage of victims will admit to lying. The victim hasn't lied in less than 5 percent of my cases. The case will move forward if the victim insists it happens. The victim makes or breaks a case.

Consistent with the "guilty until proven innocent" approach, these statements from LAPD and LASD detectives focus primarily on the victim's consistency in retelling the story without consideration of: (1) their power as gatekeepers to the criminal justice system; and (2) the impact of sexual assault–related trauma on victims' ability to recall information.

Uncooperative Victims

When asked about uncooperative and hostile victims, LAPD and LASD interviewees' responses differed in the extent to which they empathized with and inherently believed victims. This is important because, depending on an officer's attitude and efforts, he or she may prematurely close a case on grounds that the victim is uncooperative. The following are examples of detectives' statements that implied what may be termed an "innocent until proven guilty" approach to victims:

> Victims can be uncooperative, yes, but not hostile. Most people want to solve the problem, but when someone is uncooperative it is for a reason. They have some type of agenda that explains why they're uncooperative. Or it could be they just don't want to deal with it anymore. It doesn't mean they're lying.

An LASD detective emphasized that the process of reporting can impact a victim's cooperation:

> I try to explain why it is important to have their cooperation. I say that I understand victims will often blame themselves but the incident happened because of the suspect and not because of anything they did. Plus there are patrol officer issues: victims will say it took too long. They just want to go home and shower and get some sleep and be alone but they had to wait for the deputy; then he's male, and then they have to wait for a female deputy, and then be transported to one of our exam centers. Then we drive them to the facility and interview them. The biggest complaint is the time it took or they feel the deputies didn't believe them, and I think that has to do with the training. You have to handle sex crimes questioning and investigation different than you would a house being broken into.

Similarly, an LAPD detective commented on the need to educate victims about the process:

> Usually my first contact is over the phone. They have already met with patrol officers, SART [Sexual Assault Response Team] nurses, advocates. As of yet I have not had any problem with people talking to me. I explain that I work sex crimes exclusively. I try to explain the process as victims have unrealistic expectations about how long things take. I try to be very low key because they tend to be anxious. I reinforce the services that are available to them. I try to explain the process; the more they know the better. I know the advocates at the local rape treatment center reasonably well and they will call me if they have a victim who is particularly anxious or hostile. I had a victim who was a chronic alcoholic and was being victimized multiple times. I tried to get her help for her alcoholism, which was leading to her victimization.

Detectives offered insight as to why a victim might be initially reluctant or uncooperative, and emphasized that "You don't just sit them down and hit them with questions." A detective encapsulated it as follows:

> Child abuse and sex crimes are not the types of cases that just anyone can work. It has to be someone who has an interest in these types of cases. I have been an officer for 15 years and I think that the worst kinds of cases are those that involve child molestation, elder abuse, and sexual assault. But I don't want to work property crimes. I want to work crimes where I can really help people. That is what makes my day and makes me want to come to work every day. If you don't feel that way, you should not be working these kinds of cases.

The following responses echo this sentiment:

> I try to bring myself down to their level. Tell them that I have been doing this for a long time and I do it because I care. I give them my cell phone [number] and tell them that what I need now is just a brief summary of the incident and I will pick you up tomorrow and we will talk in more detail. I respond by giving that person respect and not judging her. If you are humble enough, it is okay. They may yell, but I am cool with that. They really hate everyone at that point, but why wouldn't they? Someone just violated them.
>
> You have to sit down and let them know that you really are there to help them. For example, I had a young lady who was a prostitute, HIV-positive drug user. She was hostile and would get angry when she had to repeat things. But you can get around that if you are patient.
>
> Try to make people feel like they are not bothering me, not taking up my time; try to allow them to feel that their case is important. The reality is that I have a lot of cases but to that victim this is the most important thing in her life. I try to allow them to see me as a person, someone they can talk to.
>
> Advocates are used a lot here. . . . Lately I have had a good experience with them, but previously I found they interrupted the investigation by doing a lot of that stopping to make sure she is ok. I previously found that they were a hindrance.
>
> I try to get down to the underlying issues: why is this victim saying or acting this way now, especially if recanting? Once you get into those underlying issues you can address those issues and help them to overcome them. It is easy with our caseload to just give up, but I like to ask why.

These comments suggest that detectives are aware of the impact of their behavior on victims in terms of the likelihood of cooperation with law enforcement. In conclusion, two caveats are noteworthy: (1) many victims are cooperative, but there are undoubtedly situations in which victims are uncooperative that are truly beyond police control (e.g., victims with severe mental health issues; victims who disappear); (2) the much larger gray area regarding both victim cooperation with the police and police perception of victim credibility involves adult nonstranger sexual assault cases in which the victim is either acquainted with, intimately involved with, or related to the suspect. A detective explained:

> As long as you are yourself and explain the importance of prosecuting those are the major factors [in dealing with hesitant victims]. Most situations where the victim is hostile it is [in relation to] the manner in which the assault occurred: they knew the suspect, he was a friend of a friend, and they are afraid it will bring problems in the family. [Reiterating the point.] Hostile victims are not [common], and when [victims] are [hostile,] the assault usually involves nonstrangers. You have to work around that and explain how you can fix that.

This statement highlights the importance of training police officers about the dynamics involved when a sexual assault victim is acquainted with the suspect, and the associated implications for reporting (often delayed) and cooperation with the investigation due to social interdependence, shame, fear, and self-doubt (Daly and Bouhours, 2010; Kinney et al., 2007). Taking this a step further, the following sections examine how detectives evaluate victim credibility.

False Reports

The final issue that ties in with victim credibility is false reporting. LAPD and LASD detectives were asked to comment on victims' motivations for filing false police reports based on their experience working sexual assault cases. Although they provided varying responses depending on the victim's age—whether an adult or teenager—they stated that the overarching reasons for making false allegations centered on the following: covering up for one's whereabouts, revenge, money, attention seeking, mental health issues, and prostitution-related[9] "business disputes." Some detectives, however, again emphasized the complexities of sex crimes and cautioned against a quick rush to judgment. The following statements from LAPD detectives are representative:

> We don't see many false reports, but there are some involving very young girls who for some reason believe that it is better to make up

a story about rape than to get in trouble for being out too late or going where they aren't supposed to be.

Fabricated/false crimes are not as prevalent as people seem to think. They do exist but understanding how to handle them is the nuance that is so important as a detective; deliberate deceit versus mistake of fact. For example, a girl drinks all night, wakes up in her bed, does not know how she got there, has no underwear on, and feels raw as if she had sex. Just because her DNA swab comes back saying no DNA detected does not mean a rape did not occur. Fabricated cases exist and are hard to investigate but you have to do basic detective work.

I just put a guy away for 35 years that a top sex detective who teaches for LAPD would have unfounded if [possible]. . . . There were eight pages of opinion in the report. Only reason the guy didn't get life was they feared putting the detective on the stand. The detective thought she was making it up.

Along similar lines, an LASD detective stated:

Often when done it's coming from an abusive relationship and they are worried about what their boyfriend will say to prevent getting in trouble. Or they have substance abuse problems. It's not just your average citizen that comes in and makes up a rape report. They usually all have some kind of history or problem.

In terms of adult victims, the most frequent reasons cited by detectives for filing false reports are to either cover up infidelity or to act out in revenge as a woman scorned. One LAPD detective described false reporting as inherently about "Marital discord, boyfriend/girlfriend, or husband/wife not getting along. The husband wants to have control of the wife and she goes out and meets someone. Whenever you have relationships you will have problems." Other detectives commented along similar lines:

The number one issue is custody issues; going through a divorce and the husband and wife are fighting for custody of the kids. All of a sudden the wife will report that the husband touched the child in her private parts or the wife will claim that her husband raped her so that she will get custody of the kids. . . . And then there is just plain old revenge. Usually they are upset and trying to lash out and get revenge. Some people just want attention and are missing something at home. Some know the system and know that they can get benefits if they report a crime such as help in relocating and medical care. To the normal person, you don't want to go through the SART exam, but some people do; it is a sacrifice they are willing to make to get out of the chaos.

> I had a woman who claimed that she was assaulted by a
> UPS worker because she thought that she was not getting enough
> attention from her husband. We had the canine unit out and devoted
> enormous amounts of resources to the case. In that case the city
> attorney did file [charges for filing a false police report] on her.
>
> It can be something as minor as an argument, a domestic
> violence (DV) situation in which partners are having problems,
> and if the suspect hits his wife a lot of times we see it that to
> get back at him she will make a false police report and get him
> put in jail for the weekend. We've had DV cases in which we
> have caught women on tape telling the suspect why they filed
> the police report. If we honestly feel the victim is lying we will
> test the victim's credibility by making a pretext phone call. So
> he may hit her and then she may take it a step further and state
> she was raped.

Finally, detectives described the prototypical false report of sexual assault as involving either an adult or teenage female. They stated that the most frequently occurring reasons for teenage girls to file false sexual assault reports revolved around not wanting to get in trouble at home related to a missed curfew, ditching school, or staying out all night; runaways; or covering up consensual sex, as evidenced in the following responses:

> I had one, a young girl who wanted to report that she had been raped.
> She started giving me the circumstances and I told her it sounded like
> it came from a movie. We traced the steps and she started to laugh
> and she said, "Ok I lied to you but here is the reason why." Not all of
> it was made up, but she was never even touched by that guy. She did
> it because she got in an argument with her father and didn't want to
> be home and wanted to get back at him. A report hadn't been taken.
> She was 15 [or] 16 and had a boyfriend and wanted to do whatever
> she wanted. She alleged a stranger did it.
>
> Sheer attention. I have had victims who just like the attention that
> they are getting. If I figure out that that is what is going on, I will put
> the fear of God into that room to have them tell me the truth. I have a
> high caseload and it makes me furious if someone takes my time
> away from legitimate victims. I will call them on that. We don't arrest
> them but I do threaten them with "the bill": "If I find out that you are
> lying, from this moment forward your parents will get a bill from the
> city for the time that I have spent on the case, for the composite
> arrest, for all of the other resources that were wasted on this case."
> That is when the truth will come out.

I'm always interested in reporting mechanism, how it came to light. For example did the assault just occur and the victim called 911, or is someone three months pregnant and starting to show and needs an alibi as to why they're pregnant so they tell their mother or boyfriend they were raped? The timing, mechanism, why and how it comes to law enforcement's attention, [are] very telling. We had a child abuse case I'm suspicious of. The girl is 13 and developmentally delayed. Her mother became suspicious and grilled her daughter and the girl denied but she kept pressing the girl until the girl made a disclosure. The police were called, a report was taken, and before we could follow up the mother continued to grill the girl and now more disclosures have come out. Did it happen? I don't know. I haven't investigated yet, but [I find it] suspect. It could be an overzealous parent who was maybe abused as a child and is highly sensitive and telegraphing their concerns onto their children. It's apparent she's not taking no for [an] answer and they're not going to let the kid leave without saying something happened. Is it possible she was not molested and was doing it willingly and not by force?

In summary, detectives reported that victim credibility is ascertained by the evidence, self-presentation, and consistency in describing the incident. Many detectives emphasized the passion and unique skill set required to investigate this form of victimization and thus were oriented toward an "innocent until proven guilty" assessment of victims, whereas others emphasized the ubiquity of alcohol, illegal drugs, prostitution, and infidelity, which oriented them more toward a "guilty until proven innocent" assessment of victims. This is important because our analyses of 2008 case files revealed the majority of female victims in our samples from both law enforcement agencies were not using alcohol or illegal drugs during the alleged incident, were not sex workers, and provided consistent statements to the police. Considered together, this underscores that the seminal task for detectives as "advocates for the truth" (a term used by many LAPD detectives to describe their job) is to disentangle the context of nonstranger suspect-victim relationships because they are the most frequently occurring suspect-victim relationship that they encounter, and to formulate conclusions via comprehensive investigative skills as opposed to preconceived notions or first impressions of whether an incident involved consensual versus nonconsensual sex.

In the next section, we describe findings from interviews with DDAs with respect to working with victims. We begin by describing interviewees' perceptions of the challenges for victims when reporting a sexual assault, followed by their strategies for building rapport and assessing victims' credibility. We conclude the chapter with interviewees' recommendations for improving the criminal justice response to sexual assault.

DDAs and Victim Credibility

Challenges for Victims When Reporting

Interviewees stated that the primary difficulty faced by victims when reporting a sexual assault is the criminal justice system itself; specifically, being believed by law enforcement and prosecutors and the procedural requirements such as the multiple interviews and testifying in front of the defendant that are necessary to successfully prosecute. Many noted that specialized training is critical for criminal justice personnel who work with these types of victims and cases, and, when lacking, makes already difficult cases impossible to prosecute. For instance, a DDA stated: "Educating initial responding officers is important because they don't always know what kinds of questions to ask. One officer asked the victim whether she had an orgasm, which I found very offensive." Another stated:

> I don't see why there would be an obstacle to reporting a crime. I know that psychologically there may be obstacles like fear or shame of being judged because maybe they're a barmaid or prostitute. But in our culture in this day and age, at least with LASD, they're open; they'll investigate, even if the case is seemingly weak. They'll go and put [in] effort and investigate. Even if I reject a case because it is so weak, they will still be there for the victim.

Others commented that the biggest challenge for victims is "the fact that they are doubted and scrutinized and questioned in a way you're not prepared for in normal life. It is never flattering." Similarly, another answered: "Everything that happens once you report it. People have no idea about what's going to happen. People do not understand the system is not set up to streamline the process. You're dragged to patrol, to the detective, to the SART exam, to the DA's office. You have no control." Reiterating the issue of believability, a prosecutor stated: "Probably the most difficult thing is they want to be believed and they want someone to believe in their case. The process is long and they are attacked sometimes by the defense. They are made to look like bad people who asked for what happened to them." Other challenges noted by prosecutors include: "Talking about it with multiple people; the SART exam is not a pleasant thing; the risk that a case is not going to be filed even though you made a report; being grilled over and over again." Another interviewee emphasized that it is not pretty. Regardless of the victim's age, it is difficult. The suspect gets a lawyer. If he gets a good one it makes a difference. As a victim you may find there isn't enough evidence. With drug cases it is gone; sleeping overnight and reporting it the next day—it is too late. Sometimes we are pretty certain based on the description that they were drugged but you cannot prove it. So they are disappointed. But that's nothing compared to if we file. If we file, you're in it, and that means you've been through several interviews, an exam, you have to testify at [the] prelim, you have to testify at trial, and it is very stressful. They have to relive it and brace themselves for cross-examination, which often involves mocking. They get called names and a lot of women choose not to do it.

Another challenge for victims, according to prosecutors, is the slow pace of the court process. For instance, an interviewee stated:

The main problem is the length of time it takes to endure the process. If it goes to trial it could take over one year and that is some of the faster cases. The suspect has the right to a preliminary hearing within ten days, but it seldom happens within that timeframe. When there is a lack of information, it is impossible to get to victims. Marsy's law [the Victim's Bill of Rights of 2008] provides for sending more info to victims, but victims sometimes do not like that as it can be retraumatizing. And depending on the type of case there can be pressures from within families. For example, today I had a 50-year-old woman told by her 70-year-old father to "stop causing trouble and to just forget about it." There she was, blamed again.

Emphasizing believability and shame, other DDAs stated:

People don't believe them. They're accused of being at fault. Teens say they didn't report because Mom doesn't believe them and still doesn't. There is a lack of support at home. These people [suspects] approach victims with low self-esteem. These kids do not have that, and that translates into adult relationships. They choose men who are not their advocates, because they were not raised in homes where parents, siblings, and friends teach them to put themselves first and to not let people disrespect them. We [the DDA and their peer group] look out for each other at bars, and while being out. These victims more often than not do not have a core group of people. Predators see that they have no friends with them and take advantage of that. They don't report because of that.

With both the physical as well as the sexual, people do not assault children and partners in public with witnesses. It is always a private and secret thing. Often it is hard to prosecute because people will say it is only circumstantial evidence, so for prosecutors especially, these are difficult. You have to mine your case for nuanced details to build a case. People don't always have the time because it's a one-on-one, but if you search and search and search you will find something. Witnesses in family situations will not come to court. They find it difficult, so therefore, "Suzy must be lying," etc. It's different with strangers, but when it's your daughter and your boyfriend is doing it to your daughter, you think your daughter is lying because she does not like your boyfriend. People do not want to come to court because the defendant is related to them and they think the victim must have some agenda.

Given these challenges, some prosecutors emphasized the importance of victims' advocates: "Victim advocates [help to overcome the challenges]. One of the good things about the process for the victim is they get to tell their story and have other people believe them and reach out to them. I always use the victim advocates." Echoing the need for supplemental support of victims in these types of cases, another interviewee stated: "Even for adults it's a trying process. You can get them to prelim, but going through it at trial is a difficult psychological process for them. Handholding is a critical part of this." Finally, echoing this sentiment, an interviewee stated a need for victims to use the services that are available to them:

Counseling, mental health services, and relocation services are often underused. Victims do not want to take part in it. I am not a fan of psychiatry, but this is about having someone neutral to talk about it and listen to you and not judge. Many victims do not have this as an outlet, and pushing it aside and not dealing with it [are] not good for them. Victims need to know the services are available and critically important.

Assessing Victim Credibility

I look at every statement previously given and every action taken all the way through my interview and ask different questions of the victim. We have to look for motive. People lie all of the time, people lie about sex crimes, and we need to see all circumstances. I look at defendants' prior conduct in terms of victims' credibility, if this is a person who repeatedly preys on the victim; I mean arrests and convictions.

I explain to jurors that no two victims will act the same way. It is important for jurors to understand because they think a victim should be a certain way. People expect the victim to be sobbing. Some will smile out of nervous habit, and some will be straight-faced, which can work against them. I look for corroborating evidence. Victims may rely on the crutch of "I don't remember," [which is the] same thing you might get from a suspect when they say something and then are presented with evidence that tells another story. If something does not make sense to you, then it will not make sense to a defense attorney. The prefiling interview must be done from the perspective of a defense attorney to try and fill those holes before we get to her explaining what happened.

The two most prominent—and often overlapping—means through which prosecutors interviewed during this study reported ascertaining victim credibility are gut feelings and the consistency in the victim's account of what happened. Closely associated with consistency is the victim's demeanor, which interviewees described as critical in relation to the totality of evidence. As one prosecutor noted:

> By the time they get here we have weeded out cases in which people might be lying. The majority of cases where I have found out they were lying, they are very few and most often teenagers. Or they involve mentally ill victims. I look at the evidence and make that evaluation, and I will not put them through that when I know there is no chance ever it will work with a jury.

The following examples are representative of the "gut feeling" approach to determining victim credibility:

> A lot of it is a hunch. Any DA in any unit has to rely on their intuition and common sense, and the better DAs are probably those who do that more. If things don't make sense, I challenge victims in the way that the defense will—things I think a jury would want to know and the defense would attack. If they explain that satisfactorily then I believe them.
>
> Inconsistencies. Not so much those, but more gaping holes where they can't answer questions. Or the more you talk, the more info comes out. Office policy is a prefiling interview to evaluate their credibility. You talk to so many people that you start to see from their responses and demeanor whether they're credible. It's mostly a feeling you get. For example, [citing an earlier case where the victims lied], you would ask them questions and get to a certain point, and all of a sudden they don't know anything, the house they went to, the

friends who were there, etc. Often they'll say, "My friend saw this but she doesn't want to get involved."

Consistency in their story. I've never been raped or abused, but there has to be consistency, and there has to be something about their demeanor. By just being older you can tell whether someone is lying. It is also a gut, also the probability of it possibly happening. Also being older and just having more experience. You also have to gauge whether there is a motive to lie.

Some of it is a gut thing, but a lot should depend on the evidence. Is it consistent with the evidence? Is it dispelled? Motive becomes critical with the victim because sometimes a victim gets angry with a partner because they are cheating and they make allegations that things happen so you have to get to the bottom of that and make sure there are no ulterior motives.

It's a feeling you get when interviewing with them. Most victims will be inconsistent in terms of patrol, detective, to DA. It's about evaluating how she answers. It's more of a gut feeling.

Your gut. After 15 years it's just my gut. You can go through a checklist, can you corroborate things. It's also how you interview. "What were you watching on TV, if watching TV?" There's corroboration that proves a crime and then there's a corroboration that brings a ring of truth. Most young people put themselves in harm's way. They ditched, saw [a] movie, met at [a] park and drank. They were drinking locos [alcohol mixed with an energy drink] and doing blunts [hollowed-out cigars filled with marijuana]. It is easy to confirm that stuff.

Instinct and whether facts make sense given the situation and the evidence: if they have a secondary motive for falsehood such as trying to punish the suspect in any way. I'd say the victim is not being truthful in 1 in 40 cases. For the most part they're being truthful. This isn't really something you make up. There are the teen cases where they lie to stay out of trouble when caught skipping school, coming home late, and suddenly there is a claim of sexual assault. But a 12-year-old saying they were molested, it's so [seldom that] I don't believe them, it's [more a case of] whether we can prove it.

I sit across the table from them and try to figure out whether they are telling the truth and would a jury believe them. How do they react to the questions, do they appear to be withholding info? I have had victims with rap sheets and records, and it does not mean that they are not victims worth fighting for.

That is a tough one to answer. A lot of it is just your gut feeling about the victim and the story she tells and whether the victim looks you in the eye. For example, I've interviewed victims who look you in the eye until you ask if they were drinking or using drugs at the time of the incident. They say no but they won't look at you. If the story doesn't make sense and doesn't match what the other witnesses said, I tend to question whether the victim is telling the truth. It's not an exact science.

It's a gut thing: consistency in the story, honesty in other things. Sometimes you can tell if they're telling the truth if they're honest about things that they wouldn't otherwise need to tell. Some things they disclose you wouldn't exactly want a stranger to know; if they give info readily every time you ask them a question. Basically I cross-examine them when interviewing them, and I ask them what a defense attorney would ask. I say, "I don't want to offend you but this is what a defense attorney would say." And I'd say, "This doesn't make sense. First you said this and now you're saying something else." In the end I'm not judging based on [whether she made] a bad decision, I just want to know what happened. Often these women will make poor decisions and use bad judgment and if you ask them to articulate why they did what they did, it might not be the same choice you would make, but if you ask them those questions—why did you get in the car with this stranger—they say, "I needed to go to the bathroom, [and] he looked like a nice guy." It's the way they give the answer, if they can answer right away without thinking about it. And to tell you the truth I can't think of any cases where I haven't believed my victim 100 percent. When they come in to sit with us I believe they're telling the truth; the only problem is we don't have corroboration. I think the ones that are lying don't return the detective's phone calls.

The second theme in responses focused primarily on victims' demeanor and consistency as opposed to a gut feeling:

As a more senior DA once said to me, "You don't have a truth barometer." I look at whether the story makes sense and whether the victim has any motive to lie. For example, is it a divorce case with custody issues and now all of a sudden there is the issue of sexual molestation by the father? I also look at the victim's body language, but you have to be careful about that because you don't know this person and how she normally behaves. A victim may have a very blank attitude and flat affect but that does not mean that she is not telling the truth. Some victims can just shut down and not show any emotion when retelling what happened.

We do prefiling interviews of all of the sex crimes victims so that we can evaluate it. Demeanor: you can talk to someone and see if they are able to make eye contact, if they respond the way you think that they should respond. The ability to recollect detail: the truth is always the truth but there are many variations on a lie. When you have the opportunity to interview someone in person, you can assess their credibility. But I have not come across a lot of cases where I thought that the victim was lying. We typically reject because of insufficient evidence. Those who lie are those who recant as a result of threats and pressure. We get more of these than those who lie about what happened.

I evaluate based on [whether] they can corroborate what they are saying. I look for people searching for facts in their heads. I don't like when people are not willing to accept a change when confronted with inconsistencies. I emphasize how serious these charges are, and before we can charge, much less convict, I need to know the whole story. I look at their demeanor and whether the story makes sense.

I tend to believe what they tell me. I can think of only one time where I sat with a victim who started telling me she was pregnant, that it was triplets; she [says] she hadn't gone to the doctor but she just knows. Until they say something that is completely off, I think, who would want to sit here and go through all of this? I believe them until I have a reason not to. Whether they look [me] in the eye; do they seem genuinely scared? Are they worried about other things? Texting?

For me, as I am talking to them I try to see if they're telling the truth. One victim I had started to gag and throw up when talking about the oral cop. Are they crying at the right time? Do you know what I mean? That sounds terrible. I don't know if there is a science to it but I base it on how I feel overall when talking to them. I voir dire this with jurors saying, "How do you expect a victim to look?"

I'd like to have some injuries, anal things, torn clothing; a girl who goes immediately to the police; a SART exam; she's totally emotionally devastated. I'm very precise on cross-examination. One of my criteria is if they show emotion, but not hard and fast because some don't cry. They must be consistent. [I tell victims]: "I need to know if you have done anything, I just need you to be honest." [I establish victim credibility] by seeing if she stays consistent and doesn't change. If the testimony of one witness is to be believed, the jury can convict. In terms of going to trial it's better to offer probation or three years' state prison. Isn't that better than going to trial and something funky happening with the victim?"

Usually I do what I assume jurors do. I look at the victim, the facts of case, and body language. There have been times where a victim comes in and gives a bizarre story—[for example,] the victim said the Holy Ghost said he would rape her—and even then I would look at the detective and ask for more corroboration. I look at what she says, and I question her thoroughly, the way a defense attorney would, to see if she has all the answers. Is she crying? Is she calm? Is she angry? Does she have a reason to be vindictive? Is there a divorce pending? I dismissed a teen case in which the victim alleged her stepfather raped her and that he was the father of her child. I do the same thing that any human would: listen, and see if the facts make sense.

I'm not a lie detector. It's the same routine in terms of picking a jury. How do you know you are picking the right people? You don't. You make educated guesses. Sometimes it's obvious they are lying, and it doesn't make sense. And it doesn't flow right. Basically, if you're a trial lawyer, you are cynical about what anybody tells you. People lie, and sometimes they lie to help themselves, or to hurt someone, but the reality is when they come in here and they are interviewed. We all do interviews here. It is really up to us individually as to whether we believe the witness is going to be able to take the stand and be believable. Sometimes they have all the right things to say but their demeanor is such that they are a big problem to put on the stand; . . . they are inarticulate or have social issues. Some of the homeless people are like that.

Finally, a couple of interviewees emphasized that a corroboration requirement in place at the district attorney's office specific to sexual assault cases protects against victims who are not credible:

[I] never know for sure if the victim is telling the truth. I can say that I believe the victim but I wasn't there so I can't know for sure. That is why we have this corroboration requirement so that we are not basing it on her word alone.

I try not to make the focus whether I believe someone or not. If I absolutely did not believe the victim, I would not file. But usually it is the converse: you believe someone but there isn't any corroboration so you can't file charges.

In short, prosecutors' two main strategies for assessing victim credibility focused on a gut feeling and on victims' consistency and demeanor in describing what happened. Many emphasized the prefiling interview as an important opportunity to assess the victim's credibility, which ultimately plays a role in charging decisions. In the following section we examine the strategies employed by prosecutors to build rapport with sexual assault victims.

Establishing Rapport

> The use of advocates is helpful. Our job is to prosecute the case and
> keep the victims involved in the cases. Victims often have so many
> other issues they need to deal with: therapy, housing, doctors. Thank
> God for victim advocates because they assist with all of that. They
> are awesome because they can deal with those issues directly, getting
> [victims] through it, holding their hand in court, so they're not alone
> with the defendant's family in court. When a victim comes in I
> initially speak about school, work, pets—like you do with anyone
> else. I talk with them about what you have in common, and usually
> it goes from there. I will usually talk about mundane things. I always
> tell them, "This will be really hard, it will be uncomfortable, and
> court will be very difficult. You can always call me with any
> questions. From now until the end of your case you're going to
> [be in touch with] me."

A deputy-in-charge (DIC) of a VIP unit stated that the best way to establish rapport with victims and minimize inconsistencies is to have a "rollout"
program in which a lawyer and a detective interview the victim and go
through the initial report at the same time:

> Instead of LAPD or LASD doing a two-hour interview after a two-
> to three-hour SART exam and the detective then having to bring the
> victim for another hour and a half interview with me, it is much more
> effective to send a lawyer from my unit with a detective and the
> victim can go through one report. It is also better for the victim to
> see the lawyer and the investigator as one team from the beginning,
> and we can make counseling referrals then as well.

The majority of responses emphasized that victims are seldom uncooperative and rapport building requires making the victim feel at ease:

> The key for me, what I try to do is to listen. Let them be heard. Try
> to speak to them on whatever level they are on. Try to understand their
> background before getting into all of the details about the traumatic
> incident that they are reporting. You have to try to get them to open
> up to you because they feel comfortable enough to trust you. Many of
> our victims do not trust anyone because they have been abused for so
> long. I use the victim advocates a lot. If the victim has made a good
> connection with the first responding officer, I will bring that officer in
> on the interview. Whatever it takes to create some type of trust, that is
> what we need to do. If that first line can't adequately speak to these

people, then the case is done before we even start. One thing I have been trying to express to the officers that I deal with is that they need to be better trained in that area. This is especially true of the DV cases. The responding officer should audio-record the initial interview, because we know that in a DV case the victim is likely to recant and if we don't have that initial statement recorded the case is dead. But even if the victim is uncooperative, if we have that initial statement we can file and use that to get a conviction.

We all have different personalities. I try to put them at ease but there are times when you can't. I think I am successful and I think they want to talk to me. I am a good listener and I always let them say everything they want to say. They have to have confidence that they have been heard.

Just talk to them. Do not be judgmental. Let them know it is not their fault and they were right to report it and our office and the agencies will do whatever it takes to assist them. We don't only interview the nonrejects or rejects. It takes time and they have to be willing to do it.

I acknowledge it is difficult for them and I try to talk about something else even for [a few] moments beforehand. I think that easing them into the process is helpful. One thing I tell them is my burden: "There are times where I might believe you but not file the case." Maybe it is just me, but I encourage them not to let the person win; that they can have a great life and not hinge success based on whether I can get prison out of this or whether the jury believes you. I have been fortunate in that I think victims respond well to me.

It is important to meet face-to-face and try to treat them as you would want to be treated; that they are not just another case in my caseload. Acknowledge [that] what they are going through is one of the most horrible they will hopefully ever go through and that you care for them as well as the case. I care about securing a conviction but I won't do it at any cost to them. They matter.

With kids: I ask about school, what they like to do; teenagers, sort of the same; grownups: "How are you? Do you want some water?" It is sort of hard because we are under time constraints so we don't get to have the soft build-up that would be nice for them.[10]

We have a Hispanic base; I think they can relate to me. I also talk about the fact they're not in trouble. You are here because something happened to you. I think the biggest fear with women is they are intimidated by me as a male and the officer who is a male. I try to tell them I am not intimidating; as a DDA I am here for you.

I just try to be honest with everybody. With young adults I try to be honest and empathize with what they've been through but sometimes you have to ask hard questions. I like to use [the guideline that] in my perfect world every victim would get justice but in the real world other people make decisions. Victims like to know what's coming. I'm in court every day so it's comfortable for me, but not for many people. It's important to make yourself available because victims are going to have questions before, during, and after the process. It's important to be honest and to recognize they're going to be frustrated and embarrassed and nervous, and all of those things are OK because this is not easy.

I ask them questions about themselves that don't have to do with the crime. I answer any questions they have; I tell them things about myself. I try to find things in common between us. I try to make them feel comfortable and safe and in control. I let them make small decisions: where to sit, where to have the interview; small things to make them feel in control of their surroundings and situation. I always ask if they want to have someone with them, but I discourage it if there is a prior relationship because it might impact what they disclose. Advocates are good, but the more people in the room, in their mind [it amounts to] the more people could be judging them. I try to just have the detective sit back. I always tell them I will not judge them, to just tell me the truth, it doesn't matter. I'm not going to judge why you did something; I just need to know why. Lots of victims make poor choices and they do things that don't make sense. But once you have them explain their thought process all of a sudden it makes total sense. You maybe wouldn't have done it that way, but when they explain it you get it. The key is to ask questions about why they do things that don't make sense to us.

It is different with every victim in terms of age and socio-economic status. You cannot speak the same way with different people. With teens, you cannot speak to them like they are children; it insults them by doing so. You have to try to explain to them what is going to happen as if they are adults. With adults, you have to keep in mind where the person is coming from. A professional at a tax firm walking to her building needs different treatment than [a] set of prostitutes who were raped at gunpoint in terms of the language used, how you describe the next step, and your expectations.

It depends on whether they know the defendant, or if a relative, because as time goes on they start feeling bad for them, or conflicted. I make sure they stay on with me, that I have their current information, if they are [absent from] court. That happens a lot. Often in context of DV they start to go backward.

Sometimes where there is a current sexual assault and you find a prior case and you bring in a prior sex crime victim you get resistance from them . . . because of a crappy DA or police officer. . . . Unless she disappears, gets lost, or we can't find her. I won't reject a case if it was up to filing standards. That in and of itself is not a reason to reject.

Another DDA noted the opposite with regard to victim cooperation as a reason to reject: "I will explain, depending whether I think I have enough to file, they have to testify. If they won't cooperate that is a reason to reject." This is a potentially problematic strategy if a prosecutor fails to recognize his or her role in fostering victim cooperation, as explained by some LAPD and LASD detectives:

> I try not to take it out on them personally. I let them know that I think they may not be truthful and they should come to court and tell the judge the truth.
>
> If I can't break them I will bring in the victim advocate. They are usually female. If they are combative and uncooperative from the beginning usually the officer will give me a heads up. I will tell the advocate and they will talk to the victim before they talk to me because I get seen as part of law enforcement. Advocates are a very, very important figure in our ability to deal with recalcitrant victims. Not that we are buying their testimony, they understand that we are here to help them. They are a huge role in turning victims.
>
> It depends on age. If it's an adult and it's a custody case, you don't have much time to establish rapport. A lot of it is built as the case moves toward trial. I always call my victims back. They have my cell phone number. I am also totally honest with them. If I think that it is going to be a tough case, I don't sugar-coat things. I tell them straight that it is not going to easy and that they are going to be grilled about their behavior.
>
> I just try to be straightforward with them. I know that we are busy but if you sit down and give them your time, they appreciate that. If you tell them that you are here to get the truth and that you are not going to judge them. That is my approach.
>
> As early as the prefiling interview, I make sure that they know that this is difficult and embarrassing but that it also is a therapeutic process. I tell them that testifying at the prelim is essential. It is a show of power to the defendant and signals that he is not going to get away with this. [I say,] "He took your control away from you by doing this, but now you are going to get it back."
>
> I also like to take them to court, to introduce them to the judge and the staff and let them see the setting . . . they are going to be in, especially with kids. With adults, I walk them through the entire process and explain in detail what is going to happen.

> Our policy is that the victim, if available, should testify. Some people think that you don't want to give the defendant an opportunity to cross-examine the victim early on but I think that it works to our advantage. With an adult sex victim, especially if it is a stranger rape, we want to talk about it anyway with them. I tell them why they are here, what we are doing, and what the process is. It is another interview not because we don't believe them, but because this is the process: you tell your story so that we can file the case and move forward.

In summary, the majority of DDAs interviewed for this project took responsibility for setting a straightforward tone with the victim in an attempt to establish rapport. Many noted that high caseloads and staff turnover make it hard to spend as much time with victims as they would like, and—similar to some of their law enforcement counterparts—one strategy noted to address this was extensive use of advocates. The final portion of this chapter describes LAPD, LASD, and LA DDA interviewees' ideas about how to increase the successful prosecution of sexual assault in the criminal justice system.

How to Increase the Successful Prosecution of Sexual Assault

> Have detectives and DAs dedicated to the job who are patient, nonjudgmental, and come into it believing victims and looking for ways to find corroboration. I find that if a detective already has an opinion it affects the investigation.—DDA

We concluded interviews by asking respondents to provide insight about how to increase the successful prosecution of sexual assault. The most frequently emerging themes were more training specific to interviewing victims, interrogating suspects, crime scene investigation, a more timely return on crime lab analyses, and a clarified policy on the use of DNA evidence, specifically in relation to its value in nonstranger cases. In addition to LAPD detectives' overwhelming request for more training[11] and investigative resources such as tape recorders, they stated a need to increase the senior department leadership's overall regard for sex crimes. As one detective noted:

> Everyone is so busy we are throwing detectives into the deep end. We need detectives who want this assignment. They must understand how different it is from other types of investigations. There is so

much more emotion involved than even in homicide. We need more emphasis on training courses as well as mentors in the field; that is the biggest thing missing in so much investigator work. We need to work hand-in-hand with newer detectives. These are skills that are lost as the department skews younger as a whole. Fifty percent of the department has under five years on the job. That's a nightmare.

Others noted that the problem starts with that first report taken by a patrol officer: "I worked 17 years of patrol. We do not have any training for report writing. There is not enough training on report writing. The report writing and interviewing skills are not there."

Another common statement among LAPD detectives was the need for specialization as a sexual assault detective:

Detectives should have to apply to work in a sex unit. There should be standardized, specific training. A lot of cases are lost because detectives do not know enough about how to investigate sex crimes, the elements. I had a new detective who made a comment after working at another division saying, "I get these girls who drank and then they want to report rape and what am I supposed to do?" She had never heard about rape by intoxication. At a lot of divisions they just throw someone in there who isn't interested and won't do a good job. It takes a detective who understands victimology, the layers to these cases, and not everyone wants to do that. It's hard to get people to work the sex table. Some don't want to deal with people, they just want the property crimes.

Echoing the sentiment that a specialized skill set is critical, another LAPD detective added: "Interviewing is an emotional drain. It is tough to do a lot of serious case interviews in one week. I had to buy my own tape recorder. It would be helpful to have critiques. To have a professional tell you how you are doing." One LAPD detective offered a way to make training more accessible to sexual assault detectives:

The thing about training is that we're so busy. You should provide it on a Saturday or Sunday, or make it a regular work assignment so you won't get bombarded by cases or going to court. When we have quarterly training we often miss because we have a custody or court. You should bring the training to the division at that table or within the bureau. Bring training to the people and make it more convenient for investigator. The focus of training should be: (1) Making procedures consistent because every division is doing something different with [the] DA's Office when it comes to filing; (2) Ever-changing situations with DNA. With in-car cameras they came and gave training. Once a month, someone from SID [the Scientific Investigation Division] should go to every division and bureau and discuss problems with request forms, cases, etc., so they don't have to deal with an audit six months later to talk about what we're missing. We need monthly training but please bring it to the detectives.

Something else LAPD detectives requested was easier accessibility to polygraph machines than the current three-week wait: "Now it takes three weeks to get a polygraph, whereas doing it immediately lessens the likelihood they'll [suspects] change their mind. You really only get one chance and you want to catch them off guard because once they're on to you they're going to tell you no." Another added:

> We have the sexual assault exam to tell injuries, but those don't necessarily tell that a rape happened. Polys [polygraphs] would be great if they were immediately available. Resources are inconsistent citywide. We have more sex assault detectives. In manpower we have more here. Normal stuff, like tape recorders. We all don't have the same stuff.

"The DNA process needs to be a lot faster," noted another, describing a practical consequence of the current pace of business:

> We need to be able to get a quicker response upon sending something to the lab. When we have to wait two to six months for results to verify a suspect that makes things a little difficult. I have a case now where [the] victim was raped, drinking vodka [and] Red Bull [an energy drink], passed out, and awoke in an abandoned apartment. No one saw anything, and she does not recall how she got there. The last thing she remembered was dancing on the dance floor and [then] awaking the next day. We are still awaiting the results.

Other LAPD detectives concurred:

> We need to increase the turnaround time for some of these saliva samples we turn in as sometimes they take up to six months. We are being asked to get a confirmation sample [for] what has already been confirmed. It is an unwritten policy from [the] DA's Office. If we get a notice that identifies John Smith as an offender in [a] particular rape and we interview and arrest him and we feel there is enough and we go to court, eventually the DA's Office is going to ask for a saliva sample to confirm what is being reported to us. Often they want that

up front so there is no question it is him, but that delays their job a lot. When asked to do confirmation and the suspect [is] in prison we have to do [a] swab, search warrant, a search warrant log, and all of that paperwork. If that was eliminated it would save detectives a lot of time.

The amount of time it takes to get back DNA is way too long. When we submit for examination, it takes four months just to get it assigned to a DNA expert, and another three to four months to get it analyzed. That's eight months once you submit before getting anything back, if you're lucky.

Another detective explained that DNA is ultimately not a factor in case processing because "It takes a year and a half to get results. They [advocates] argue with us about what needs to be tested. They want to test unfounded and old cases instead of current cases where we need them. Murder is the first priority [in DNA analysis] but you would think rape would be second." LAPD detectives' final area of emphasis with respect to increasing the successful prosecution of sexual assault focused on aspects of LAPD leadership and bureaucracy; specifically, a need to centralize sexual assault investigations citywide, and for senior leadership to treat sexual assault more seriously. The following statements are emblematic:

Sexual assault needs to be more of a priority. Working homicide in this department is major status. But sex cases, nobody cares. At divisions there are tables, Auto, Theft, etc. D-IIIs. There are Divisions where there isn't a head D-III. More value is put on auto cases than victims in sex cases. There needs to be a supervisor that cares.

I believe in centralization as the only proper way to handle sex investigations. Otherwise you constantly have detectives taken away to support other investigations. It is the only way to achieve effective mentorship and it promotes a tremendous resource of unit knowledge. It is amazing how much you learn when you read a report assigned to one detective and someone else says, "Hey I had something like that last month," and all of a sudden you're putting a case together. . . . But captains in a division do not want to lose their resources; it undermines their castle. Egos get involved.

We need to access more resources: supplies, vehicles, evidence recovery kits, access to analysts, prioritizing analysis of rape kits, entering DNA into CODIS [the FBI's Combined DNA Index System]. City attorneys take a long time to make filing decisions regarding misdemeanors. Every investigator should have a camera and digital recorders. Everyone on my table wants to be there so they bought their own. But it raises problems with discovery when LAPD employees use their own phone for pictures. When making a policy like that, Major Assault Crimes, Sex, Burglary, should each have a camera on their desk. It would be nice if each division [was] hooked up to sound and camera. Older stations do not have that.

I've been a part of two centralized units. The philosophy is good but it has to be done right. It needs to start with a few core detectives who are experienced and take in a few more and let it grow over time. The last one was a disaster because they threw everyone in with no resources so it was doomed to fail. It must be a multidisciplinary approach with the district attorney, city attorney, counseling, and SART nurses, so the victim doesn't have to go through so many interviews. It should be centralized, but not the way this department has done it.

Centralizing sex [crimes] citywide is needed but someone has to monitor the quality and standards of all bureaus to ensure they meet the criteria of what is done. The detective bureau chief should oversee it. We cannot have the same players come in and run it like a district where they think it is their empire and they are not accountable to the chief of police. And there should be one standard as far as sexual assault investigations regardless of where you are in the department. You should get a standard level of service across the city.

The same attention and resources should be afforded to all of the divisions and that doesn't happen realistically. You can't control who comes in, but there should be equality of resources. [When the] bureau was centralized in 2003 we could recognize patterns better; filing and clearance rates were better. We had more personnel for [a] search warrant. If we wanted to run 290 sweeps on sex registrants we didn't have to rely on asking another table. It is such a benefit for our victims. Everyone worked all of the divisions.

Turning to the LASD, whose sexual assault investigations for victims under 18 are already specialized, the most frequent responses were to have the Special Victims Bureau (SVB) investigate all sexual assaults, not just those involving victims under 18.[12] The Special Victims Bureau was repeatedly cited throughout district attorney interviews as the "gold standard" for sexual assault investigations, in contrast to the station level, where detectives receive very limited training specific to sexual assault and investigate whatever type of crime report is sent their way. An SVB detective stated:

I've never been a station detective but we have a policy that we interview everyone in person. The station level goes by the initial report from the deputy. We have more resources available to us. They have the same, but we have them quicker, such as the polygraph, sexual assault exams, and the crime lab, and we have more pull to get things done quicker. Patrol station detectives deal with all types of crimes, not just sexual assault. We have more advantages because we get sent to more trainings and our investigations are more thorough.

Another detective emphasized the need for crime scene investigators who specialize in sexual assault so when a sexual assault is reported: "crime scene units would be readily available. The big thing is the time of reporting. It can either make your case or wipe it out." Noting the high volume of teen and adult sexual assault cases at the station level, another LASD detective stated:

> We have a very high caseload so it limits what we can do with any particular case. There are so many cases and too few of us. I have between 30 and 40 cases at any one time. There is another female detective and we handle all of the cases. Even if the case is assigned to a male detective there is always a female detective present. They push to try to have a female involved one way or another. It seems to help the victim.

The following statements are emblematic of both SVB and station-level LASD detectives:

> All sex crimes should fall under Special Victims Bureau. All rapes need to be in the hands of detectives who want to deal with these cases. You might have a good detective at a station that is going to a sergeant [for supervision] that deals with burglaries and robberies, but our sergeants, lieutenants, and captain understand the dynamics better. I can't control the DA's Office, but we can control how we do things here at LASD. DAs will say, "Why don't you [Special Victims Bureau] take the [adult] rape cases as well?"
>
> We need to increase training across the board on interviewing. Cops don't get enough training on interviewing, and not just suspects, but on understanding victims. We send them to interrogation to interview suspects, but there's not enough in terms of how to deal with rape victims. Specialized units are the answer. In a specialized unit the first year you will be drowning, the second year you will start doing the dog paddle, and the third year you're swimming laps.
>
> More investigators and a specialized unit for adult sexual assault. We really do need to specialize in these cases. It would be beneficial to the people we serve if we had a specialized unit for all types of sexual assaults. Training is needed to investigate these types of crimes. All law enforcement agencies should have specialized

training, if not a specialized unit. We have too many cases and therefore we are forced to triage the cases.

They should establish a unit similar to Special Victims that just handles adult rapes. Right now they are at the station level and we are handling lots of different types of crimes. If I had an assignment that focused just on sexual assault I would have more time to do a solid investigation. Not to say that we don't do a good job now, but we can't give 100 percent given the current situation.

More training classes as far as interviewing goes. We can never have enough training. And a specialized unit to work adult sexual assault. Since it is specialized that is what you deal with all of the time, and you can have someone in the same office that you can talk to about the case. It helps to have a bigger pool of support that you can talk to about strategies.

If we could send our lab results and speed up the process of getting DNA results back. It now takes months. When you have a case where there is not a named suspect and no charges pending they outsource those and it takes months to get the results back. If we had our own unit that handled sexual assault, a Special Victims Unit for adults. We are not case specific, and if we had a unit they would become really savvy and know the ins and outs of how to handle those kinds of cases.

LASD detectives overwhelmingly referenced a need for a more efficient DNA evidence policy and process and a need for training in interview and interrogation skills to increase the overall quality of sexual assault investigations:

Training for detectives. When I got this assignment I did not receive any training and had to learn from other detectives. I did not even know how to package the sexual assault kits or where to bring them; I had to learn this all on my own. Getting DNA more quickly would really help. I think that it takes five to six months to get the results. I have had cases go forward without it being ready but the DA will extend the date for case completion until it is ready.

A fresh complaint or reporting immediately helps a lot. A quality first report with a quality patrol officer building the foundation a detective can work off. Not prejudging the case because of how the woman was dressed or the circumstances of how the assault took place. A prompt sexual assault exam and getting the victim treated immediately with quality personnel that get the ball rolling without all of the blame and other issues that can go along with sexual assault [all are] key to a good investigation.

The crime lab needs to analyze evidence immediately, and more detectives. We should have teams working on one case. That's helpful because people think differently. One person's mind may think one way and overlook things. I think working in teams is good for interviews and evidence retrieval. I'm the type of person who would enjoy having another person in case I overlooked something.

It would be great to have another detective working these cases with me. It's important to have another detective working the case with you so you can relieve stress and have someone to bounce ideas off. The department is already testing every sexual assault kit. I think they are wasting a lot of money. I had to do an audit of every case from 1999 through the present, and after going through the majority of cases I didn't find one instance where the detective who handled the case had made a mistake, [so] because of that I now get all of the DNA returns. In 100 percent of the cases so far the identity of the suspect was never in question from the beginning. They've wasted all of this money when he was interviewed and the case was submitted to the DA.

We need the DNA analyzed much more quickly. If I have a rape victim, she may be cooperative at first but not as the case drags on. DNA is huge. I had a very, very brutal rape involving two offenders who raped the victim at gunpoint. She ended up identifying someone within three months and the suspect failed a polygraph. But the victim was a little bit flaky and some of what she was telling us did not make sense, and we really needed the DNA to clarify what happened. I just got the results back and that was a December of 2009 case. There were no findings of male DNA either vaginally or rectally. There was DNA from three males on her neck but none matched the suspect I had in custody initially.

Finally, one LASD detective focused the need for improvement on the LA County DA's Office:

If there is a place where progress could be made it would be the DA's Office by assigning special DAs to these types of cases. VIP is a façade. We only have one DA, but the problem is there's only one of her and eight of us that work 100 cases each per year. . . . The big problem is the burden of proof and to surmount that is tough. I don't know what more can be done. The DA is hard-pressed with time and resources. Our filing VIP DA I think . . . files everything [that] can possibly [be filed]. And they've helped us some. Over the years it used to be [that] an uncorroborated child case without a confession or physical evidence would not get filed. We've come a long way now.

We use victim testimony and suspect behavior. An investigator changed that with the head DA. They said if you can successfully prosecute one of those we'll change that policy. That was 1989 [or] 1990. That helped us with smaller kids because the earlier policy gave us a challenge to be able to qualify these victims for interviewing. The DA's Office has come a long way, but with the rape cases of teens I honestly don't know, using our burden of proof. I'll use the DA as the scapegoat because they have serious issues with [the] number of cases they are trying.

Turning now to DDAs' recommendations for increasing the successful prosecution of sexual assault, they overwhelmingly emphasized a need for: (1) only those people who want to work these types of cases to be assigned to them; (2) specialized sex crimes training; (3) better front-end investigations by law enforcement with regard to interviewing and evidence collection; (4) faster processing from the crime lab in sexual assault cases; and (5) juror education. Tied to the notion that only those who want to work these cases should, one DDA noted: "I was working in [a branch] 18 years ago and a judge said that a prostitute cannot be raped. There is still a prevalent attitude that a wife cannot be raped." Another DDA also spoke to the dynamics of victim blaming and stated the pathway for change is to

fix the rape shield law. I think the only loophole is that even if the evidence does not get introduced the defense is not precluded from asking about it. Victims are the ones who are put on trial. There is inconvenience, their privacy is invaded, they are held up for scrutiny, and they are shamed, sometimes by their own family members.

Another attorney commented how these dynamics extend to the mindsets of jurors:

Jurors have a lot of misconceptions about what a sex crime victim is going to look like and sound like. Many believe that there is going to be injury and there is going to be DNA. We can try to get this across during jury selection, but judges often don't give you enough time to do this. One thing I always ask is whether they can convict based on just one person's testimony. When they step into the box it's like they lose common sense and they expect more than they would in any other type of case. The second thing would be detective training. They send people in here who don't know what they are doing. They seem to have a difficult time finding people who are willing to do sex crimes.

Along these lines, another DDA stated:

> I've stopped looking at people as promiscuous. If young ladies go
> out then they have to live with the consequences of drinking. I think
> it is wonderful that we have nurses who encourage reporting; maybe
> it will make boys afraid. But if she doesn't report right away, [and
> connect with] SART right away, then all of these things are
> questioned. And it's not their fault. Jurors make a victim toe the
> line that's been created by the media, movies, and books. It creates
> a scenario where women go through horrible things but can't get
> back at him through the legal process.

A problematic consequence of this, as explained by another DDA, is a continued distinction between how any evidence in stranger versus nonstranger cases is processed: "If we had patrol officers who understood the big picture and crime lab technicians who followed up quickly. If it's a known suspect they do not rush. If a stranger comes up it's a higher priority. If it's his word against hers they are lower priority." This is particularly problematic given a head deputy's reflection about the infrequency of stranger cases: "Each lawyer in my unit might have one stranger case out of 149 open cases." Another common distinction noted by both detectives and district attorneys is the seriousness accorded to homicide investigations relative to sexual assault, which translates into a discrepancy in resources. A DDA commented: "We need to be better with physical evidence and crime scene investigation. There's a whole team of investigators in homicide that are canvassing for witnesses, doing forensics, and taking pictures. If we did that with sexual assault it would be better for prosecution." Similarly, a few attorneys described ways that law enforcement could strengthen their investigations:

> Law enforcement needs to do more investigation into the defendant
> and his past because I think for most of these victims they are not the
> first for these guys, it's just that we don't know. If we had other
> victims to corroborate it would help. The only other way to get our
> prosecutions better is to have better victims. Without good victims
> cases don't get filed. I had bad victims in the party girl case, but I had
> enough victims to show the defendant is bad. You can overcome these
> things with a thorough investigation.
>
> Quicker DNA processing. We have cases that are filed and we are
> still waiting for DNA. I would like to have photos of everything and
> audiotaping the initial interviews with the cops and the SART nurse
> because reading the notes is not as good as viewing the video. SART
> nurses always tape-record them and these are great. Detectives don't

always do this but it is nice when they do. And photos for everything help paint a picture for the jury.

All suspects who are interviewed should be videotaped. We want the jury to see how they react as well as hear their words. Some agencies do it and some detectives will do it, but it just does not happen enough. We can't fabricate evidence and I can't change who my victims are and make them someone they aren't when they walk into court.

It's those first hours that are critical and most cases are mishandled. This is no offense to patrol officers but there is a lack of training and understanding. We aren't there in the first 48 hours. By the time cases come to us the damage has often been done and we can't un-ring the bell. The things I'm asking a detective to do weeks and weeks later they should do immediately. Many detectives do not understand what happens in the courtroom. When my detectives go through a case with me I make them list through the case with me. They say, "Oh my God, this is what you need to do," and from then on they are a different detective. Many haven't been through a trial and they don't get the burdens and hoops we have. They just feel, "Oh, the DA is lazy and can't file and won't do [the] job." They don't understand the onerous burden we're doing. Often I'm calling regarding a 288(C)(1) saying: "I need you to ask the defendant how old he is because I need a ten year age difference. Ask the defendant how old he thought victim was." Otherwise how do I prove he knew she was a certain age?

Given this is the computer age and considering victims are young and perps [perpetrators] are not usually 70-year-old guys, all of these people have computers. There must be more forensic evidence on these computers. Detectives and DAs need to be more computer savvy. We have cell phones and Blackberries but prosecutors and law enforcement are still stuck in the 1980s before all of this popped up and [yet] evidence is out there on the Internet. [The perps are] young people who are computer savvy, and we should be computer savvy too.

It takes a long, long time, especially with LAPD, to get DNA tested. We need to have the ability to get physical evidence more quickly because the evidence will disappear if you don't strike while the iron is hot. And, for example, if the victim said that she bit the defendant the detective should take photos.

Other interviewees emphasized funding related issues and the need for outreach to communities, as demonstrated by the following:

One problem is that since Prop 69 we take DNA samples from felons but samples just sit around. If all samples were entered into CODIS, LA County would have one solve per day on cold hit cases; this was what the media coverage said from Prop 69 ads. It is shameful that samples are sitting around and not being entered into the system and there is a responsibility to victims to do that. Funding for that should be a huge priority and that it is not is disturbing. More education is needed out there. Victims need to know what they need to do, for example, in drug and alcohol-related cases. If the victim knows there is only a six-hour period [to detect the rapist's drug in their system] they will be more likely to report immediately. If they are unsure, they should report anyway and get that sample. Many SART nurses recommend taking a urine sample yourself. That creates chain-of-evidence problems but it's better than nothing. I had a friend ask me to prepare a presentation about date rape [for] a Catholic school [wanting to educate students] about drug rapes. They never got back to me and my feeling was it was too graphic and [their reaction] was denial-based. They didn't want this kind of presentation in the school yet it is the precise thing that it going in this age group. It globally speaks to a need for education.

We need better equipment. [For example,] media carts in the courthouse are broken or missing a cable. We've made some progress technologically. We should have a paralegal assigned to us because huge parts of our cases are based on past behavior. We use time building cases by looking backward. A victim advocate is critical to play the gap when the DDA is not available. The victim advocate needs to be there watching the defendant. When the victim holds up [testifies articulately and consistently] at prelim, defense attorneys know they have something to be scared of. Some of my colleagues need to be better trained as to how to use victim advocates. They are an underused and undervalued aspect of the office.

I need more people desperately. For example, I am trying to do a domestic violence rape currently and you can't prepare a case with two-minute increments. I realized there was a prior victim. The guy had been calling her from jail and they were having one-hour-long conversations. The cases I am working on I do not have enough time to attend to. I've been working early morning through late evening every night and I have a new trial starting on Wednesday of a rapist who raped the 65-year-old woman he befriended. He has six prior arrests for rape.

The problem we have is lack of outreach. How to fix that? We do not know who to target. Victims are unaware that they should report.

I have victims who report only when they see on TV that a crime is discussed. Schools should be outreaching and educating. Outreach is very bad, especially in this community. Gangs and drugs [are] the focus here; sexual assault is not discussed as much. Parents do not know or they are doing it. Often they are not English speakers and not comfortable with the system. [We need] a better showing on law enforcement's part in the community to show there is an effort to get these victims justice.

Finally, a head deputy called for a change in how the district attorney's office gets involved in sexual assault cases:

We need roll-outs where DAs go to the SART exam. The DA needs to be a part of the investigation from the beginning. You can pin down on the victim right away. The initial story when injuries are fresh is the best story. Victims need to be educated. By the time we get a case we hear he has done it a bunch of times but never reported. Education. If we did roll-outs victims would not be revictimized and traumatized by [the] process.

This statement is representative of the feelings of many detectives and DDAs, who longed for a streamlining of the investigative process to both maximize the effective use of resources and better serve sexual assault victims. It is similar to the reasoning of LAPD detectives, who called for centralization of sex crimes throughout Los Angeles, and the LASD detectives, who stated the Special Victims Bureau should investigate all sexual assault cases, not just those involving victims age 18 and under. While larger city and county economic conditions and subsequent budget cutbacks are beyond the control of LAPD, LASD, and the LA County DA, each agency's leadership does have control over how to best use available resources and is uniquely positioned to effect change. We return to this in Chapter 8.

Conclusion

This chapter began by describing LAPD and LASD detectives and LA County DDAs' perceptions of the challenges that sexual assault victims face when reporting to law enforcement. It also examined interviewees' self-reported strategies to establish rapport with sexual assault victims and evaluate their credibility, and their recommendations for increasing the successful prosecution of sexual assault. Across all dimensions, respondents trended in two main ways: first were those who evidenced passion for working sexual assault cases and highlighted the nuances and complexities of these cases. They emphasized the importance of a thorough investigation, the need for good interview and interrogation skills, and that victims seldom lie. Conversely, the second group was more likely to express skepticism about nonstranger sexual assault and emphasize stranger rape or cases involving children as "real" rape. They were also more likely to focus on victim consistency from the initial report to the follow-up without consideration of how the treatment of victims or the pathways through which law enforcement collects information may generate the very inconsistencies that are cited as reflecting on victim credibility. The next chapter turns to patterns in case attrition and outcomes.

Notes

1. GHB is short for gamma-hydroxybutyric acid.
2. "Six-pack" is police jargon for a photo lineup done so that victims and witnesses can identify a suspect.
3. An LAPD deputy chief described sentiments such as this as "having a fire in the belly" to work these kinds of cases.
4. Our analysis of 2008 case files revealed that the majority of female sexual assault victims older than age 12 did not report the sexual assault immediately: 25.8 percent of females older than age 12 who reported a sexual assault to LAPD and 20.5 percent who reported to LASD did so within one hour of its occurrence.
5. Our analysis revealed that the majority of victims in our sample provided consistent statements to law enforcement. Specifically, 20 percent of the LAPD female victims and 11.8 percent of LASD female victims gave inconsistent statements.
6. Our analysis of 2008 case files revealed that the majority of female sexual assault victims did not have a criminal history. Specifically, only 12.4 percent who reported to LAPD and 3.2 percent who reported to LASD had a criminal record of some sort.
7. The term 5150 refers to an involuntary psychiatric hold authorized under Section 5150 of the California Welfare and Institutions Code.
8. Our analysis of 2008 case files revealed that 7.8 percent of female sexual assault victims in our sample who reported to LAPD and 1.7 percent who reported to LASD were sex workers.
9. To clarify, by raising the issue of "business disputes" detectives were not categorically asserting that simply by virtue of being a prostitute one cannot be raped. Rather, they drew a distinction between cases in which suspects prey on prostitutes because they are vulnerable and cases in which a prostitute and a john agree to sex for a price, it occurs, and then he refuses to pay her. With no civil recourse given its illegality, prostitutes will sometimes reach out to the police for help in the context of a rape report.
10. This quote comes from a DIC of a VIP unit, who stated that [he or she] does all of the prefiling interviews and the lawyers working in their unit have about 30 cases each, which is "probably about 10 cases too many for each of them."
11. In response to this study, senior LAPD leadership developed a one-week sexual assault school that all sex crimes detectives must complete.
12. As we discuss in Chapter 8, this is one of the changes that was implemented in response to our study's findings and recommendations.

4

Case Attrition
and Case Outcomes

One of the enduring realities of sexual assault is that very few cases result in the arrest, prosecution, and conviction of the suspect. In many cases—especially those in which the suspect is a stranger to the victim—a suspect is not identified. In cases in which a suspect is identified, the police will not necessarily make an arrest, and in cases in which an arrest is made, the prosecutor will not necessarily file charges. Sexual assault cases in which charges are filed can be dismissed if the case falls apart or the victim fails to show up for court proceedings, and cases that go to trial can result in acquittals. Although these patterns of case attrition are common in all types of felonies (Vera Institute of Justice, 1981), they are particularly pronounced in sexual assault cases, which often involve traumatized or uncooperative victims, delayed reporting, and inferences about the victim's character or reputation and behavior at the time of the incident. As numerous researchers have pointed out (Estrich, 1987; LaFree, 1989), the likelihood of case attrition will be especially high in cases in which the victim and the suspect are acquaintances or intimate partners.

In this chapter, we examine the outcomes of sexual assaults reported to the Los Angeles Police Department (LAPD) and the Los Angeles County Sheriff's Department (LASD). Our objectives are to document where in the process attrition is likely to occur and to identify the factors that predict whether the suspect will be arrested and prosecuted. We begin by examining longitudinal data on all sexual assaults reported to the two law enforcement agencies from 2005 through 2009. We then focus on cases that were reported in 2008. We use the richer and more detailed data that we collected on these cases to create a descriptive profile of sexual assaults reported to the LAPD and the LASD and to model case outcomes.

Case Attrition:
Sexual Assaults Reported from 2005 Through 2009

As explained in Chapter 1, each law enforcement agency provided us with data on all sex crimes that met our selection criteria and that were reported from January 2005 to December 2009, and the DA's Office provided us with outcome data on cases that resulted in the arrest of at least one adult suspect. There were 10,832 cases reported to the LAPD and 3,301 cases reported to the LASD. Of the cases reported to the LAPD, 5,031 (46.4%) were the Uniform Crime Reporting (UCR) Part I Index offenses of rape and attempted rape, and 5,801 (53.6%) were sexual batteries (n = 4,721) or other sex crimes (i.e., sexual penetration with a foreign object, n = 202; oral copulation, n = 496; sodomy, n = 363; unlawful sex, n = 9; and sex with a child, n = 10). Of the cases reported to the LASD, 2,269 (68.6%) were the UCR Part I index offenses of rape or attempted rape and 1,040 (31.4%) were sexual batteries (n = 410) or other sex crimes (i.e., sexual penetration with an object, n =214; oral copulation, n = 303; and sodomy, n = 113). In this section we first focus on the outcomes for the Part I Index offenses of rape and attempted rape. We then discuss the types of cases that were excluded from the UCR definition of forcible rape that was in effect during this time period[1] and provide descriptive data on the outcomes of these cases.

Case Outcomes for 2005 to 2009: LAPD

The outcomes for the 5,031 rapes and attempted rapes reported to the LAPD are shown in Figure 4.1. Most cases were either cleared (N = 2,300; 45.7%) or the investigation was still continuing (N = 2,185; 43.4%); there were only 546 cases (10.9%) that were unfounded by the police during this five-year period. Of the 2,300 cases that were cleared, the majority were cleared by exceptional means (33.5% of all cases) rather than by arrest (12.2%). Of the 616 cases that were cleared by arrest, 591 resulted in the arrest of at least one adult suspect. The prosecutor filed charges in 486 (82.2%) of these cases and charges were declined in 105 cases (17.8%). Although this is a higher charging rate than is found in most studies of prosecutorial decisionmaking in sexual assault cases, it reflects the fact that the LAPD (and the LASD) present "problematic" cases to the district attorney (DA) for a prearrest filing decision. As discussed in detail in Chapter 2, if the DA believes that the case does not meet their filing standard of proof beyond a reasonable doubt, the case is "rejected" before the suspect is arrested and is then cleared (inappropriately) by exceptional means. As we explain in more detail in Chapter 6, use of this prearrest charge evaluation process and overuse of the exceptional clearance reduces the LAPD's arrest rate and increases the charging rate for cases that result in an arrest.

The fact that the DA screens out sexual assault cases in which the evidence does not meet the standard of proof beyond a reasonable doubt is reflected in the conviction rate, which is 80.2 percent; 349 defendants pled guilty, 35 were convicted at a jury trial, and 5 were convicted at a bench

Figure 4.1 Case Outcomes for Rapes and Attempted Rapes Reported to LAPD, January 2005–December 2009

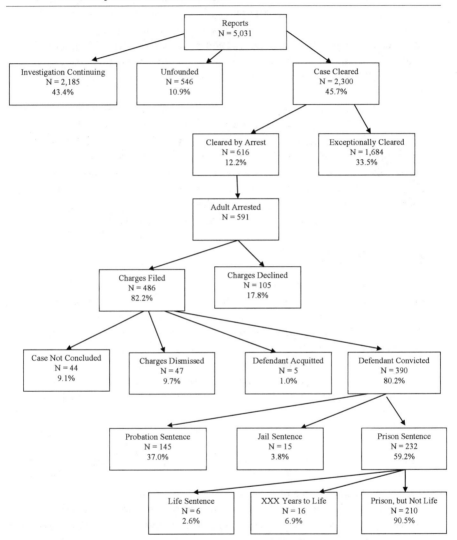

trial. Only five defendants were acquitted at trial and charges were dismissed in 47 cases (9.7% of all cases in which charges were filed); an additional 44 cases (9.1%) were still open at the time that the data were provided to us. Of the 390 defendants who were convicted, the majority (59.2%) was sentenced to prison and received a sentence for a fixed term of years rather than a life sentence or a sentence of some number of years to life. Over a third (37.0%) of the convicted defendants were sentenced to probation and 15 (3.8%) received a jail sentence.

Another way to conceptualize the pattern of case attrition is to calculate the proportion of cases that "survive" successive stages of the process. Using this approach, only 11.7 percent of the 5,031 rapes and attempted rapes that were reported to the LAPD during this five-year time period were cleared by the arrest of an adult suspect, 9.7 percent resulted in the filing of charges by the prosecutor, 7.8 percent resulted in a conviction, and 4.6 percent resulted in a prison sentence. As these data make clear, the locus of case attrition resides in the decision to arrest (or not).

Case Outcomes for 2005 to 2009: LASD

A somewhat different pattern of results is found for the 2,269 UCR Part I rapes and attempted rapes reported to the LASD from 2005 through 2009 (see Figure 4.2). In contrast to the LAPD, which cleared or solved fewer than half of the cases, the clearance rate for the LASD was 88.3 percent; there were only 224 cases (10.6%) in which the investigation was continuing and only 24 cases that were unfounded. The LASD's unusually high clearance rate reflects both a higher arrest rate (33.9% versus 12.2% for the LAPD) and greater use of the exceptional clearance (54.4% versus 33.5% for the LAPD).

There were 614 adults arrested for rape and attempted rape and charges were filed in 405 (66.0%) of these cases. Although the charging rate for suspects arrested by the LASD is lower than the rate for suspects arrested by the LAPD, it is nonetheless higher than the rates reported in other studies. Again, this reflects a process that weeds out "problematic cases" before an arrest is made. Of the 405 LASD cases in which charges were filed, the conviction rate was 78.1 percent. This is very similar to the rate for LAPD cases (80.2%). The sentences imposed on convicted defendants who were arrested by the LASD also were almost identical to those imposed on convicted defendants arrested by the LAPD. Over half of the defendants were sentenced to prison for a fixed term of years and just over a third were given probation sentences.

In terms of the cases that survived from one stage of the process to the next, 27.1 percent of the 2,269 rape and attempted rape cases that were reported to the LASD during the five-year time period were cleared by the

Figure 4.2 Case Outcomes for Rapes and Attempted Rapes Reported to LASD, January 2005–December 2009

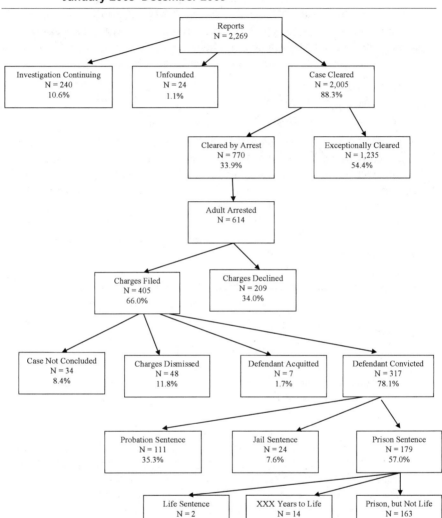

arrest of an adult suspect, 17.8 percent resulted in the filing of charges, 14.0 percent resulted in a conviction, and 8.4 percent resulted in a prison sentence. As was the case with outcomes for the LAPD, these figures illustrate that most cases are filtered out at the arrest stage of the process. Because the arrest rate for the LASD is three times higher than the rate for the LAPD, the proportions of cases that survive successive stages also are larger.

Reports Not Included in the
Pre-2012 UCR Definition of Rape

Prior to 2012, the *UCR Handbook* (FBI, 2004) defined forcible rape as "the carnal knowledge of a female forcibly and against her will. Attempts or assaults to commit rape by force or threat of force are also included; however, statutory rape (without force) and other sex offenses are excluded." The fact that rape was defined as "carnal knowledge" meant that acts that did not involve penile-vaginal penetration—including sexual penetration with an object, oral copulation, and sodomy—were not included as Part I offenses but as "other sex offenses" in Part II of the "crimes known to the police." Also not included were reports of sexual penetration with an object, oral copulation, and sodomy, which were the "secondary crimes" that accompanied reports of Part I crimes such as robbery, burglary, and aggravated assault. Despite the fact that most experts would categorize sexual penetration with an object, oral copulation, and sodomy as crimes that fall within the definition of rape/sexual assault, the antiquated definition used by the FBI for Uniform Crime Reporting purposes prior to 2012 meant that these serious sex offenses were combined with the less serious sexual batteries (i.e., fondling or touching with sexual connotation) as Part II "other sex offenses."

The implications of excluding these crimes from the definition of forcible rape are illustrated by the data provided in Table 4.1. From 2005 to 2009, the LAPD received 5,031 reports of rape and attempted rape; they received 1,061 reports of oral copulation, penetration with an object, and sodomy. If these "other sex offenses" were included in the forcible rape category, the number of reports of forcible rape received by the LAPD during this five-year time period would increase by 21 percent (from 5,031 to 6,092). The figures for the LASD are similar. From 2005 to 2009, the LASD received 2,269 reports of rape and attempted rape; they received 630 reports of oral copulation, penetration with an object, and sodomy. Including these "other sex offenses" in the forcible rape category would have increased the number of reports of forcible rape received by the LASD by more than 27 percent (from 2,269 to 2,899). Stated another way, 17.4 percent of the reports received by the LAPD and 21.7% of the reports received by the LASD during these five years were reports of penetration with a foreign object, oral copulation, and sodomy.

Table 4.1 Reports of Sex Offenses, LAPD and LASD, 2005–2009

	N	%
Reports Received by LAPD		
Rape or Attempted Rape	5,031	82.6
Sexual Penetration with a Foreign Object	202	3.3
Oral Copulation	496	8.1
Sodomy	363	6.0
Reports Received by LASD		
Rape or Attempted Rape	2,269	78.2
Sexual Penetration with a Foreign Object	214	7.4
Oral Copulation	303	10.4
Sodomy	113	3.9

Case Characteristics and Case Outcomes: Cases Reported in 2008

The data discussed thus far provide an overview of the outcomes of rape and attempted rape cases reported to the two law enforcement agencies from 2005 to 2009. However, these data do not address questions regarding the characteristics of cases that were reported to the agencies or the outcomes of various types of cases. We use the detailed data collected from the redacted case files provided by each agency to describe the characteristics of victims, suspects, and cases and to provide more complete descriptions of case clearances or outcomes.

Victim, Suspect, and Case Characteristics

The victim, suspect, and case characteristics for the 2008 cases are presented in Tables 4.2 through 4.4. As shown in Table 4.2, the typical victim (both agencies) was a Latina in her mid-20s. Substantial numbers of victims reported that they were drinking or drunk at the time of the incident, but the number reporting use of illegal drugs was low. Most victims were not engaged in any type of risky behavior at the time of the incident (other than use of alcohol) and the number of victims with documented mental health issues noted in the case file was low. Nearly half of the victims suffered some type of collateral injury during the assault and stated that they resisted the suspect both verbally and physically. Most victims did not report the crime within one hour. In terms of the victim's willingness to cooperate with law enforcement, Table 4.2 illustrates that a substantial proportion of victims was able to identify the suspect by full name and address (39.8% of those who reported to the LAPD and 59.8% of those who reported to the LASD) and were cooperative during the investigation of the crime by the police (56.3% for LAPD and 72.5% for LASD). Very few victims recanted

Table 4.2 Victim Characteristics in Rape and Attempted Rape Cases, 2008

Victim Characteristics	LAPD (N = 273)[a]		LASD (N = 410)	
	N	%	N	%
Background Characteristics				
Age (mean)	27.4		25.6	
Race/Ethnicity				
Caucasian	65	23.9	87	22.0
Hispanic/Latina	127	46.7	191	48.2
African American	74	27.1	97	24.5
Asian American/Other	6	2.1	21	5.3
Credibility Factors				
Criminal record	34	12.4	13	3.2
Gang affiliation mentioned in report	11	3.9	3	0.7
Drinking at time of incident	80	29.3	97	23.8
Drunk at time of incident	66	24.1	67	16.3
Using illegal drugs at time of incident	20	7.4	27	6.6
Passed out (not drugged)	41	15.0	43	10.5
Walking alone late at night	30	10.9	8	3.4
Accepted a ride from a stranger	24	8.9	8	3.4
Mental health issues	34	12.6	33	8.1
Sex worker	21	7.8	4	1.7
Injured during assault	119	43.6	193	47.1
Inconsistent statements to police	54	20.0	48	11.8
No physical or verbal resistance	74	27.3	81	19.8
Verbal resistance only	47	17.1	76	18.5
Physical resistance only	28	10.3	32	7.8
Verbal and physical resistance	124	45.3	221	53.9
Reported within one hour	71	25.8	84	20.5
Cooperation with Law Enforcement				
Identified suspect by full name and address	109	39.8	245	59.8
Cooperative during police investigation	154	56.3	296	72.5
Recanted her allegation	26	9.4	21	5.1
Moved residences after the assault	43	15.8	25	6.1
Did not want suspect arrested	29	10.6	37	9.1

Note: a. Weighted sample of cases.

their allegations and only about 1 in every 10 indicated that they did not want the suspect arrested.

The suspect characteristics for the rape and attempted rape cases are shown in Table 4.3. We do not present data on the sociodemographic characteristics of suspects due to the fact that in a substantial number of cases handled by each agency there was not an identified suspect (39.7% of the LAPD cases and 15.1% of the LASD cases did not have an identified suspect). In these cases, in other words, we would have had to rely on the victim's perception of the age and race or ethnicity of the suspect.

Most of the suspects in these cases were not affiliated with a gang and most did not drug their victims prior to the alleged assault. Nearly two

Table 4.3 Suspect Characteristics in Rape and Attempted Rape Cases, 2008

Suspect Characteristics	LAPD (N = 273)[a]		LASD (N = 410)	
	N	%	N	%
Gang affiliation mentioned in report	32	11.6	40	9.8
Drugged victim	10	3.7	38	9.5
Physically assaulted victim, this incident	164	60.1	204	49.8
Weapon used	73	26.6	47	11.5
Bodily force only to subdue victim	192	70.2	333	81.2
Defense in statement to police[b]				
Consent	48	51.9	96	45.7
Incident fabricated	32	34.7	71	33.8
Incorrect identification	3	2.8	3	1.4
Admitted or confessed	10	10.7	40	19.0

Notes: a. Weighted sample of cases.
b. Of the identified suspects who gave a statement to law enforcement.

thirds (60.1%) of the suspects in the LAPD cases and half (49.8%) of the suspects in the LASD cases physically, as well as sexually, assaulted the victims during the incident that generated the police report. Most of the suspects subdued their victims using bodily force only, but more than one fourth (26.6%) of the suspects in the LAPD cases used a gun, knife, or some other type of weapon to subdue the victim. By contrast, only 11.5 percent of the cases reported to the LASD were cases in which suspects used weapons. Of the suspects who gave a statement to the law enforcement agency, the most common defense was that the sexual contact with the victim was consensual, followed by an assertion that the incident was fabricated by the complainant. Very few suspects claimed that they had been incorrectly identified and only 10 (10.7%) of the LAPD suspects and 40 (19.0%) of the LASD suspects admitted or confessed to the crime for which they were under investigation.

Table 4.4 presents the characteristics of the cases reported to each agency, as well as data on the investigation conducted by the agency. The most serious charge listed on the police report was rape (i.e., forcible rape, rape of a spouse, rape by intoxication, sodomy, oral copulation, or rape with an object) rather than attempted rape. The majority of the crimes occurred at night—that is, from 6 PM to midnight or from midnight to 6 AM. Very few of the incidents took place between 6 AM and noon.

In terms of the relationship between the victim and the suspect, the majority of the cases reported to each law enforcement agency were cases involving nonstrangers. This was particularly true for cases reported to the LASD, where more than three fourths of all cases involved victims and suspects who were nonstrangers (51.5%) or intimate partners (27.1%); only

21.4 percent of the LASD cases were cases involving strangers. By contrast, 41.0 percent of the cases reported to the LAPD were cases involving strangers, 33.4 percent were cases involving nonstrangers, and 25.6 percent were cases involving intimate partners. These differences led to similar differences in the percentages of cases in which a suspect is positively identified; 84.9 percent of the LASD cases, but only 60.3 percent of the LAPD cases had an identified suspect. Of the cases involving intimate partners, the mean length of the relationship varied from 6.2 years (LAPD) to 4.4 years (LASD); most of the suspects and victims in this category did not have a child together.

Between 40 and 50 percent of these cases were cases with at least one witness and in which some type of physical evidence (e.g., clothing, bedding,

Table 4.4 Case Characteristics in Rape and Attempted Rape Cases, 2008

Victim Characteristics	LAPD (N = 273)[a]		LASD (N = 410)	
	N	%	N	%
Rape or attempted rape charge				
Rape	234	85.6	347	84.6
Attempted rape	39	14.4	63	15.4
Time of day when crime occurred				
Midnight to 6 AM	82	30.2	57	15.0
6 AM to noon	44	16.1	77	20.3
Noon to 6 PM	61	22.4	113	29.7
6 PM to midnight	85	31.4	133	35.0
Relationship between victim and suspect				
Strangers	112	41.0	87	21.4
Nonstrangers	91	33.4	209	51.5
Intimate partners	70	25.6	110	27.1
Length of relationship (mean)	6.2 yrs		4.4 yrs	
Victim and suspect have a child	19	20.9	30	27.5
Evidence				
At least one witness	108	40.5	176	43.0
Witness corroborates victim's story	41	42.9	40	24.8
Witness corroborates suspect's story	9	16.1	13	12.5
Forensic medical exam conducted	146	53.5	203	49.8
Any type of physical evidence recovered	132	48.3	197	48.0
Characteristics of Police Investigation				
LAPD/LASD can identify suspect	165	60.3	348	84.9
LAPD/LASD interviewed suspect[b]	93	56.4	212	60.9
LAPD/LASD interviewed witnesses[c]	7	89.8	156	88.6
LAPD/LASD conducted pretext phone call[b]	12	7.2	22	6.3
LAPD/LASD got photos of victim's injuries[d]	77	64.7	160	82.9

Notes: a. Weighted sample of cases.
   b. Of the identified suspects who gave a statement to law enforcement.
   c. Of cases in which there was at least one witness.
   d. Of cases in which the victim suffered collateral injuries.

hair, fibers, blood, weapon, semen) was recovered from the scene of the crime or from the victim or suspect. If there was a witness, the witness was much more likely to corroborate the victim's testimony than that of the suspect. In about half of the cases (53.5% for LAPD and 49.8% for LASD) the victim underwent a forensic medical exam.

We collected data on a number of indicators of the steps taken by the law enforcement agency during the investigation of the crime. As shown in Table 4.4, police were substantially more likely to interview witnesses (in cases in which there was at least one witness) than suspects (in cases in which there was an identified suspect). The LAPD interviewed witnesses in 89.8 percent of the cases but interviewed suspects in only 56.4 percent of the cases; similarly witnesses were interviewed by the LASD in 88.6 percent of the cases but suspects were interviewed in only 60.9 percent of the cases. This no doubt reflects that fact that whereas suspects have a right to refuse to speak to law enforcement, witnesses do not. Although our interviews with detectives in each agency revealed that the pretext phone call—that is, a phone call made by the victim to the suspect in which the victim attempts to get the suspect to incriminate himself—was regarded as an effective investigatory technique, we found that these calls were used in a very small percentage of the cases (7.2% for LAPD and 6.3% for LASD). Moreover, the investigating officers did not always photograph the victim's injuries; in cases in which the victim suffered collateral injuries, her injuries were photographed in only 64.7 percent of the cases handled by the LAPD and in 82.9 percent of the cases handled by the LASD. (This could reflect the fact that victims claimed that they suffered collateral injuries during the assault but reported the assault after evidence of these injuries had disappeared.)

Case Clearances and Case Outcomes

As shown in Table 4.5, the case clearances for sexual assaults reported in 2008 were very similar to those for cases reported from 2005 to 2009 (see Figures 4.1 and 4.2). Nearly half (45.3%) of the LAPD cases and 89% of the LASD were cleared, either by arrest or by exceptional means. Sexual assaults reported to the LAPD were substantially more likely than those reported to the LASD to be open, investigation continuing cases or to be unfounded.

Because we had access to the case files, we were able to provide more detailed descriptive data on the 2008 cases. For example, we were able to identify cases that resulted in an arrest but that were cleared exceptionally when the DA refused to file charges (as we explain in Chapter 6, these cases should not have been cleared by exceptional means given statements in the *UCR Handbook* indicating that the exceptional clearance is to be

Table 4.5 Case Clearances by Victim-Suspect Relationship, 2008

	LAPD (N = 273)[a]		LASD (N = 410)	
	N	%	N	%
All Cases				
Cleared by arrest (adult and juvenile)	32	11.7	130	31.7
Cleared exceptionally	92	33.6	235	57.3
After making an arrest	*35*	*12.8*	*37*	*9.0*
Investigation continuing	119	43.4	38	9.3
Report unfounded	30	10.9	7	1.7
Suspect arrested (cleared by arrest + exceptionally cleared after making an arrest)	67	24.5	176	40.7
	(N = 112)		(N = 87)	
Cases Involving Strangers				
Cleared by arrest (adult and juvenile)	9	8.0	19	21.8
Cleared exceptionally	17	15.2	48	55.2
After making an arrest	*5*	*4.5*	*7*	*8.0*
Investigation continuing	71	63.4	19	21.8
Report unfounded	15	13.4	1	1.1
Suspect arrested (cleared by arrest + exceptionally cleared after making an arrest)	14	12.5	26	29.9
	(N = 161)		(N = 318)	
Cases Involving Nonstrangers				
Cleared by arrest (adult and juvenile)	23	14.3	110	34.5
Cleared exceptionally	75	46.6	184	57.7
After making an arrest	*30*	*18.6*	*39*	*12.2*
Investigation continuing	48	29.8	18	5.6
Report unfounded	15	9.3	6	1.9
Suspect arrested (cleared by arrest + exceptionally cleared after making an arrest)	53	32.9	149	46.7

Note: a. Weighted sample of cases.

used when factors beyond the control of law enforcement prevent them from making an arrest). We also were able to determine clearance rates for cases in which the victim and suspect were strangers and cases in which the victim and suspect were nonstrangers. Finally, we were able to identify cases that were rejected by the DA prior to and following the arrest of a suspect.

Turning first to the cases that were exceptionally cleared, 12.8 percent of the LAPD cases and 9.0 percent of the LASD cases were cases in which the police initially made an arrest but then cleared the case by exceptional means when the DA decided not to file charges. Adding these cases to the cases that were cleared by arrest more than doubles the LAPD arrest rate (from 11.7% to 24.5%) and increases the LASD arrest rate from 31.7 percent to 40.7 percent. Reclassifying cases where an arrest was made but the prosecutor refused to file charges as exceptional clearances, in other words, substantially reduces the official arrest rate for each agency.

The data presented in Table 4.5 indicate that cases involving strangers were cleared differently than cases involving nonstrangers. The percentages of cases that were cleared by arrest were higher for cases involving nonstrangers than for cases involving strangers for each agency; by contrast, cases involving strangers were substantially more likely than those involving nonstrangers to be categorized as open or investigation continuing. These patterns no doubt reflect the fact that cases involving strangers were less likely than those involving nonstrangers to have an identified suspect. The patterns for cases cleared by exceptional means are very different for the two law enforcement agencies. Whereas the LAPD was significantly more likely to use the exceptional clearance in cases in which the victim and suspect were nonstrangers, the LASD cleared about the same proportions of stranger and nonstranger cases by exceptional means. Table 4.5 also documents that cases in which the victim and suspect were nonstrangers were more likely to be cleared by exceptional means following an arrest and charge rejection by the prosecutor than were cases in which the victim and suspect were strangers. Thus, the effect of this (clearing by exceptional means following an arrest) is manifested most clearly in terms of the overall arrest rates for the nonstranger cases. The nonstranger arrest rate increases from 14.3 percent to 32.9 percent for the LAPD and from 34.5 percent to 46.7 percent for the LASD when cases that were cleared by exceptional means after an arrest was made are included.

Case outcomes—The decision to prosecute. The fact that we had access to the case files for the 2008 sample of cases meant that we could identify cases that were presented to the DA for a charging decision both before and after the suspect was arrested. This is important, given that detectives from both agencies frequently presented cases to the DA prior to arresting the suspect and, if the DA refused to file charges because the evidence in the case did not meet their filing standard of proof beyond a reasonable doubt, cleared the case by exceptional means. Focusing only on charging decisions that followed the arrest of the suspect, in other words, would provide an incomplete picture of the charging process in Los Angeles.

Considering cases from both law enforcement agencies, there were 356 cases in which the DA made a charging decision. As shown in Table 4.6, 143 cases (40.2 percent) were presented to the LA DA before the suspect was arrested and 213 cases (59.8 percent) were presented to the LA DA after the suspect was arrested. Of the cases presented before arrest, the DA filed charges in only 8 (6.6 percent) cases. By contrast, charges were filed in 107 (50.2%) of the cases presented to the DA following the arrest of the

Table 4.6 Outcomes of Cases Presented to LA District Attorney Before and After Arrest of Suspect

	Suspect Not Arrested (N = 143)		Suspect Arrested (N = 213)	
	N	%	N	%
LA DA Filed Charges				
Yes	8	6.6	107	50.2
No	135	94.4	106	49.8
Case Clearance Type—				
Cases Rejected by LA DA				
Cleared by arrest	0	0.0	46	43.4
Cleared by exceptional means	134	99.3	58	54.7
Unfounded	1	0.7	2	1.9

suspect. As these data indicate, a substantial proportion of rape and attempted rape cases were presented to the DA prior to the suspect's arrest, and the outcome of these cases was very different than the outcome of cases presented following the suspect's arrest.

The data presented in Table 4.6 also demonstrate that cases presented to the LA DA prior to the suspect's arrest and subsequently rejected by the prosecutor who reviewed the case were, with only one exception, cleared by exceptional means. In contrast, cases that were rejected by the LA DA following the arrest of the suspect were either cleared by arrest (43.4 percent) or cleared by exceptional means (54.7 percent). Use of the exceptional clearance is problematic for both types of cases. As discussed in more detail in Chapter 6, the *UCR Handbook* specifies that the exceptional clearance can be used only if (1) the suspect has been identified, (2) the location of the suspect is known, (3) there is sufficient evidence to support arresting, charging, and turning the suspect over to the court for prosecution, and (4) there is something beyond the control of law enforcement that prevents the arrest of the suspect. The handbook also notes that cases in which the victim refuses to cooperate in the prosecution of the suspect can be cleared by exceptional means, but only if the first three criteria are met.

Turning first to cases cleared by exceptional means without the arrest of the suspect, all of these were cases in which the identity of the suspect was known, but we do not know whether the location of the suspect was known or whether the police had probable cause to make an arrest. Even assuming that criteria 2 and 3 were met, there is still a question of whether there was something beyond the control of law enforcement that prevented them from making an arrest. In 51 of the 134 cases (38.1%), the victim indicated that she did not want the suspect arrested or was unwilling to cooperate in the investigation and prosecution of the suspect, but the victims in the remaining cases (83 of 134 or 61.9%) were willing to cooperate if charges were filed. Assuming that in these latter cases the police had probable cause to make an arrest, the cases should not have been cleared by exceptional means, given that the victim was willing to cooperate and that there was nothing beyond the control of law enforcement that prevented them from making an arrest.

The 58 cases that were cleared by exceptional means following the arrest of the suspect—34 of which were investigated by the LASD and 24 of which were investigated by the LAPD—clearly should not have been cleared exceptionally. Because these cases resulted in the arrest of the suspect, by definition there was nothing beyond the control of the law enforcement agency that prevented the suspect's arrest. These cases should have been cleared by arrest.

Case characteristics. Further evidence that the prearrest screening process is used by detectives from both law enforcement agencies to dispose of problematic cases is found in Table 4.7, which presents descriptive data on the victim characteristics, indicators of crime seriousness, and measures of evidentiary strength for cases evaluated by the LA DA before and after arrest. Cases involving victims who engaged in risky behavior at the time of the incident or who had a mental illness or mental health issues were significantly more likely to be presented to the DA prior to arresting the suspect. By contrast, more serious cases (i.e., cases in which the suspect physically assaulted the victim, the suspect used a weapon, the victim suffered collateral injury, and the victim both verbally and physically resisted the suspect) were significantly more likely to be presented to the DA after the suspect was arrested. Moreover, all four of the evidentiary factors affected whether the case would be presented to the prosecutor before or after arresting the suspect. The case was significantly more likely to be evaluated following the arrest of the suspect if the victim reported the crime promptly, if the victim was willing to cooperate in the prosecution of the suspect, and if there was physical evidence to corroborate the victim's story or connect the suspect to the crime; the number of witnesses also had a positive effect on the likelihood that the case would be presented to the LA DA following the arrest of the suspect. On the other hand, the cases presented to the DA for a charging decision prior to and following the arrest of the suspect did not vary based on the victim's age, race or ethnicity, or relationship with the suspect, or based on whether there were questions about the victim's character or reputation or whether the victim had a motive to lie. Finally, the law enforcement agency to whom the incident was reported did not affect whether the case would be evaluated prior to or following the arrest of the suspect.

Table 4.7 Rape and Attempted Rape Cases by Whether Case Was Presented to District Attorney Before or After Suspect Arrest

Victim Characteristics	Presented to DA Before Suspect Arrested (N= 143)		Presented to DA After Suspect Arrested (N = 213)	
	N	%	N	%
Age (mean)	25.92		25.67	
Race/Ethnicity				
White	45	31.5	48	22.5
African American	30	21.0	46	21.6
Hispanic/Latina	68	47.6	119	55.9
Relationship with suspect				
Stranger	19	13.3	38	17.8
Nonstranger	74	51.7	102	47.9
Intimate partner	50	35.0	73	34.3
Risk-taking behavior (% yes)	56	39.2	69	32.4
Questions about character/reputation (% yes)	24	16.8	25	11.7
Mental illness or mental health issues (% yes)[a]*	20	14.0	14	6.6
Has a motive to lie (% yes)	25	17.5	24	11.3
Indicators of Crime Seriousness				
Most serious charge*				
Rape	137	95.8	175	82.2
Attempted rape	6	4.2	38	17.8
Suspect physically assaulted victim (% yes)*	66	46.2	125	58.7
Suspect used a weapon (% yes)*	7	4.9	35	16.4
Victim suffered collateral injury (% yes)*	65	45.5	127	59.6
Type of resistance*				
No verbal or physical resistance	32	22.4	42	19.7
Verbal only	37	25.9	31	14.6
Physical only	7	4.9	16	7.5
Both verbal and physical	67	46.9	124	58.2
Strength of Evidence				
Victim reported within one hour (% yes)*	12	8.4	71	33.3
Number of witnesses (mean)*	0.63		1.21	
Victim willing to cooperate (% yes)*	91	63.6	184	86.4
Physical evidence (% yes)*	66	46.2	1332	62.0
Agency				
LAPD	52	36.4	67	31.5
LASD	91	63.6	146	68.5

Note: a. One-way ANOVA testing for differences in means between cases presented to the district attorney before and after arrest.

  * $P \le .05$.

Summary: 2008 Case Characteristics and Case Clearances and Outcomes

Our analysis of the descriptive data on the sexual assaults reported to the LAPD and the LASD in 2008 revealed that these were cases involving relatively young victims, most of whom were Latina or African American women who were assaulted by nonstrangers or intimate partners from 6 PM to 6 AM. Most victims were not engaging in any type of risky behavior at the time of the incident, including drinking, using illegal drugs, or walking alone late at night. About half of the victims stated that they suffered collateral injuries during the assault and that they physically and verbally resisted the suspect, but very few reported the crime to the police immediately. About half of the victims had a forensic medical exam. Victims generally were willing to cooperate in the investigation of the case and few recanted their allegations or stated that they did not want to have the suspect arrested. Most suspects subdued their victims using bodily force only. About half of the suspects physically, as well as sexually, assaulted their victims, but very few drugged their victims before assaulting them. Some type of physical evidence was recovered in about half of the cases, and the investigating officers assigned to the case generally interviewed witnesses (in cases in which there was at least one witness), interviewed suspects less often, and rarely asked the victim to make a pretext phone call.

Data on the cases reported to the LAPD and LASD in 2008 reveal that the LASD is substantially more likely than the LAPD to clear rape and attempted rape cases by arresting at least one suspect; the official arrest rate (that is, the rate of cases in which the final case clearance is cleared by arrest) is 31.7 percent for the LASD but only 11.7 percent for the LAPD. This may reflect the fact that the cases reported to the LAPD are about twice as likely as those reported to the LASD (41.0% versus 21.4%) to involve victims and suspects who are strangers, as well as the related fact that the LASD cases are substantially more likely than the LAPD cases to have an identified suspect (84.9% versus 60.3%).

Our results also reveal that each agency overuses the exceptional clearance; a third of the cases reported to the LAPD and more than half of those reported to the LASD were cleared exceptionally. This leads to an overall rate of cases cleared by arrest for UCR purposes of 55.3 percent for the LAPD and 89.0 percent for the LASD; both of these rates, and particularly the rate for the LASD, are substantially higher than the national average for forcible rape, which was 39.5 percent in 2006 (Federal Bureau of Investigation, 2006). As we explain in more detail in Chapter 6 of this book, each agency uses this case clearance category inappropriately in a significant proportion of cases. In fact, each agency's use of this case clearance type in cases in which an arrest is made but the DA refuses to file charges (and thus the case clearance is changed from cleared by arrest to cleared by exceptional means) artificially depresses each agency's official arrest rate. If cases in which an arrest is made were consistently cleared by arrest, the LAPD arrest rate would be 24.5 percent and the LASD arrest rate would be 40.7 percent; among cases involving nonstrangers, the LAPD arrest rate would be 32.9 percent (rather than 14.3%) and the LASD arrest rate would be 46.7 percent (rather than 34.5%). We return to this issue in Chapter 6.

Analysis of the cases presented to the DA for a filing decision revealed that cases presented to the DA before the arrest of the suspect differ in important ways from cases presented following the arrest of the suspect. In addition, cases evaluated prior to the suspect's arrest are substantially more likely than those evaluated following the suspect's arrest to be rejected for prosecution and, subsequently, cleared by exceptional means. Considered together, the data on the characteristics and outcomes of cases evaluated before and after the suspect's arrest suggest that both law enforcement agencies use the prearrest screening process to clear problematic sexual assault cases without arresting the suspect.

The Correlates of Case Outcomes

In this section we present the results of our quantitative analysis of case outcomes. We focus on the police decision to unfound the charges, the police decision to make an arrest, and the prosecutor's decision to file charges. All of our analyses are limited to cases of rape and attempted rape, broadly defined. Thus, we include cases of oral copulation, sodomy, and penetration with an object; cases in which the most serious charge was sexual battery are excluded. Our analysis of the decision to unfound is limited to cases reported to the LAPD; this is because the LASD unfounded only eight cases in 2008.

We begin with a discussion of the independent variables included in the models of case outcomes.[2] This is followed by the presentation of results from the quantitative analyses. See Chapter 2 for a discussion of the process of clearing cases in the two jurisdictions and the standards used by the DA in deciding whether to file charges.

Modeling Case Outcomes

From the 2008 case files, we collected data on more than 250 independent variables. For the analysis of case outcomes, we selected independent variables for which there was little, if any, missing data and that prior research identified as relevant to case-processing decisions in sexual assault cases. The victim characteristics include the victim's age, race or ethnicity, and relationship with the suspect; whether the victim engaged in any risk-taking behavior at the time of the incident; and whether the case file indicated that the victim had characteristics that would make police and prosecutors question her credibility. The victim's age is a continuous variable that ranges from 12 to 99 (mean = 26.03). The victim's race or ethnicity is measured by four dummy variables (white, black, Hispanic, other); in all of the analyses white victims are the reference category. The relationship between the victim and the suspect is measured by three dummy variables (intimate partner, non-stranger, stranger); cases involving victims and suspects who were strangers are the reference category. The risk-taking variable is coded 1 if the case file indicated that at the time of the incident the victim either was walking alone late at night, accepted a ride from a stranger, voluntarily went to the suspect's house, invited the suspect to her residence, was in a bar alone, was in an area where illegal drugs were sold, was drinking alcohol, was drunk, was using illegal drugs, or had passed out after drinking alcohol or using illegal drugs. We use this composite variable, rather than the individual risk-taking variables, because of the small number of victims who were engaged in any of these types of risky behavior at the time of the incident. Of the cases in which the most serious charge was rape or attempted rape, 39.1 percent (N = 254) involved some type of risk-taking behavior, typically walking alone late at night or drinking alcohol.

The character or reputation variable is also a composite of several factors that might lead officials to question the victim's credibility. This variable was coded 1 if there was information in the case file indicating that the victim had a pattern of alcohol abuse, had a pattern of drug abuse, had a disreputable job (e.g., stripper, exotic dancer), was a prostitute, or had a criminal record. There were 108 cases (16.6%) with one or more of these character issues noted in the case files. We also controlled for whether there was information in the case file to indicate that the victim had a mental illness or mental health issues (yes = 1; no = 0)[3] or to indicate that the victim had a motive to lie about being sexually assaulted (yes = 1; no = 0).[4]

Our models also include a number of indicators of the seriousness of the sexual assault. We controlled for whether the most serious charge was rape (which for these analyses includes oral copulation, sodomy, and penetration with an object) rather than attempted rape, as well as for whether the suspect used some type of weapon during the assault (yes = 1; no = 0), and whether the suspect physically as well as sexually assaulted the victim (yes = 1; no = 0). We also included a variable that measures whether the victim suffered some type of collateral injury (e.g., bruises, cuts, choke marks) during the assault (yes = 1; no = 0); this information was obtained from the forensic medical report of the sexual assault examination (if there was an examination), from the responding officer's description of the victim's physical condition, or from the victim's statements in the case file. Finally, we control for whether the victim verbally or physically resisted the suspect using a series of dummy variables (no verbal or physical resistance, verbal resistance only; physical resistance only; both verbal and physical resistance); no verbal or physical resistance is the reference category.[5]

We controlled for several variables that measure the strength of evidence in the case. The first is whether the victim made a prompt report (yes = 1; no = 0), which we define as a report within one hour of the incident.

We also included controls for the number of witnesses to the alleged assault and for a dichotomous indicator of whether the victim was willing to cooperate after the investigation of the case began (yes =1; no = 0).[6] Our final evidentiary factor is a composite measure that is coded 1 if any of the following types of evidence were collected from the victim or from the scene of the incident: fingerprints, blood, hair, skin samples, clothing, bedding, or semen.

To control for the possibility that case outcomes differed between the LAPD and the LASD, our analyses of the decision to arrest and the decision to charge included a variable indicating whether the case was reported to the LAPD (coded 1) or the LASD (coded 0). Because our analysis of the decision to unfound includes only cases reported to the LAPD, for this analysis we included a set of dummy variables measuring the bureau to which the case was reported (Central, South, Valley, West); West Bureau is the reference category.

The Decision to Unfound the Charges

As discussed in more detail in Chapter 5 of this book, both the FBI and the International Association of Chiefs of Police (IACP) have published policy statements on the decision to unfound the charges. For example, FBI guidelines on clearing cases for purposes of Uniform Crime Reporting state that a case can be unfounded only if it is "determined through investigation to be false or baseless" (FBI, 2004: 77). The handbook also stresses that police are not to unfound a case simply because the complainant refused to prosecute or they are unable to make an arrest. Similarly, the IACP (2005) policy on investigating sexual assault cases states that "the determination that a report of sexual assault is false can be made only if the evidence establishes that no crime was committed or attempted" and that "this determination can be made only after a thorough investigation" (p. 12). Both sources, in other words, emphasize that the police must conduct an investigation and that their investigation must lead them to a conclusion that a crime did not occur.

The results of our analysis of the decision to unfound the charges are presented in Table 4.8. The dependent variable is a dichotomous measure of unfounding that is coded 1 if the LAPD unfounded the charges and 0 if the investigation was continuing, the case was cleared by exceptional means, or the case was cleared by arrest. In addition to these variables, our model includes a dichotomous variable that indicates whether the victim recanted her testimony (coded 1) or not (coded 0). Together, the victim characteristics, measures of case seriousness, evidence factors, and the LAPD bureau to which the sexual assault was reported explain 66 percent of the variance in the unfounding decision.

Table 4.8 LAPD's Decision to Unfound the Charges: Logistic Regression Analysis

	B	SE	Exp(B)
Victim Characteristics			
Age	.010	.02	1.01
Race/ethnicity			
African American	.511	.67	1.67
Hispanic/Latina	−.170	.61	0.84
Relationship to suspect			
Intimate partner	**−2.68***	.82	0.07
Nonstranger	−.680	.55	0.51
Risk-taking behavior at time of incident	.556	.53	1.74
Questions about character/reputation	**1.14***	.53	3.14
Mental illness or mental health issues	**2.287***	.69	9.85
Motive to lie	−.004	.66	0.99
Victim recanted	**5.72***	.98	305.20
Indicators of Case Seriousness			
Most serious charge is rape	.891	1.04	2.43
Suspect physically assaulted victim	−.403	.53	0.67
Suspect used a weapon	−.008	.87	0.99
Victim suffered collateral injury	**−1.074***	.52	0.34
Type of resistance			
Verbal only	−.562	.53	0.51
Physical only	−2.182	1.22	0.11
Verbal and physical	.190	.58	1.21
Strength of Evidence			
Victim reported within one hour	.229	.58	1.26
Number of witnesses	.335	.20	1.40
Victim willing to cooperate in investigation	.003	.47	0.60
Physical evidence	**−1.299***	.52	0.27
LAPD Bureau			
Central	−.256	.72	0.74
South	−1.022	.76	0.36
Valley	.494	.66	1.64
Constant	−2.103	1.59	
Nagelkerke R^2		.656	

Note: *P ≤ .05 (significant coefficients are indicated in bold)

Not surprisingly, the strongest predictor of the likelihood of unfounding was whether the victim recanted her testimony; the odds of unfounding were 305 times greater if the victim recanted. Several other victim characteristics also predicted the likelihood of unfounding, even taking into account whether the victim recanted the allegations. The report was more likely to be unfounded if the victim alleged that she was assaulted by a stranger than if she reported that she was assaulted by an intimate partner. This is not surprising, given that complainants who file false reports are more likely to report being assaulted by strangers; they apparently believe that their allegations will be viewed as more credible if they conform to stereotypes of "real rape." Also not surprising is that fact that unfounding was nearly 10 times more likely if the victim had a mental illness or mental health issues that called her credibility into question. Finally, the LAPD was three times more likely to unfound the charges if there was information in the case file that raised questions about the victim's character or reputation.

The only other variables that affected the likelihood of unfounding were whether the victim suffered some type of collateral injury and whether there was any physical evidence collected during the investigation. Unfounding was less likely if the victim was injured and if there was physical evidence. Both injury to the victim and physical evidence serve to corroborate the victim's allegations and therefore make it less likely that the detective investigating the case will believe that the victim fabricated the incident.

Because we believed that some of the independent variables would have both direct effects on the likelihood of unfounding and indirect effects on unfounding through their effect on whether the victim recanted, we estimated a model of recantation that included all of the variables listed in Table 4.8. The best predictor of victim recantation was whether the victim had a motivation to lie (B = 2.778; SE = .53); recanting was 16 times more likely if the victim had such a motivation. In addition, victims who reported being assaulted by strangers were significantly more likely to recant than were victims who reported being assaulted by intimate partners (B = −1.413; SE = .74) or nonstrangers (B = −1.626; SE = .60). Thus, the relationship between the complainant and the suspect affected both the likelihood that the victim would recant (victims who said that they were assaulted by strangers were more likely to recant their testimony) and the likelihood that the case would be unfounded (unfounding was more likely if the victim reported being assaulted by a stranger than if the victim reported being assaulted by an intimate partner). By contrast, having a motive to lie did not have a direct effect on the likelihood of unfounding, but was a strong predictor of the likelihood that the victim would recant the allegations.

The Decision to Arrest the Suspect

Sexual assault cases can be cleared (or solved) for UCR purposes either by the arrest of at least one suspect or by exceptional means. Cases that are not cleared are "open" cases in which the investigation is continuing. According to the *UCR Handbook* (FBI, 2004: 79), "an offense is cleared by arrest, or solved for crime reporting purposes, when at least one person is (1) arrested, (2) charged with the commission of the offense, and (3) turned over to the court for prosecution." To clear a case by arrest, in other words, the law enforcement agency must arrest and book a suspect and turn him or her over to the prosecuting attorney for a charging decision.

Our analysis of the decision to arrest is complicated by the fact that both the LAPD and the LASD—and particularly the LAPD—interpret (misinterpret) the word "charged" in the UCR discussion of "cleared by arrest" to mean "charged by the DA." Thus, cases in which an arrest is made but the DA declines to file charges are initially cleared by arrest but the clearance is changed to cleared by exceptional means when felony charges are not filed by the prosecutor. In coding case outcomes for the project, we created two variables for "cleared by arrest." The first, which we called cleared-arrest, was coded 1 if the final case clearance was cleared by arrest. The second, which we called police-arrest, was coded 1 if a suspect was arrested, regardless of whether the DA filed charges, and was coded 0 if there was an exceptional clearance without an arrest or if the case was open and the investigation was continuing. We used this latter variable to analyze the decision to arrest or not, as it more accurately reflects police decision-making. Cases that were unfounded by the police are excluded from the analysis, as are cases in which the most serious charge was sexual battery. We analyzed all cases (n = 570) reported to the LAPD and the LASD in 2008, and we include a control for the law enforcement agency that handled the report. There were 247 (43.3%) cases in which the police or sheriff's department made an arrest and 323 (56.7%) cases that were either cleared by exceptional means or for which the investigation was continuing. We then partitioned the data by relationship type (stranger versus nonstranger) and estimated a separate model of the decision to arrest or not for each type of relationship.

Analysis of the full sample. The results of our analysis of the decision to arrest or not are presented in Table 4.9. As these data indicate, arrest decisions were based primarily on the relationship between the victim and the suspect, indicators of case seriousness, and measures of the strength of evidence in the case. In contrast, the decision to arrest or not was not based on the victim's background characteristics, character, or behavior at the time of the incident.

Not surprisingly, arrest was more likely if the victim and the suspect were nonstrangers. Compared to cases in which the victim and suspect were strangers, police were 4.89 times more likely to make an arrest if the victim and suspect were intimate partners and 3.14 times more likely to make an arrest if the victim and suspect were nonstrangers (for example, relatives, neighbors, coworkers, acquaintances). This no doubt reflects the fact that cases involving strangers are much less likely to have an identified suspect whose location is known and who can therefore be taken into custody. Of the cases involving victims and suspects who were strangers to one another, 49.4 percent had an identified suspect. In contrast, there was a known suspect in 89.5 percent of the cases involving nonstrangers and 97.7 percent of the cases involving intimate partners.

The likelihood of arrest also was affected by three indicators of case seriousness: whether the case involved a rape or attempted rape, whether the suspect used a weapon, and whether the victim suffered some type of

**Table 4.9 Decision to Arrest, Full Sample:
Logistic Regression Analysis**

	B	SE	Exp(B)
Victim Characteristics			
Age	.010	.02	1.01
Race/ethnicity			
African American	.511	.67	1.67
Hispanic/Latina	−.170	.61	0.84
Relationship to suspect			
Intimate partner	**−2.68***	.82	0.07
Nonstranger	−.680	.55	0.51
Risk-taking behavior at time of incident	.556	.53	1.74
Questions about character/reputation	**1.14***	.53	3.14
Mental illness or mental health issues	**2.287***	.69	9.85
Motive to lie	−.004	.66	0.99
Victim recanted	**5.72***	.98	305.20
Indicators of Case Seriousness			
Most serious charge is rape	.891	1.04	2.43
Suspect physically assaulted victim	−.403	.53	0.67
Suspect used a weapon	−.008	.87	0.99
Victim suffered collateral injury	**−1.074***	.52	0.34
Type of resistance			
Verbal only	−.562	.53	0.51
Physical only	−2.182	1.22	0.11
Verbal and physical	.190	.58	1.21
Strength of Evidence			
Victim reported within one hour	.229	.58	1.26
Number of witnesses	.335	.20	1.40
Victim willing to cooperate in investigation	.003	.47	0.60
Physical evidence	**−1.299***	.52	0.27
LAPD Bureau			
Central	−.256	.72	0.74
South	−1.022	.76	0.36
Valley	.494	.66	1.64
Constant	−2.103	1.59	
Nagelkerke R^2		.656	

Note: *P < .05 (significant coefficients are indicated in bold)

collateral injury. Arrest was less likely if the most serious charge was rape; it was more likely if the suspect used a weapon and if the victim was injured. In addition, the odds of an arrest were influenced by the promptness of the victim's report, the victim's willingness to cooperate, and the availability of witnesses and physical evidence. The police were 5.6 times more likely to make an arrest if the victim was willing to cooperate in the investigation of the crime (this reflects the victim's willingness to cooperate after making the report and during the investigation by the detective to whom the case was assigned); they were 3.3 times more likely to make an arrest if the victim reported the crime within one hour. The likelihood of arrest also increased as the number of witnesses increased and if there was some type of physical evidence collected from the crime scene or from the victim or suspect.

Analysis of data partitioned by relationship type. The relationship between the victim and the suspect influenced the likelihood that the police would arrest the suspect; cases involving victims and suspects who were intimate partners or nonstrangers were significantly more likely to result in an arrest than were cases involving victims and suspects who were strangers. To determine whether the factors that affect the likelihood of arrest varied by relationship type, the next step in the analysis was to partition the data by relationship type and estimate separate models of the likelihood of arrest for cases involving intimate partners, other nonstrangers, and strangers.

The results of our analysis are shown in Table 4.10. It is important to point out that none of the victim characteristics affected the likelihood of arrest for any of the three relationship types. Moreover, the indicators of case seriousness and evidentiary strength had differential effects on the three types of cases. Beginning first with the cases in which the victim and suspect were strangers, the odds of arrest were affected by only two variables—whether the victim made a prompt report and the number of witnesses to the incident. Arrest was 3.6 times more likely if the victim reported the crime within one hour, and the odds of arrest increased as the number of witnesses increased.

Turning next to cases involving nonstrangers, the results of our analysis reveal that the strongest predictors of arrest are measures of the strength of evidence in the case. Arrest is significantly more likely if the victim of a nonstranger sexual assault is willing to cooperate with police and prosecutors during the investigation of the crime, if the victim reported the crime promptly, and if there are witnesses or physical evidence that can corroborate her allegations. In contrast, the likelihood of arrest in cases involving intimate partners is influenced by the seriousness of the crime—arrest is substantially more likely if the suspect used a weapon and if the victim suffered some type of collateral injury. In these cases, the willingness of the victim to cooperate in the investigation also has a positive effect on the odds of arrest.

The Decision to Prosecute the Suspect

Our analysis of the decision to prosecute the suspect is complicated by the prearrest charge evaluation process used by both the LAPD and the LASD; each agency presents cases to the DA for charging decisions both prior to and following the arrest of a suspect. To account for the two contexts of charge rejections, we therefore created a three-category variable: charges

Table 4.10 Decision to Arrest, Victim-Suspect Relationship: Logistic Regression Analysis

	Strangers	Nonstrangers	Intimate Partners
Victim Characteristics			
Age	1.04	0.98	0.99
Race/ethnicity			
African American	1.09	1.74	0.43
Hispanic/Latina	1.47	1.01	0.76
Risk-taking behavior at time of incident	1.75	0.80	0.35
Questions about character/reputation	0.96	1.14	0.87
Mental illness or mental health issues	0.23	0.49	0.67
Motive to lie	1.40	1.22	2.27
Indicators of Case Seriousness			
Most serious charge is rape	0.65	**0.21***	0.41
Suspect physically assaulted victim	1.00	1.88	1.19
Suspect used a weapon	2.65	2.36	**9.07***
Victim suffered collateral injury	2.49	0.98	**2.61***
Type of resistance			
Verbal only	0.34	0.52	1.62
Physical only	2.16	0.91	2.29
Verbal and physical	1.83	1.46	2.20
Strength of Evidence			
Victim reported within one hour	**3.60***	**5.70***	2.74
Number of witnesses	**1.66***	**1.56***	1.16
Victim willing to cooperate in investigation	3.20	**20.74***	**2.36***
Physical evidence	0.79	**2.38***	1.95
Law enforcement agency			
LAPD	0.86	1.32	0.98
Nagelkerke R^2	.41	.52	.36
No. of cases	131	262	159

Note: Coefficients presented are exp(B); significant coefficients are indicated in bold.
*$P \leq .05$

rejected before arrest; charges rejected after arrest; and charges filed. Included in the first category are cases in which the suspect was not arrested and the case was cleared exceptionally as a result of a rejection by the DA during the prearrest charge evaluation process. The second category includes cases in which the suspect was arrested but the DA declined to file charges, and the third category includes cases in which the suspect was arrested and the DA filed charges. In creating this variable, we excluded (i.e., coded as missing) cases (N = 267) that were unfounded, open cases in which the investigation was continuing, and cases that were exceptionally cleared but were not referred to the DA for a charging decision. We analyzed the trichotomous charging variable using multinomial logistic regression, which allowed us to contrast cases in which the DA filed charges with (1) cases in which the DA rejected charges during the prearrest charge evaluation process and (2) cases in which the DA rejected charges after the suspect was arrested.

The results of our analysis, which are presented in Table 4.11, reveal that different variables affected the two indicators of charge rejection. Beginning with the prosecutor's decision to reject charges during the prearrest charge evaluation process, we see that the likelihood of charge rejection was determined by a mix of victim characteristics, indicators of crime seriousness, and measures of the strength of evidence in the case. Prosecutors were more likely to reject charges in cases involving older victims, victims who engaged in some type of risky behavior at the time of the incident, and victims who both verbally and physically resisted the suspect. In fact, charge rejection during the prearrest charge evaluation process was nearly three times more likely if the victim had engaged in risk-taking behavior and was more than twice as likely if the victim resisted the suspect verbally and physically (as opposed to no resistance). The likelihood that the prosecutor would reject the charges during the prearrest charge evaluation process also was affected by the most serious charge and by the suspect's use of a weapon; the prosecutor was 7.5 times more likely to decline to file charges if the most serious charge was rape rather than attempted rape and was substantially less likely to decline to file charges if the suspect used a gun, knife or other weapon during the commission of the crime. Charge rejection also depended on the strength of evidence in the case. Prosecutors were significantly less likely to decline to file charges if the victim reported the crime within one hour, if the victim was willing to cooperate with law enforcement as the case moved forward, and if there was physical evidence recovered from the victim or from the scene of the crime. Finally, the likelihood of charge rejection decreased as the number of witnesses increased.

The results for the analysis of the decision to reject charges following arrest are very different. In fact, only three variables—whether the victim had a motive to lie, whether the suspect used a weapon during the commission of the crime, and whether the victim was willing to cooperate with the investigation—influenced this indicator of charging. In cases in which a suspect was arrested and in custody, the odds of charge rejection were higher if the victim had a motive to lie about the incident; the odds were lower if the suspect used a weapon and if the victim was willing to cooperate with law enforcement officials.

The Correlates of Case Outcomes: A Summary

Our quantitative analysis of the case outcomes revealed that the likelihood that the case would be unfounded, the likelihood that the suspect would be arrested, and the odds that charges would be rejected by the DA were affected by a mix of case characteristics and victim characteristics. None of these outcomes, on the other hand, was affected by the bureau (in the case of unfounding) or agency (in the case of arrest and charge rejection) that

Table 4.11 Charging Decisions in Rape and Attempted Rape Cases: Multinomial Logistic Regression Analysis of Three-Category Charging Variable, LAPD and LASD, 2008

	Charges Rejected Before Suspect Arrested			Charges Rejected After Suspect Arrested		
	B	SE	Exp(B)	B	SE	Exp(B)
Victim Characteristics						
Age	**0.04***	.02	1.04	0.02	.02	1.03
Race/ethnicity						
African American	−0.60	.49	0.55	−0.70	.47	0.50
Hispanic/Latina	−0.56	.39	0.57	−0.68	.38	0.51
Relationship with suspect						
Intimate partner	0.40	.54	1.49	0.39	.49	1.48
Nonstranger	0.59	.49	1.80	0.17	.45	1.19
Risk-taking behavior	**1.02***	.39	2.78	0.44	.36	1.55
Questions about character/reputation	0.86	.56	2.35	0.87	.54	2.38
Mental illness or mental health issues	1.07	.64	2.92	1.01	.64	2.73
Motive to lie	1.15	.61	3.15	**1.60***	.59	4.97
Indicators of Crime Seriousness						
Most serious charge is rape	**2.02***	.61	7.54	0.33	.45	1.40
Suspect physically assaulted victim	0.12	.36	1.13	.56	.35	1.76
Suspect used a weapon	**−1.78***	.56	0.17	**−0.95***	.45	0.38
Victim suffered collateral injury	−0.44	.34	0.65	−0.15	.33	0.86
Type of resistance						
Verbal only	0.07	.51	1.07	−0.22	.52	0.80
Physical only	−0.72	.75	0.49	−0.49	.68	0.61
Verbal and physical	**−0.88***	.44	0.41	−0.62	.43	0.54
Strength of Evidence						
Victim reported within one hour	**−1.65***	.47	0.19	−0.02	.35	0.98
Number of witnesses	**−0.27***	.12	0.76	0.01	.10	1.01
Victim willing to cooperate	**−3.13***	.57	0.04	**−2.25***	.55	0.10
Physical evidence	**−0.87***	.36	0.42	0.28	.35	1.32
Case Handled by LAPD	0.03	.36	1.03	−0.38	.35	0.68
Number of cases			371			
Nagelkerke R^2			.46			

Note: *P ≤ .05 (significant coefficients are indicated in bold)

investigated the crime; the victim's race or ethnicity; whether the suspect physically, as well as sexually, assaulted the victim; or the type of resistance offered by the victim.

Our analysis of the LAPD's decision to unfound the report revealed that the likelihood of unfounding is affected by victim characteristics and by factors (collateral injury to the victim and physical evidence) that can corroborate the victim's allegations of sexual assault. The most powerful predictor of unfounding is whether the victim recanted her allegations. This is not surprising, given comments made by detectives who were interviewed for this project (see Chapter 2). Although many stressed that recanting was neither a necessary nor a sufficient condition for unfounding the report, others stated that they would unfound only if the victim recanted her testimony and admitted that the incident was fabricated. Even after taking whether the victim recanted into account, however, we still found that the victim's relationship with the suspect, the victim's character or reputation, and whether the victim had some type of mental health issue affected the odds that the report would be unfounded. Moreover, the relationship between the victim and the suspect influenced both the likelihood that the victim would recant (there was a greater likelihood if the victim stated that she was assaulted by a stranger) and the likelihood that the case would be unfounded (there was a greater likelihood if the victim said she was assaulted by a stranger rather than an intimate partner).

Our findings suggest a few things about victims who make false allegations of sexual assault: (1) many, but not all, eventually recant; (2) their allegations are eventually unfounded; (3) they believe that their allegations will be more credible if they conform to societal stereotypes of real rape— that is, rape by a stranger. They also suggest that in attempting to determine whether a report is false and therefore should be unfounded, detectives also consider the character or reputation of the victim (is she a prostitute? does she work as an exotic dancer or stripper? does she have a history of alcohol abuse or illegal drug use?), as well as whether the victim has mental health issues that might have led her to fabricate the incident and whether there is evidence (either physical injury to the victim or some type of physical evidence collected from the victim or the scene of the alleged incident) that can corroborate her allegation of sexual assault.

The results of our analysis of the decision to arrest also highlight the role of the relationship between the suspect and the victim. We found that law enforcement is more likely to make an arrest if the sexual assault was committed by someone known to the victim, but this largely reflects the fact that cases involving nonstrangers are more likely to have an identified suspect. In fact, when we examined the percentage of cases with identified suspects that resulted in an arrest, we found that the arrest rate was identical (44.2%) for cases involving strangers and cases involving nonstrangers and was only slightly higher (50.6%) for cases involving intimate partners. The key factor, in other words, is not the relationship between the victim and the suspect but the ability of the victim or the police to identify the suspect.

Our results also provide some evidence in support of arguments that arrest is more likely if the rape is an aggravated rape in which the suspect used a weapon or the victim suffered collateral injury. However, we found no evidence that arrest is affected by legally irrelevant characteristics of the victim—the victim's race or ethnicity did not influence the likelihood of arrest and arrest was not affected by whether the victim was engaged in risky behavior at the time of the incident, had a motive to lie about the incident, had a mental illness or mental health issues, or if there were questions raised about her character or reputation. In fact, and not surprisingly, the strongest predictors of the likelihood of arrest were variables related to the strength of evidence in the case—whether the victim reported promptly (a prompt report means a greater likelihood of collecting physical evidence from the victim or the crime scene), whether the victim was willing to cooperate with the investigating detective, the number of witnesses, and the availability of some type of physical evidence to corroborate the victim's testimony and connect the suspect to the crime.

Our analysis of the data partitioned by relationship type revealed that none of the victim characteristics affected the likelihood of arrest for any of the three victim-suspect relationship categories: Arrest did not depend on the victim's race or ethnicity, age, or factors that might cause the investigating officer to "blame" the victim or question her credibility. Rather, the odds of arrest reflected the strength of evidence against the suspect (cases involving strangers and nonstrangers), the willingness of the victim to cooperate with law enforcement officials (cases involving nonstrangers and intimate partners), and the seriousness of the crime (cases involving intimate partners).

We found a different pattern of results when we analyzed the trichotomous charging variable. The relationship between the victim and the suspect, which affected both the likelihood that the case would be unfounded and the likelihood that the suspect would be arrested, did not play a role in the charging decision. Prosecutors did not take the victim/suspect relationship into account in deciding whether to file charges, either during the pre- or postarrest charge evaluation process.

We also found that different variables affected the two types of charging decisions. For example, three victim characteristics (i.e., the victim's age, whether the victim engaged in risky behavior at the time of the incident, and whether the victim resisted the suspect both verbally and physically affected the likelihood of charging during the prearrest charge evaluation process, but only one victim factor (whether the victim had a motive to lie about the incident) affected charging during the postarrest charge evaluation process. Whether the victim was willing to cooperate with law enforcement during the investigation of the crime affected both types of charging decisions, as did the suspect's use of a weapon. On the other hand, the promptness of the victim's report, the number of witnesses, and whether physical evidence was recovered influenced charging decisions only during the prearrest charge evaluation process.

These findings suggest that law enforcement officials present "problematic" cases to the DA prior to making an arrest and, when the DA determines that the evidence in the case does not meet the standard of proof beyond a reasonable doubt or that the victim's cooperation is unlikely, they clear the case by exceptional means. In other words, cases in which the victim engaged in risky behavior at the time of the incident are likely to be screened out before law enforcement makes an arrest, as are cases in which the victim did not resist the suspect or failed to make a prompt report, cases in which there is a lack of physical evidence to corroborate the victim's story, and cases without any witnesses who can attest to the victim's allegations. This is confirmed by the fact that none of these factors affected the likelihood of charging once the suspect had been arrested.

The problematic nature of cases rejected by the DA (either before or after the suspect is arrested) also is illustrated by the type of defense put forth by the suspect in the case. Although not all suspects were interviewed, those who were interviewed typically claimed either that the sexual contact with the victim was consensual or that the incident was fabricated. However, the cases rejected by the prosecutor were substantially more likely than those in which charges were filed to involve a suspect who put forth a consent defense: 56.7 percent of the cases rejected during the prearrest charge evaluation process and 53.4 percent of the cases rejected following arrest of the suspect involved a consent defense, compared to only 36.8 percent of the cases in which the prosecutor filed charges. By contrast, 33.3 percent of the suspects in the cases in which charges were filed made incriminating statements and/or admitted committing the crime, compared to only 4.5 percent of the suspects in cases rejected prior to arrest and 10.2 percent of the suspects in cases rejected following arrest. Cases in which charges were rejected by the DA, in other words, were more likely than those in which charges were filed to be "he said/she said" cases in which the victim claimed that she was sexually assaulted and the suspect claimed that the sexual contact was consensual.

Notes

1. In 2012 the definition of forcible rape was changed to "penetration, no matter how slight, of the vagina or anus with any body part or object, or oral penetration by a sex organ of another person, without the consent of the victim." This broadened definition includes oral copulation, sodomy, penetration with an object, assaults of male victims, and assaults of female victims by female offenders.

2. As noted in Chapter 1, the case files were coded by the two coprincipal investigators and by a graduate student who was trained by the coprincipal investigator at California State University, Los Angeles. During the process of coding the case files, we had numerous conference calls in which we discussed how to code particular variables.

3. This variable was coded 1 if the case file indicated that the victim was currently or had been in the past a patient at a mental health facility, that the victim was taking medication for a mental health problem, or if a family member or friend stated during an interview with the responding officer or the detective that the victim had a mental illness or mental health issues.

4. Information about whether the victim had a motive to lie was obtained either from the victim's statement, the interview of the victim by the investigating officer,

or the statement of witnesses. Examples of the types of statements found in the case file regarding the victim's motive to lie are the following: "all informants interviewed said the victim fabricated the incident because her parents found out she was sexually active," "victim was angry with suspect because he would not give her crack cocaine," "the victim was angry that the suspect returned to his wife," "the victim is involved in a custody dispute with the suspect," "victim was angry with suspect because he broke off the affair with her," "victim did not want her mother to find out what she did," "victim was cheating on her husband with the suspect," "suspect (victim's boyfriend) was flirting with another woman at a party," "suspect has nude photos of victim and victim found out that suspect has another girlfriend," "the girls were afraid that they would get in trouble for coming home late."

5. The type of resistance was obtained from the victim's statement, which was recorded in the case file. We originally coded six types of verbal resistance (cried, screamed, refused/protested/said stop, attempt to dissuade/fool, calls names/denigrates suspect, passive/saying nothing) and five types of physical resistance (fled/attempted to flee, resisted/struggled, fought (hit, scratched, bit), used a weapon to defend, passive/did nothing to resist). Because there could be multiple types of verbal and physical resistance, we coded verbal resistance 1 if the case file indicated that there was any type of verbal resistance; similarly, we coded physical resistance 1 if the case filed indicated that there was any type of physical resistance.

6. Whether the victim was willing to cooperate with the detective assigned to the case was determined from the case file. If the victim was uncooperative, it would be noted in the file by the investigating officer (I/O). For example, the I/O might have noted that he or she had attempted to contact the victim but the victim refused to talk (either via telephone or in person), that the victim stated that she did not want anything to happen to the suspect or that she did not want the suspect arrested, that the victim said (giving a variety of reasons) that she did not want to take the case to court, that the victim stated that she was no longer interested in pursuing a criminal prosecution, or that the victim refused to participate in a prefiling interview with the DA's Office.

5

False Reports

Ultimately, the criminal justice system and those writing about the issue of rape have dealt poorly with the issue of false allegations. Given the legal and societal prominence of this subject, it is a failure that should be addressed.

—Philip N. S. Rumney (2006: 158)

In June 2010, the *Baltimore Sun* reported that the Baltimore Police Department led the country in the percentage of rape cases that were deemed to be false or baseless and thus were unfounded. According to the report, from 2004 through 2009 about a third of the rapes reported to the police department were unfounded, a rate three times the national average. Also in June 2010, the *New York Times* reported that New York police commissioner Raymond W. Kelly had appointed a task force to look into the handling of rape complaints and to recommend new training protocols for dealing with victims of sexual assault. The review was prompted by complaints from rape victims, who said that their allegations of sexual assault were unfounded or downgraded to misdemeanors. These news stories—along with others regarding the mishandling of rape cases in Milwaukee, Cleveland, New Orleans, and Philadelphia—culminated in a September 2010 U.S. Senate Hearing convened by Senator Arlen Specter to examine the systematic failure to investigate rape on the part of police departments nationwide. Testifying at the hearing was Carol E. Tracey, executive director of the Women's Law Project, who said, "It's clear we're seeing chronic and systemic patterns of police refusing to accept cases for investigation, misclassifying cases to non-criminal categories so that investigations do not occur, and 'unfounding' complaints by determining that women are lying about being sexually assaulted" (US Senate, 2010).

Allegations that "women are lying about being sexually assaulted" are not new. In fact, Sir Matthew Hale, an English judge, opined in the seventeenth century that rape "is an accusation easily to be made and hard to be proved, and harder to be defended by the party accused, tho never so innocent" ([1736] 1971). Estimates of the number of false reports vary, with one study (Kanin, 1994) reporting that 45 of the 109 (41%) rape complaints

133

received by a Midwestern police department were false and another (Thei-lade and Thomsen, 1986) concluding that the false reporting rate was only 1.5 percent. A comprehensive review of research examining the prevalence of false reports in the United States, the United Kingdom, Australia, New Zealand, and other countries noted that estimates varied from 1.5 percent to 90 percent (Rumney, 2006). These variations reflect differences in the way false reports are defined and measured, as well as differences in the relia-bility and validity of the research designs used to evaluate false reports. According to Lonsway, Archambault, and Lisak (2009: 2), "When more methodologically rigorous research has been conducted, estimates for the percentage of false reports begin to converge around 2–8%."

In this chapter we evaluate sexual assault cases that were unfounded by the Los Angeles Police Department (LAPD) in 2008. Using qualitative and quantitative data from redacted police case files and from interviews with LAPD detectives, we determine whether the unfounded cases involved false allegations by victims and, if so, what motivated victims to file false reports. We begin with a review of research on the prevalence of false alle-gations of rape.

Prior Research on False Reports

One of the most controversial—and least understood—issues in the area of sexual violence is the prevalence of false reports of rape, which Lonsway (2010) referred to as "the elephant in the middle of the living room" (p. 1356). Estimates of the rate of false reports vary widely, with some re-searchers concluding that the rate is 30 to 40 percent (Jordan, 2004; Kanin, 1994) or higher (see Rumney, 2006) and others finding that the rate is 2 percent or lower (Brownmiller, 1975; Kelly, Lovett, and Regan, 2005; Theilade and Thomsen, 1986). Noting that those who work in the field of sexual violence are continually asked to comment on the number of reports of rape that are false, Lonsway (2010) stated that recent research findings from studies that use appropriate research designs suggest that the rate of false allegations is low and concluded that "there is simply no way to claim that 'the statistics are all over the map.' The statistics are actually now in a very small corner of the map" (p. 1358).

Conflicting conclusions regarding the prevalence of false allegations of rape reflect a lack of conceptual clarity, a confounding of police decisions to unfound and false reports, and inappropriate research strategies. Many researchers (Jordan, 2004; Kanin, 1994) either did not explicitly explain how they defined a false rape allegation or used a definition that is incon-sistent with policy statements by the Federal Bureau of Investigation (FBI) and the International Association of Chiefs of Police (IACP). As explained in Chapter 4, both sources emphasize that the police must conduct a thorough investigation and that their investigation must lead them to a conclusion that a crime did not occur.

A related problem concerns the assumption that rape cases unfounded by the police are, by definition, false allegations. There are two problems with this. First, Uniform Crime Reporting (UCR) guidelines state that a case can be unfounded if it is "false *or* baseless" (emphasis added). Although sometimes used interchangeably, these terms—"false" and "baseless"—do not mean the same thing. According to Lisak and his colleagues (Lisak et al., 2010), a report is false if "the victim deliberately fabricates an account of being raped"; it is baseless if "the victim reports an incident that, while truthfully recounted, does not meet . . . the legal definition of a sexual assault" (p. 1321). Consider a case in which a complainant, believing that "something happened" while she was passed out at a party, reports a rape to the police but the investigation conducted by the police uncovers no forensic or other evidence that a crime was committed; the victim's allegation would be baseless, but not deliberately false. The second problem with conflating unfounding with false allegations is that researchers have documented that police unfound sexual assault reports inappropriately; they categorize as unfounded complaints involving complainants who engaged in risky behavior at the time of the incident, complainants who are unwilling to cooperate in the prosecution of the suspect, or complainants who delayed reporting (Kelly, Lovett, and Regan, 2005; Kerstetter, 1990; Konradi, 2007; McCahill, Meyer, and Fischman, 1979). If a police agency is using unfounding to dispose of problematic—but not false—cases, to assume that unfounded cases are false allegations is obviously misleading.

A third problem plaguing research on false rape reports is that many studies simply rely on the classifications made by law enforcement agencies. That is, they take at face value the conclusion of law enforcement that a complaint is false or baseless and therefore should be unfounded. Kanin's (1994) widely cited study, for example, determined that a complaint was a false report based on the police department's classification of the case as a false allegation. Similarly, a British Home Office study (Harris and Grace, 1999) of rape cases reported to the police in England and Wales relied on police classifications of complaints. As Lisak and his colleagues (Lisak et al., 2010) note, studies that rely on law enforcement categorizations "are unable to determine whether those classifications adhere to IACP and UCR guidelines and whether they are free of the biases that have frequently been identified in police investigation of rape cases" (p. 1322).

Although the prevalence of these definitional and methodological problems calls the findings of much of the extant research on false rape reports into question (Rumney, 2006), there are a number of recent studies that use appropriate research designs and that thus provide more credible estimates of the number of false reports. For example, a British Home Office study (Kelly, 2010; Kelly, Lovett, and Regan, 2005) of case attrition in rape cases used multiple sources of data to analyze cases that were "no-crimed" (equivalent to unfounding in the United States) by the police. The researchers found that cases in the no-crimed group included both false allegations, which constituted about 8 percent of the rape cases reported to the police, and cases in which there was no evidence of an assault (which included both cases that were reported by a third party and cases involving complainants who had no memory of an assault but reported to the police because they feared that "something" had happened). In about half of the cases that were designated as false reports, the information provided by the police contained an explanation for why the complaint was deemed to be false—in 53 of the cases the complainant admitted that the allegation was false, in 28 the complainant retracted the allegation, in 3 the complainant refused to cooperate in the investigation, and in 56 the police determined that the complaint was false based on the lack of evidence (Kelly, 2010: 1349). Cases in which the complainants admitted that the allegations were false were described by the police as cases involving motives of revenge against a current or former partner, a desire to hide consensual sexual activity with other men from a current partner, or, in the case of young girls, an attempt to avoid confrontations with parents about being sexually active.

Because the authors' review of the case files revealed that policy statements regarding false complaints were not always followed, they coded the complaints that were designated by the police as false allegations as either "probable," "possible," or "uncertain." They then excluded the cases that were coded "uncertain" (i.e., cases "where it appeared victim characteristics had been used to impute that they were inherently less believable") and recalculated the rate of false reports to be 3 percent of all cases reported to the police (p. 1350). The authors of the study concluded that "a culture of suspicion remains, accentuated by a tendency to conflate false allegations with retractions and withdrawals, as if in all such cases no sexual assault occurred" (p. 1351).

Similar conclusions were reached by Lisak and his colleagues (Lisak et al., 2010), who analyzed case summaries of every sexual assault reported to the police department of a major university in the Northeastern United States from 1998 to 2007 (N = 136). The author and three co-investigators used the IACP guidelines to independently determine whether a report was a false report. A complaint was categorized as a false report "if there was evidence that a thorough investigation was pursued and that the investigation yielded evidence that the reported sexual assault had in fact not occurred" (Lisak et al., 2010: 1328).[1] The research team concluded that only 8 of the 136 cases (5.9%) were false reports; these 8 cases were also designated as false reports by police investigators. In three of these cases the complainant admitted that the report had been fabricated, in one the complaint provided a partial admission of fabrication and there was other evidence that a crime did not occur, in three the complainant did not admit that the allegation was fabricated but the police investigation produced evidence that the crime did not occur, and in a final case the complainant recanted but evidence that the allegation was fabricated was ambiguous. Lisak and his coauthors (2010) concluded that the results of their study "are consistent with those of other studies that have used similar methodologies to determine the prevalence of false rape reporting" (p. 1329).

Although the Kelly, Lovett, and Regan (2005) and Lisak et al. (2010) studies help to fill a void in the literature, more research clearly is needed. Neither of these studies, despite being methodologically superior to much of the extant research, provides definitive answers to questions regarding the prevalence of false rape reports. Kelly and her colleagues examined complaints reported to the police in England and Wales, and it is questionable whether their results can be generalized to the United States; moreover, in half the cases designated as false allegations, the police did not explain why the complaint was deemed to be false. The generalizability of Lisak et al.'s findings (2010) is also called into question, given that they examined rapes reported to a university police department. Another limitation of this study is that the authors did not have access to the complete case files; rather, the police department provided case summaries and the research team met with officials from the department, who brought the case files with them and who referenced the files if questions arose regarding the appropriate categorization of a case.

In building on and extending the research conducted thus far, we respond to Rumney's (2006: 155) call for "research that examines how and why police officers determine that particular allegations are false." We examined the case files for a random sample of sexual assaults unfounded by the Los Angeles Police Department (LAPD) in 2008 to determine whether the complaints unfounded by the police were false reports. We used the detailed quantitative and qualitative data collected for this study to determine the prevalence of false rape allegations reported to one of the largest law enforcement agencies in the United states, to categorize complainants' motivations for filing false allegations of rape, and to identify the decision-making criteria that LAPD detectives use in deciding to unfound a rape complaint.

Research Design and Methods

In this chapter, we analyze quantitative and qualitative data on 81^2 sexual assault complaints that were unfounded by the LAPD in 2008. The data were extracted from case files that were provided by the LAPD and from which all information that could be used to identify the complainant, the witnesses, the suspect, or the law enforcement officers investigating the case was redacted. We supplemented the data from case files with information gleaned from interviews with LAPD detectives who had experience investigating sexual assaults. During June and July 2010, we interviewed 52 detectives from the LAPD's 21 divisions.[3] During the interview, we asked respondents a series of questions regarding the decision to unfound the report: the standards they use in making this decision, whether complainants have to recant the allegations in order to unfound the report, whether certain types of cases have a higher likelihood of being unfounded than others, and whether officers ever unfounded a case for reasons other than a belief that a crime did not occur. Respondents also were asked what would motivate someone to file a false report and how they determined whether the report was false.

Categorizing Cases as False or Baseless

In this chapter, we attempt to determine, first, whether sexual assault reports unfounded by the LPAD were false or baseless reports, and, second, for cases determined to be false reports, to identify the factors that motivated victims to file a false report. Following Lonsway, Archambault, and Lisak (2009: 4), we define a false report as "a report of a sexual assault that did not happen." Consistent with both FBI guidelines for clearing cases and with the IACP model policy on investigating sexual assault cases, we categorized a case as a false report only if a thorough investigation led the police to conclude that the allegation was false and that no crime had occurred. In order to categorize a complaint as a false report, in other words, the case file had to include evidence indicating that the complainant deliberately fabricated the allegation of sexual assault. We categorized as "baseless" cases that were unfounded by the police after an investigation revealed that no crime had occurred but there was also no evidence that the complainant had intentionally lied about the incident.

To determine whether the allegation was a false report, each case file was reviewed by one of the principal investigators for the project (Spohn) and by two research assistants, both of whom were doctoral students in the School of Criminology and Criminal Justice at Arizona State University. Each of them independently categorized the report as a false report, a baseless report, not a false report, or a case in which it was not clear whether the report was false or not. Within the "false report" category, cases were subdivided into (1) cases in which the complainant recanted and there was evidence in the case file to support a conclusion that a crime did not occur and (2) cases in which the complainant did not recant but the case file contained either evidence that the crime did not occur or no evidence that the crime did occur. In many of the cases in which complainants recanted, the complainant provided an explanation for the false report; either the complainant indicated that she had a motive to lie (we discuss these motivations later) or she admitted that the sexual contact with the suspect was consensual. Regardless of whether the complainant recanted, we looked for evidence that would support a conclusion that a crime did not occur: witness statements, video evidence, or physical evidence that clearly contradicted the complainant's statement. In one case, for example, the complainant reported that she was abducted from a fast-food restaurant's parking lot, but video surveillance cameras did not record anyone being abducted during the time frame provided by the complainant. In another case, the complainant stated that she called 911 and reported that she had been sexually assaulted, but there was no record of the call. There also were a number of cases in which the complainant had mental health issues, and others where family members or witnesses stated that the complainant was not being truthful or there was evidence that she had made false reports in the past.

The second category of unfounded cases are cases that were determined to be baseless; that is, there was no evidence that a crime had occurred but the complainant did not deliberately fabricate the account. Included in this category are cases in which complainants believed that they might have been sexually assaulted when they were under the influence of drugs or alcohol; these cases were unfounded when the forensic medical exam revealed no physical evidence of a sexual assault or witnesses testified that they were with the complainant and that an assault did not occur.

The "not a false report" category was subdivided into (1) cases in which the complainant recanted but there was evidence that her recantation was motivated by fear of retaliation by the suspect, pressure from the suspect or the suspect's family or friends, or lack of interest in proceeding with the case, and (2) cases in which the complainant did not recant, there was evidence that the crime did occur but that prosecution would be unlikely because of the complainant's behavior at the time of the incident, the complainant's lack of cooperation, or lack of corroboration of, or inconsistencies in, the complainant's statement, and these factors were noted by the investigating officer as reasons for unfounding. The cases that fell into the "not clear whether the report was false or not" category included cases that the LAPD should have investigated further before making a decision regarding case clearance and cases that the researchers could not categorize. After independently categorizing the cases, the researchers met to review their decisions and to discuss in more detail the few cases (N = 8) in which there was disagreement about the way the case should be categorized. The interrater reliability for these 81 cases was 90.1 percent.

We want to emphasize that we did not assume that complainants who recanted their testimony or retracted their allegations had filed a false report. We assumed, like Raphael (2008), that "just because the victim recants does not mean that the abuse did not happen" (p. 371). A case in which the complainant recanted was categorized as a false report only if there was independent evidence that a crime did not occur and there was no indication in the case file that the complainant's recantation was motivated by fear, pressure, or a belief that prosecution would not be in her best interest.

Findings

Unfounding and False Reports

As shown in Table 5.1, we categorized two thirds (67.9%) of the unfounded cases as false reports, either because the complainant recanted and there was evidence that a crime did not occur (N= 31; 38.3%) or because there was evidence that the crime did not occur or no evidence that the crime did occur, even though the complainant did not recant (N =24; 29.6%). Five cases were determined to be baseless, but not false. Only 10 cases (12.3%) were deemed not to be false reports; eight of these were cases in which the complainant recanted but there was evidence that her recantation was motivated by fear, pressure, or a lack of interest in moving forward with the case, and only two were cases in which the complainant did not recant and there was evidence that a crime did, in fact, occur. We were unable to categorize the remaining 11 (13.6%) cases as false reports or not; most of these (N = 8) were cases where the research team concluded that the LAPD should have investigated further prior to making a decision regarding the appropriate case closure.

One conclusion that can be drawn from these data is that the LAPD is clearing sexual assault cases as unfounded appropriately most, but not all,

Table 5.1 Cases Unfounded by LAPD (N = 81)

	N	%
False Report	**55**	**67.9**
Victim recanted and there was evidence that the crime did not occur	(31)	(38.3)
Victim did not recant but there was evidence that the crime did not occur or no evidence that the crime did occur	(24)	(29.6)
Baseless Report	**5**	**6.2**
Case unfounded because it was baseless but not fabricated		
Not a False or Baseless Report	**10**	**12.3**
Victim recanted but there was evidence that the recantation was motivated by fear, pressure, or lack of interest in continuing with case	(8)	(9.9)
Victim did not recant and there was evidence that the crime did occur	(2)	(24.4)
Unclear Whether Report Was False, Baseless, or Neither	**11**	**13.6**
LAPD should have investigated further before closing the case	(8)	(9.9)
Unable to categorize	(3)	(3.7)

of the time. Stated another way, three quarters (74.1%) of the cases that were cleared as unfounded were cases in which there was evidence that a crime did not occur and that the complainants, for various reasons, either filed false reports of sexual assault or sexual battery (false allegations) or reported a rape because they believed that they had been assaulted while under the influence of illegal drugs or alcohol (baseless complaints). Although there were some cases that appeared to require additional investigation before clearing, there were only 10 cases where we concluded that a crime did occur and therefore the case should not have been unfounded. These data also reveal that recantation by the complainant is not required to unfound the case. Of the 81 cases that were unfounded, only 45 (55.6%) were cases in which the complainant recanted.

Because the 81 unfounded cases are not a random sample of all cases reported to the LAPD in 2008, we cannot use the unweighted data to determine the proportion of all 2008 reports that were false reports. To determine this, we used data that were weighted by the proportion of cases from each division and, within each division, the proportion of cases from each case closure type.[4] Using these data, 4.5 percent of all cases reported to the LAPD in 2008 were false reports: 2.2 percent were cases in which the complainant recanted and there was evidence that a crime did not occur, and 2.3 percent were cases in which the complainant did not recant but there was evidence that a crime did not occur. This is consistent with Lonsway, Archambault, and Lisak's (2009: 2) conclusion that although one cannot know with any degree of certainty how many sexual assault reports are false, "estimates narrow to the range of 2–8% when they are based on more rigorous research of case classifications using specific criteria and incorporating various protections of the reliability and validity of the research."

In the sections that follow, we provide qualitative data to illustrate the types of cases in each category. We begin by highlighting the characteristics of the cases that were deemed to be false reports, followed by a description of one of the cases categorized as baseless. This is followed by a discussion of the cases that were categorized as not false reports and the cases that the researchers concluded the LAPD should have investigated further before clearing them. We conclude with a discussion of the motives of complainants who filed false reports.

Unfounded Cases That Were
False Reports or Baseless Allegations

False reports. Descriptive statistics on the 55 unfounded cases deemed to be false reports are presented in Table 5.2. In all but 10 of these cases, the complainant reported that she had been raped; only 5 cases involved attempted rape and only 5 were reports of sexual battery (i.e., fondling or

Table 5.2 Cases Categorized as False Reports (N = 55)

	N	%
Characteristics of Incident or Case		
Type of crime		
Rape	45	81.8
Attempted rape	5	9.1
Sexual battery	5	9.1
Suspect used a gun or knife (% yes)	9	16.4
Number of suspects		
One	41	74.5
More than one	14	25.5
Complainant injured in some way (% yes)	18	32.7
Relationship between complainant and suspect		
Strangers	27	49.1
Nonstrangers	20	36.4
Intimate partners	8	14.5
Aggravated rape[a] complaint (% yes)	43	78.2
Suspect's initial contact with complainant		
Immediate attack	16	30.8
Offered complainant a ride or forced complainant into vehicle	10	19.3
Attack while complainant was passed out or asleep	5	9.6
On a date or at a party	4	7.7
Offered money or drugs to complainant	4	7.7
Propositioned complainant for sex	3	5.8
Complainant reported the crime within one hour (% yes)	14	25.5
Complainant verbally and physically resisted the suspect (% yes)	21	38.2
Complainant had a forensic medical exam (% yes)	27	49.1
Complainant recanted the allegations (% yes)	31	56.4
Complainant Characteristics		
Complainant has mental health issues (% yes)	20	36.4
Complainant is younger than 18 (% yes)	12	21.8

Note: a. An aggravated rape complaint is an allegation of forcible rape that involved a suspect who used a gun or a knife, more than one suspect, or collateral injury to the victim (see Estrich, 1987).

touching the complainant). In most cases the complainant did not report that the suspect used a gun or knife, but in one fourth of the cases the complainant stated that she had been attacked by more than one suspect and in a third of the cases the complainant stated that she had been injured during the assault. Half (49.1%) of the allegations involved suspects who were strangers to the complainant. We used these characteristics to determine the number of false reports that were allegations of aggravated rape; that is, allegations of rape in which the victim claimed that she was attacked by a stranger, the suspect used a gun or knife, she was attacked by more than one suspect, or she suffered collateral injuries in the attack (for a discussion of the concept of aggravated rape, see Estrich, 1987; Kalven and Zeisel, 1966). We found that more than three quarters (78.2%) of the false reports involved allegations of aggravated rape. This suggests that complainants who file false reports believe that their accounts will be more credible if they conform to the stereotype of a "real rape."

There was little consistency in complainants' accounts of the suspects' initial contact with them: in 16 cases it was described as an immediate attack and in 10 the complainant stated that she was offered a ride or forced into a vehicle. Other complainants stated that they were attacked while asleep or passed out, that they encountered the suspect on a date or at a party, or that the suspect approached them by offering money or drugs or by propositioning them for sex. Most complainants did not report the crime within one hour; more than a third (38.2%) indicated that they resisted the suspect both verbally and physically. About half of the complainants underwent a forensic medical exam and more than half eventually recanted the allegations. Of the 55 complainants, 20 had mental health issues; only 12 were under the age of 18.

Although these descriptive statistics provide an overview of the types of false reports handled by the LAPD, a more detailed picture can be painted using the qualitative data from the cases files. In one case, for example, the complainant told the police that she was walking alone at 2:30 in the afternoon when a white van pulled up alongside her and the driver asked her if she needed a ride. She said that she did and got in the vehicle. The suspect then parked the van under a freeway overpass. According to the complainant:

> The suspect kissed her on the mouth and she asked him, "What are you doing?" The suspect stated, "I think you're pretty," and kissed her again. The suspect then locked the doors of the van and stated, "Let's stay here a while." She replied, "I need to go home." The suspect then reached into her clothing and touched her vagina with his hands. The suspect told her to remove her underwear. She said, "No, this has gone far enough." The suspect then brandished a knife and said, "Bad things will happen if you don't cooperate. Pull your underwear down." Thinking that she did not have a choice, she cooperated. The suspect pulled his pants down and penetrated her vagina with his penis. She was unsure if the suspect ejaculated. The suspect asked her where she lived and drove her to her residence, which took 25 minutes.

The complainant subsequently told her therapist that she had been sexually assaulted and her therapist insisted that she report the crime to the police. The investigating officer took the complainant to the alleged crime scene, pointed out the camera that was located there, and told her that they would be able to get the suspect's license plate number from the video footage. At this point, the complainant admitted that the incident was fabricated. She told the officer that she "sometimes initiates sexual liaisons with older men when she is depressed and that was the case in this incident." She said that all of the sex acts were consensual, that no force or weapon was used, and that she had reported the incident to her therapist to garner sympathy.

In this case, the complainant retracted her allegations of sexual assault when it became clear that the police would be able to identify the suspect's car using video footage from the alleged scene of the crime. The complainant told the police that the suspect was a stranger and stated that she did not know his name or where he lived, but apparently realized that the consensual nature of her encounter with the suspect would be revealed if the police contacted him.

Just over half of the cases labeled as false reports involved complainants, like the one in the previous case, who recanted their allegations. In the case described next, the complainant did not recant but there was no evidence that a crime occurred. The complainant, who was homeless, stated that she was sleeping in her car, a Honda Civic, and at some point during the night she woke up with two naked men in the car with her. She said that they drugged her with the "date rape drug" and that both suspects then penetrated her with their penises. She also said that this had happened several times before with the same suspects, but she had not reported those incidents. She indicated that she did not know their names or where they lived, but that she could identify them if she saw them again. The forensic medical exam did not reveal any findings consistent with the complainant's account of forced sexual intercourse.

In the explanation for why this case was unfounded, the investigating officer wrote,

> Based on the totality of the circumstances in this case, including a lack of medical evidence, victim's lack of memory, victim's claim of prior unreported incidents with the same suspects, the physical challenge of a 6'2" and a 5'11" suspect assaulting the victim in a Honda Civic, the victim's unresponsiveness to contact efforts, and a total lack of any evidence to corroborate the victim's unsupported allegation, there is no corpus of a crime and this report is unfounded.

We categorized this case as a false report based on the implausibility of the complainant's assertion that she was sexually assaulted by two tall naked men in a small compact car, the lack of any forensic or physical evidence to support her allegations of being drugged or sexually assaulted, and the fact that she alleged that the same thing had happened several times in the past.

Unfounded Cases That Were Baseless

Our review of the case files revealed only five unfounded cases that were baseless—that is, these cases did not involve deliberate fabrications by the complainant. Rather, the complainants in these cases believed that they had been sexually assaulted or that "something" had happened to them. One complainant stated that she was raped while under the influence of drugs at a rave concert, a second reported that she was sexually assaulted after she and a friend left a club with two men who offered to drive them home but who instead took them to an apartment and plied them with drinks, and the third claimed that someone at the drug rehabilitation facility where she was staying raped her while she was sleeping. In the other two cases, the complainants were developmentally delayed and did not appear to understand the concept of rape.

In the first case, the 18-year-old complainant stated that she smoked marijuana and took two ecstasy pills while attending a rave concert. She said that while she was on the dance floor, a man walked up to her, sprayed her in the eyes with some type of liquid, and said, "I had a mask on, so she doesn't know it was me." She said that people were staring at her and stated, "I felt weird. I think someone did something to me. I think that someone raped me." She said that she did not remember having sexual intercourse with anyone, but thought that she might have blacked out. She told her friend—who was with her at the concert and who told the investigating officer that she was "100% positive that XXXX was not sexually assaulted at any time while we were at the rave"—that she decided to report the crime to the police "just to be on the safe side." Because the complainant believed that she might have been sexually assaulted and did not intentionally fabricate the assault, we categorized the case as baseless rather than false. The other four cases categorized as baseless were very similar.

Unfounded Cases That Were Not False Reports

Most of the 10 cases that we determined were not false or baseless reports were cases in which the complainant recanted but it was clear that the complainant's recantation was motivated by fear of reprisal from the suspect, pressure from the suspect or his family or friends, or the complainant's lack of interest in pursuing prosecution of the suspect. For instance, one case involved an allegation of sexual assault against a physician; the complainant retracted the allegation but the investigating officer noted in the follow-up report that she did so only after being told that the suspect would go to jail if he was identified and prosecuted. In another case, the complainant told the investigating officer that the suspect, a friend from school, threatened her with a knife and after sexually assaulting her said, "You better not tell anyone 'cause my homies will get you and I know where you stay." Although the complainant did eventually recant and told the police that no one had threatened her or coerced her to change her story, we categorized this case as "not a false report" based on the fact that the complainant gave a very clear account of the incident, used the same words to describe the incident to the patrol officer and the investigating officer, and appeared to be concerned that the suspect would get in trouble. Moreover, the investigating officer presented the case to the DA for a prearrest filing decision, which suggests that the officer may have believed that the victim had been assaulted. A third case in this category involved a complainant and suspect who had been married for seven years. The suspect accused the complainant of cheating on him, punched her in the face, and left the house; the rape occurred when he returned home the next morning after being out all night drinking. The complainant recanted the allegations of physical and sexual assault, despite the fact that she had a black eye and bruises on her arms and that one of her children told the officer that the victim's injuries "came from the beating she got." The complainant stated that she fell over an unknown object in the house and that her husband did not hit her or force her to have sex with him. In this case, it was clear that the complainant either was afraid of the suspect or had reconciled with him.

One of the more troubling cases that we categorized as not a false report involved a complainant who stated that she was assaulted by a man she had been dating for three months; the forensic medical exam revealed tissue damage to the complainant's rectum that was consistent with her allegation of forced anal intercourse and an eyewitness identified the complainant's boyfriend as the person who physically and sexually assaulted her. Notwithstanding this evidence, the complainant eventually recanted her testimony and identified another man as the person who assaulted her.

> The victim was at home with her young son when the suspect, whom she had been dating for three months, arrived. She let him in, they began to argue, and their arguing woke the baby. The suspect then bit the baby five times in the face, stomach and legs, hit the victim on the head and demanded that she make breakfast for him. The suspect became upset with the victim, pushed her out of the kitchen and made his own breakfast. After he finished eating, the suspect pushed the victim on the bed and demanded sex. The victim attempted to push him away, but he said, "Bitch, you don't got no choice." The victim told the suspect that she would call the police if he forced himself on her; he replied, "If I go to jail, I'll get someone to kill you." The suspect choked the victim until she was close to passing out and raped her. The suspect then went to sleep; the victim stated that she did not call the police because she was afraid of the suspect and his threat that he would have someone kill her if she did. When one of the victim's friends arrived at her house, she told her that the suspect had beaten her, but she did not tell her about the rape. The suspect woke up, demanded that the witness leave, and when she would not, threw the TV on the floor, smashing it. The suspect then kicked a hole in the wall and left the apartment. The victim locked the door and called the police.
>
> At the police station, the victim named another man as the suspect and picked his picture out of the photo line-up. The witness, however, stated that the suspect was not in the photo line-up. She said that the man

who raped the victim was her (the victim's) boyfriend, who was a member of the street gang "Rollin 60's" in South Los Angeles.

Four days later, the victim came to the police station and said that she fabricated the incident. She said that her boyfriend kicked a hole in the wall and she could not get the apartment manager to repair the damage unless she had a police report. When the investigating officer asked the victim how the baby received the bite marks that she claimed in her initial report were inflicted by the suspect, she said that she always bites her son in play and that she was the one who bit her baby.

We categorized this case as "not a false report" for several reasons, the most important of which was the fact that there was corroboration of the complainant's allegation of sexual assault: the forensic medical exam provided physical evidence consistent with the complainant's allegation of forced anal intercourse; the complainant made a fresh complaint to the witness, who identified the suspect as the person who assaulted the complainant; and the baby had bite marks consistent with the complainant's testimony regarding the suspect's behavior. The fact that the suspect was a known gang member and that he hit the complainant and threatened to kill her if she told the police that he had sexually assaulted her suggests that the complainant's recantation was motivated by fear of the suspect. This is confirmed by the fact that the complainant told the police that she did not call them when the suspect fell asleep because she was afraid of him and by the fact that the complainant's assertion that "she always bites her son in play" is not credible.

Another case in which the complainant recanted but there was evidence that a crime did occur involved a young woman who claimed that she was sitting at a bus stop at 10:30 PM when she observed a Hispanic male exit a bus that had stopped near where she was sitting. According to the complainant's report:

> The suspect began walking in her direction and whistled to get her attention. The victim ignored the suspect but he came up to her, sat down next to her, and asked her "How much?" When the victim attempted to stand up, the suspect grabbed her, forced her to sit down, pulled an orange boxcutter out of his pocket, opened the blade, and grabbed the victim by the hair. The victim attempted to scream, but the suspect held the boxcutter to her throat and said that if she screamed he would kill her. He then pulled the victim to an empty lot near the train tracks and raped her. The suspect then walked away and the victim walked home and took a shower. The next day she made a police report. She said that she delayed reporting because she was afraid of retaliation from the suspect.
>
> The investigating officer talked to the victim's mother, who expressed doubt that the incident had happened. She said that her daughter is a habitual liar and that she (mother) did not become aware of the incident until two weeks after it allegedly happened. She said that she talked to the victim on the phone and the victim told her she was on her way to the doctor

to find out if she was pregnant but did not want to talk about it with her mother. She would only say that she had been raped by "a Latino man with a boxcutter."

When the investigating officer talked to the victim, the victim became upset and said that she did not want to talk about the incident because it brought back bad memories. When the officer persisted she said, "If I say nothing happened will you leave me alone?"

Although the mother's belief that the incident was fabricated might have led us to categorize the case as a false report, the investigating officer noted in his report that he had information about a similar attack in the same part of the city—in that case, the suspect used the same MO (modus operandi) and was arrested for attempted kidnapping. The investigating officer prepared a photo lineup that included the picture of this suspect and explained to the complainant that there was a similar incident involving another complainant and that the LAPD wanted to determine if the same suspect attacked her. When the officer began reading the photographic lineup admonition to the complainant, she became upset and asked, "Why am I going to look at pictures if I told you nothing happened?" The complainant then got up and left the police station. The officer stated in the report, "Based on the victim's statements and her refusal to cooperate, this report will be unfounded."

The fact that the police had information about a similar incident involving a different complainant, coupled with the fact that the complainant reported the incident within a day of its occurrence and seemed to have second thoughts about pursuing the case, calls into question the conclusion that a crime did not occur. It appears that the complainant wanted to put the incident behind her and was not willing to cooperate in the police investigation, and that this led the police to unfound the report.

In contrast to these two cases in which the complainant recanted her testimony, in a third case categorized as not a false report the complainant did not recant. This case involved two 18-year-old friends who attended a concert at the Staples Center. After the concert, they were approached by three Latinos, who offered them a ride home. They agreed but instead of taking them home, the suspects drove to a liquor store to buy alcoholic beverages and then drove the complainants to a home in the valley. The suspects offered the women drinks, as well as cocaine and marijuana, and both initially refused. Eventually the complainant accepted a drink; she stated that she became intoxicated after drinking half of the drink and does not remember everything that happened after she accepted the drink from one of the suspects. She told the officer that

she went into the bathroom (which was attached to one of the bedrooms) and when she emerged she was surprised to find the suspect in the bedroom.

She stated that the suspect grabbed her waist and turned her around. He then began to kiss her. He pulled her pants down as he then pushed her onto the bed. She stated that she was scared and was unable to do anything except cry. She was pushed onto her stomach by the suspect, who then commenced penile-vaginal penetration. At some point, she heard the door open. She was still crying. She observed suspect-2 enter the bedroom. She advised that she was now "blanking out." She remembers a penis in front of her face and someone's hands attempting to push the penis in her mouth. As the unknown suspect attempted to force oral copulation, the victim pushed away, forcing the suspect that was penetrating to stop. As she sat up, she noticed that suspect-1 and suspect-2 were in the room. Suspect-1 then asked, "Why are you crying?" She observed them become nervous and rush out of the room.

All of the facts in the case were confirmed by the witness (the complainant's friend), who did not drink the alcoholic beverages offered to her. She reported that the complainant was crying when she exited the bedroom and that the suspects hurriedly left the location. The two women called a friend to pick them up and on the way home the complainant told the witness that she had been raped by suspect-1 and possibly by suspect-2. The complainant told the same story to the nurse during the forensic medical exam.

The complainant and the witness reported the crime to the police and the police arrested the two suspects and charged the first suspect with rape and the second with indecent exposure. The case file notes that suspect-1 had a prior arrest for domestic battery and that suspect-2 had previous arrests for disturbing the peace, burglary, carrying a concealed weapon, and driving under the influence. Male DNA recovered from the complainant during the forensic medical exam matched DNA taken from the suspect. The DA reviewing the case refused to file charges, on the ground that there was no corroborating evidence and that the complainant consented.

The day before the investigating officer presented the case to the DA, . . . [the officer] reinterviewed the complainant, who told the officer that she was very confused by the incident and that she now blamed herself "for letting it go too far." She changed her story, saying that the suspect did not use force as she originally said. She said that when she started crying loudly and told the suspects to stop, they stopped. According to the officer, "After subsequent reflection [*sic*] on the incident, she decided that neither of the 2 suspects had crossed the line and committed a crime against her." After the DA rejected the charges, the investigating officer presented a summary of the case to [the] supervisor. The supervisor then concluded that the complainant had recanted her testimony and changed the case clearance from cleared by arrest to unfounded.

This case is unusual, in that the report was unfounded after the suspects were arrested and charged by the police. Clearly, the investigating officer initially believed that a crime occurred. The complainant and the witness, who were interviewed separately, gave nearly identical testimony about the incident and DNA that matched suspect-1 was recovered from the complainant. Moreover, the investigating officer presented the case to the DA for a filing decision the day after the complainant, during the second interview, changed her story. The unfounding decision appears to be based on a belief that the complainant would not cooperate in the prosecution of the suspects rather than a belief that a crime did not occur.

Unfounded Cases That
Should Have Been Investigated Further

There were eight cases that the research team believed should have been investigated further. We believed that the evidence is these cases was ambiguous and that the investigating officer should have continued the investigation until these ambiguities could be clarified. Although a number of these cases involved complainants who were under the influence of alcohol or illegal drugs at the time of the alleged assault, most also involved witnesses who might have been able to corroborate the complainant's allegations but who were never interviewed. Several of the cases involved complainants whose allegations appeared credible, but who either could not be located or decided that they did not want to proceed with the case. There were no identified suspects in any of these eight cases. Considered together, these case characteristics suggest that the complaints were unfounded because the officers investigating them believed that a suspect was not likely to be identified and arrested and that the complainant was not likely to cooperate even if a suspect was identified. Unfounding was used as a way to clear—or dispose of—these problematic cases.

Motivations for Filing False Reports

The findings discussed thus far suggest that most, but not all, of the cases unfounded by the LAPD were either false or baseless. To further illuminate the nature of the false reports, we read through each case file to identify the factors that motivated complainants to make false allegations. The procedures we used to identify complainants' motivations for making false reports were similar to those used to determine whether the unfounded cases were false reports. Two members of the research team read through the case files to identify possible motives and then independently categorized each case. Based on the typologies discussed in Kanin (1994) and Kelly, Lovett, and Regan (2005), we began with three motivations for filing a false complaint. The first, which we label "avoiding trouble/alibi," involved either (1) young girls who fabricated a sexual assault to avoid the consequences of missing curfew, drinking or using drugs, or engaging in consensual sex, or (2) older teens and adult women who made up a sexual assault to cover up consensual sexual activity with someone other than a current partner. The second motivation is labeled "anger/revenge." Included in this category are cases in which the complainant used a false allegation of sexual assault to retaliate against a current or former partner, typically after the partner broke up with or cheated on the complainant. The third motivation, which we label "attention seeking," involves complainants who fabricated a sexual assault to gain attention or sympathy from family and friends, as well as those who invented an assault in order to get medical treatment or medication. As we reviewed the case files, we identified two additional motivations, which we labeled "mental health issues" and "guilt/ remorse." Many complainants, particularly those who did not recant, had mental health issues (e.g., schizophrenia) that made it difficult for them to separate fact from fantasy. Included in the "regret/guilt" category are complainants who engaged in consensual intercourse but, as a result of guilt or remorse regarding their behavior, claimed that they had been sexually assaulted by their consensual partners. As we discuss in more detail later, many of the complainants deemed to have made a false report involved overlapping motivations—for example, complainants with mental health issues who fabricated a rape as a means of garnering attention or because of remorse over consensual sexual intercourse or young girls who made up a rape both to avoid trouble with their parents or guardians and to draw attention to themselves.

As Table 5.3 shows, we were able to categorize all but five of the false reports according to at least one motive; whereas 22 complainants had only one discernible motive, 28 had two or more motives. Twenty-two cases

Table 5.3 Motivations for Filing False Reports[a]

	N	%
Provide an Alibi or Avoid Trouble	22	**40.0**
Victim missed curfew or was breaking the law	(13)	(23.6)
Victim was unfaithful to partner	(9)	(16.4)
Anger or Revenge	13	**23.6**
Attention or Sympathy	23	**41.8**
Medical	(6)	(10.9)
Personal	(17)	(30.9)
Mental Illness	18	**32.7**
Regret/Guilt	7	**12.7**
Victim Never Alleged Rape	2	**3.6**
Unable to Classify	5	**9.1**
Multiple Motives	28	**50.1**

Note: a. Motivations are not mutually exclusive.

were categorized as "avoiding trouble/alibi"; there were 13 cases in which the complainant fabricated the sexual assault to avoid trouble of some type and 9 cases involving complainants who made up a sexual assault to cover up the fact that they had cheated on their partners. There were 13 cases in which the complainant made up a rape allegation to retaliate against a partner, family member, or friends, and 23 involving complainants who filed false rape reports to garner attention or sympathy from family and friends or because they needed medical treatment or access to medication. In 7 cases the false allegation of rape was motivated by the complainant's guilt or remorse as a result of engaging in consensual sex. Finally, a total of 18 cases involved complainants with mental health issues; many of the complainants in these cases had multiple motivations. Next we provide descriptions of each category and examples of the types of cases that each includes.

Avoiding Trouble—Providing an Alibi

Many of the false reports in the "avoiding trouble/alibi" category involved adolescent complainants who missed curfew or skipped school and then claimed that they had been abducted (often from a bus stop) and sexually assaulted so as to avoid a confrontation with parents or guardians over their behavior. For example, one case involved a complainant who told the police that she was waiting for a bus at 11:30 at night when an unknown male drove up and asked her if she needed a ride. According to the complainant,

> She said yes and got into the suspect's vehicle. She told the suspect where she needed to go, but he went the wrong way. They then stopped at a house and the suspect asked the victim to come in with him, stating, "Come on, I am going to turn you into a woman." He then attempted to kiss her and to pull down her pants. She bit him on the face, got out of his vehicle and fled on foot. She said that the suspect did not pursue her.

We categorized this case as motivated by the complainant's desire to avoid trouble because the complainant, when confronted by the investigating officer regarding her honesty, recanted and stated "she lied about being raped because she was too afraid to say that she was with her boyfriend, which led her to miss her curfew." In addition, the complainant's vague description of the suspect, inability to identify the location where the incident occurred, and statement that she escaped by biting the suspect in the face are all red flags, which cast doubt on the truthfulness of this report (see McDowell and Hibler, 1987, for a description of red flags).

There were nine cases in which the complainant was cheating on her partner and attempted to cover up her indiscretion by either accusing the new partner of rape or claiming that she was sexually assaulted by an unknown suspect. For example, one case involved a complainant who had been engaging in an ongoing extramarital relationship with a coworker. The complainant claimed that the suspect raped her twice and took pictures of her to blackmail her if she told anyone. She said that after the second assault she told her husband what had happened. Three days later, the complainant, who had a black eye and a swollen lip, reported the assault to the police. During the investigation of the case, the complainant changed her story repeatedly, saying first that her relationship with the suspect was platonic but then admitting—after being told that the suspect's neighbor reported that the complainant was seen repeatedly at the suspect's residence—that she had consensual sex with him on several occasions after the initial assault. She also admitted that her husband was responsible for her black eye and other injuries. The investigating officer interviewed the suspect, who stated that he had consensual sexual intercourse with the complainant on numerous occasions and denied raping her in his car or his house.

During a follow-up interview, the investigating officer confronted the complainant with the inconsistencies in her story. He wrote, "At this point, I told her I didn't believe she had been raped. I told her that I was going to present the case to the city attorney to see if he was interested in filing charges against her. XXX and I took a short break to discuss whether we were going to arrest her." When they resumed the interview, the complainant admitted that the sexual activity with the suspect was consensual. She recanted the rape allegations, told the investigating officer that she filed the false report so that her husband would not find out about the extramarital affair, and apologized for lying, saying, "I didn't mean to cause so much trouble and I regret that I did."

The Angry Complainant Seeking Revenge

Fourteen of the false reports involved complainants motivated by anger and a desire to seek revenge against partners, ex-partners, friends, or family members. Some cases involved complainants with mental health issues who were angry at family or hospital staff for forcing them to take medication. An example of this motivation is a woman diagnosed as bipolar who refused to take her medication. When her parents insisted that she take the medication, she became upset, threw items around the house, and physically assaulted her father. She then claimed her father had raped her while her mother watched. Her mental illness, coupled with the fact that her mother witnessed her outburst, led the investigating officer to unfound the report.

Other cases in this category involved the so-called woman scorned. These were complainants who were angry after a fight with a partner or after a partner broke up with them and who claimed that they were sexually assaulted as a way to retaliate. One such case involved a woman who met the alleged suspect on a dating website and delayed reporting for two months.

> The victim said that she met the suspect on the Internet and arranged to meet him at Denny's. She states that she met him and that she left with him and that they went to a motel, where he penetrated her vagina with his finger and raped her. She said that she has called the suspect several times since the incident but he refused to speak to her; one time he did speak with her but called her a prostitute. During the follow-up interview with the investigating officer, it came out that the victim had met the suspect on prior occasions; this was not the first time they had met.
>
> When interviewed without her father in the room, the victim started to cry and said, "I didn't know he would get arrested, and I had a plan to die." When the officer asked whether the suspect hurt her, she stated, "No, he just made love to me and dumped me." When asked why she made these allegations against the suspect, the victim stated that "she felt sad since he had just dumped her after making love to him." When the investigating officer re-interviewed the victim, she admitted having sexual intercourse with the suspect but stated that it was consensual and that he had not forced her. She said that she lied because the suspect has not called her since their meeting.

In this example, the complainant admitted that she fabricated the rape and indicated that she did so because she was upset that the suspect did not want to have further contact with her. The investigating officer interviewed the suspect, who stated that he did not go to the meeting with the victim because her online profile did not match her real appearance. Regardless of whether the suspect met the complainant, the fact that he discontinued contact with her made her angry and led her to make up the rape allegation.

Attention Seeking

Cases in the "attention seeking" category involved both cases in which the complainant filed a false report to get medical attention or medication and cases in which the complainant used the rape allegation to garner attention or sympathy. Only six cases were primarily motivated by a desire to seek medical attention or a need for medication. Some complainants fabricated rapes because they needed, but could not afford, some type of medication or because they wanted to be admitted to a psychiatric facility. Other complainants filed false rape reports to obtain pregnancy tests or general physical exams. One such case involved a young female who had missed curfew and was sexually active. She stated that she was sexually assaulted by three unknown males and feared she was pregnant. Although the complainant provided detailed descriptions of the suspects, the location of the alleged incident was a major thoroughfare and no witnesses were present. When questioned by the investigating officer about the truthfulness of her statements, she recanted and stated that she had engaged in consensual sexual intercourse and feared that she was pregnant or had a sexually transmitted disease. Her statement provided a clear motive for fabricating the rape, as she told the investigating officer that she feared her mother would find out about her consensual relationships and would be upset if she was pregnant.

Many of the complainants who filed false rape allegations because they needed medical treatment or medication also had documented mental health issues. For example, in one case a distraught woman was found by police near a pay phone.

> The victim was threatening to commit suicide and said that she had been held against her will and forced to have sex all night. She said that she and an unknown black male had been smoking crack cocaine in his vehicle. Sometime during the night, the suspect verbally threatened the victim and demanded oral copulation. The victim, fearing for her safety, complied. She would not provide any additional info or explain how she ended up near the pay phone. The victim later stated that she was not sexually assaulted and only reported that she was because she had run out of psych meds and wanted to be placed on a 5150 [72-hour] hold so that she could get access to psych meds.

The vagueness of the complainant's description of the suspect and the location of the incident, combined with her inability to answer the investigating officer's questions, led the researchers to conclude that this was a false report. The complainant also recanted her statement, providing the rationale for filing the report as the desire to gain access to medication for her mental illness. The case file also notes that the complainant is homeless, which likely influenced her inability to obtain treatment for her mental illness.

One of the most common motivations for filing a false report was a desire for attention or sympathy from family, therapists, or the police. Many of these cases involved complainants who had histories of making false reports, were described as known liars by family or friends, or explicitly stated they liked the attention they received as a result of reporting the rape. Several cases also included complainants with mental health issues, in which the desire for attention may have been due to symptoms of their illness. These cases will be reported in more detail in the section that follows. For now we focus on those cases in which complainants without documented mental health issues were seeking attention. In the first case, the teenage complainant appears to have fabricated the rape to avoid trouble due to missing her curfew.

> The victim stated that she was kidnapped by two Hispanic men driving a gray car as she waited for a bus (was going to a friend's house) at 10:30 in

the morning. She cannot remember anything else until 10 pm that night, when they pushed her out of the vehicle at the same location where they kidnapped her. The victim was angry that her mother called police and said that she cannot remember anything during the 12-hours that she was with them. She refused medical treatment.

When questioned by the investigating officer about the inconsistencies in her story and the fact that it was highly unlikely she would not remember what happened during a 12-hour time span, the complainant recanted. The complainant stated that she spent most of the day at the beach alone and returned home late because of traveling by bus. She then stated that "after telling her mother and sisters that she was kidnapped, they expressed great concern and gave her more attention" and that "the attention made her feel good." Although the complainant may not have initially sought out attention when she left her home that morning, the attention expressed by her family acted as reinforcement for the lie she told.

Guilt/Remorse

Cases falling under the "guilt /remorse" category include those in which the complainant engaged in consensual sexual intercourse and later felt guilt or regret about her behavior. Some of these cases involved complainants who had been drinking or who were under the influence of drugs at the time and who therefore may have been slightly impaired. However, these complainants exhibited no significant memory loss and reported a sexual assault due to guilt or remorse, rather than to "be on the safe side." Some of these complainants may not have wanted to engage in the sexual activity, but they stated that they did not resist or say no to the suspects. Others had sexual experiences that were painful or unpleasant, but were nonetheless consensual. One example of a "consensual/regret" case involves a teenaged complainant who stated that

> she was forced into the McDonalds restroom by two suspects (ages 15 and 16), who fondled her and forced her to orally copulate one of them. She told a few friends what happened and the next day at school her friends jumped one of the suspects and a fight ensued, the police were called, and one of the bystanders told the police that XXXX had raped their friend. During the interview with the victim, the investigating officer asked her what he would see when he looked at the video from McDonalds—would he see her walking willingly into the bathroom with the two boys? When she was asked if she ever told the boys no, she said that she did at first, but that she then went along with everything.

In this case, the investigating officer interviewed one of the suspects, who stated that he and his friend engaged in playful flirting with the complainant prior to the event and that he believed that the complainant had consensually engaged in oral copulation. The complainant later recanted and "finally admitted that she wasn't forced to do any of the sexual acts on XXXX and XXXX, and that even though she didn't want to do it, she did agree." The recantation, combined with the suspect's statement, led us to categorize this as a false report with the motivation of regret. The complainant appeared to believe that the "playful flirting" had gone too far, but did not cry out or physically resist the suspects.

Another case involved a complainant who had been out drinking with a friend and was offered a ride home by two suspects that she met at the nightclub. After the suspects drove the complainant and a witness (her friend) to an apartment, the suspects offered both women more drinks. As both were intoxicated and the witness indicated that she passed out, there was some confusion as to what then happened. The witness remembered seeing the complainant in a closet with one of the suspects, and the complainant did not explicitly remember saying no to the suspect's advances. Because there was ambiguity about what happened, the investigating officer asked the complainant to make a pretext phone call to the suspect. During the call, she asked the suspect what happened. He replied:

> "Don't you remember? You were the one that initiated the sex. You asked me if I had a condom. I said yes and you asked me to put it on." The victim then told the suspect that she felt bad because she felt that she had been taken advantage of. The suspect said, "I'm sorry you feel that way. I totally thought you were into me. We need to hang out so you can see that I'm not a bad guy."

Although the complainant expressed regret about the sexual activity, both her own account and the suspect's account describe consensual sex and no physical or verbal resistance by the complainant. The suspect further stated that the complainant took an aggressive role in initiating the sexual activity, as she led him into the closet and got on top of him. After talking with the suspect, the victim hung up the phone and said: "Detective, I want to drop the charges. I know he didn't rape me. It was consensual."

The Importance of Mental Health Issues

Mental health issues played a significant role in many of the false reports, with over one third of the cases (N = 18) involving complainants whose fabrications resulted at least in part from some type of mental illness.[5] In some cases, complainants' mental conditions were noted in the case file but these conditions did not appear to play an important role in motivating them to file false reports. However, in other cases, the complainant's mental illness clearly was the motivating factor that led to the false report—either due to hallucinations and delusions, a reduced mental capacity to understand the nature of sexual acts, or a desire for attention as a symptom of her condition. For example, one case involved a victim who was living at an assisted living facility and who fell asleep fully clothed. According to the investigating officer who wrote the follow-up report:

> The victim woke up at 2:30 am and observed a black man in her room. She said that her eyes were covered by cloth and she immediately fell asleep. When she awoke at 5:30 she observed that her pants had been pulled down to her ankles and her legs spread apart. She also observed a needle injection wound in her arm. When she urinated she observed semen coming out of her vagina. There was no evidence of forced entry into her room.
>
> Officers interviewed the manager at the facility, who told them that the victim suffers from delusions and claims that she has been raped, assaulted, and that people are entering her room and removing her property. This was confirmed by the victim's daughter.
>
> The investigating officer met with the victim, who stated that she had been sexually assaulted every day for the past three years. She stated that every gang member in the city had raped her. She was unable to give a coherent account about the incident under investigation. She kept repeating that she had been raped and beaten by every gang member in the city.

This case was classified as a false report for several reasons. The complainant stated she had been raped multiple times and she had filed three very similar false reports within the past 18 months. She also could not describe the incident, other than stating that she woke to find a black man in her room. Her daughter and her doctor confirmed that she suffers from delusions and the forensic medical exam did not show any physical evidence that a sexual assault had taken place. The needle mark found on her arm was due to a blood draw the previous day, which also casts doubt on her statement. It appears that her delusions and desire for attention are symptoms of her mental illness, which led her to file multiple false rape reports.

Examples of Cases with Multiple Typologies

Many of the cases categorized as false reports involved complainants with multiple motives for filing reports. Although some of these complainants had mental health issues, as well as a desire for retaliation or need for attention, others involved overlapping motivations that were not related to the complainant's mental state. In this section we focus on these types of cases, which present different circumstances for each complainant. The complainant in the first example thought she was being interviewed by a prospective employer. She met him in his car and they discussed an open position for a nanny before the conversation turned more personal.

> The suspect said he would marry her on Monday if she would come live with him. The victim and suspect then moved to the victim's vehicle,

where he began to rub and suck her breasts. He then took her to a motel and attempted to rape her (could not get an erection); put his fingers in her anus. The victim and suspect then got dressed and left motel.

When asked if she had done all of these things voluntarily, the victim said she had. The victim asked if there was any law against the suspect making promises of paying her bills and marrying her then reneging on his promise. The I/O [investigating officer] then asked the victim "why she really made this report." She said that she made the report because she wanted to be medically examined; she was fearful that the suspect had diseases and she did not want to catch any. She said that she had participated voluntarily and did not want the I/O to tell her boyfriend about what she had done.

We categorized this as a false report in which the complainant displayed several motivations for filing: She engaged in consensual sex, as she never attempted to stop the suspect or resist him, and believed that he would marry her and pay her bills. It seems that she was angry at the suspect for failing to follow through on his promises, which led her to file the false report. She was also motivated by the current situation she was in; she had gotten back together with her boyfriend and did not want him to know that she had cheated on him with the suspect. Relating to this desire to avoid trouble, she sought medical treatment because she feared that she might have contracted a sexually transmitted disease. Thus, these three overlapping motives—avoiding trouble as a result of cheating, seeking medical attention, and anger and a desire for revenge—were the deciding factors in the complainant's decision to make a report of rape.

A second case with multiple motives involved a complainant who displayed several of the so-called red flags associated with false reports, such as declining a forensic medical exam, an unwillingness to describe the attack during the second interview, and a description of overt physical resistance during the incident (McDowell and Hibler, 1987). The complainant was riding the bus at night:

returning home after drinking at Club 6065. She got off the bus and was approached by the suspect, who began pulling her hair and telling her that she was a "dirty Mexican bitch." He pushed her down and she saw that his erect penis was out—he told her to suck it and she did. The victim said that she removed his penis and began striking suspect in face; the suspect then ripped the victim's necklace from her neck and attempted to remove her pants. The victim stated that she continued to punch the suspect in the face in attempt to get away from him. When officers went to the scene, they found human hair on the ground and a brown belt in the grass (consistent with her story).

When the investigating officer told the victim that he needed to talk to the witness (the friend who picked her up), she said "I don't want you to talk to her. I did not really tell her what happened." When the witness was finally put on the phone, she said that "XXXX is a chronic liar. Two weeks ago her car was repossessed. My son has a car that just sits at my house. She asked me if she could use it. I told her no. She told me she hated taking the bus and asked me if she could use the car. I refused. The night that this took place, she called me all night. She was drunk. She told me she was attacked and needed a ride. After the cops left, she asked if she could have my son's car. She told me she was never going to ride the bus again because of this." The witness also said, "I knew she was lying from the beginning, but once she said that I knew she made up the story so that I would let her have my son's car."

This case presented several motives that the complainant may have had for filing the false report. As the witness stated, the complainant was upset about not being allowed to use the car, and may have created this story out of anger and in order to get her way. She also told the witness, police, and friends at the bar she frequents several different stories. The investigating officer believed that the complainant manufactured this story desiring attention from others. Because she told many different people she knew about the incident, and they expressed concern for her, this motive seems plausible. Initially the researchers were in some disagreement regarding whether to categorize this case as a false report, as the evidence found by police of hair and a belt added credibility to the complainant's story. Yet the fact that the witness stated that the complainant is a chronic liar and the lengths the complainant went to in order to gain access to the complainant's son's car suggest that she may have planted the evidence to corroborate her story.

Discussion

Our examination of cases unfounded by the LAPD was designed to determine whether these reports were false or baseless and, for those that were determined to be false, to identify the factors that motivated complainants to file false allegations of sexual assault. We found that about three fourths of the unfounded cases involved false or baseless allegations; the remaining cases were either clearly not false reports or were ambiguous cases that the research team felt should have been investigated further before being cleared. Most of the false reports involved allegations of aggravated rape and in about half of the cases the victim underwent a forensic medical exam and eventually recanted the allegations. Complainants' motivations for filing false reports, which fell into five overlapping categories, included a desire to avoid trouble or a need for an alibi for consensual sex with someone other than a current partner, a desire to retaliate against a current or former partner, a need for attention or sympathy, and guilt or remorse as a result of consensual sexual activity. Finally, many complainants also had mental health issues that made it difficult for them to separate fact from fantasy.

These results suggest that the LAPD is appropriately clearing cases as unfounded most, but not all, of the time. Generally, the investigating officers are following UCR guidelines and are unfounding cases only after an investigation leads them to conclude that the allegations are false or baseless; they typically do not use the unfounding decision to clear—or dispose of—problematic cases. Nonetheless, there were 10 cases with compelling evidence that a crime did occur: physical evidence from the forensic medical exam or witness statements that corroborated the complainant's allegations, injuries to the complainant that were consistent with her account of the assault, or evidence recovered from the scene of the crime. In most of these cases, a number of which involved complainants and suspects who were intimate partners or acquaintances, the complainant recanted but it was clear that her recantation was motivated by fear of the suspect, pressure from the suspect or his family and friends, or a lack of interest in pursuing the case. It appears that the victim's recantation or lack of interest in prosecuting the suspect led the investigating officer to conclude that the allegations, while not false, were not provable and that the case therefore should be unfounded. Coupled with the fact that there were an additional eight cases that we believed should have been investigated further, this suggests a need for additional training on the decision rules for unfounding sexual assaults.[6] Patrol officers and sex detectives need specialized training to understand the complexities of sex crimes and the interview skills that are critical to build rapport with victims and maximize the likelihood of the most forthright self-disclosure.

Further evidence of this need for training comes from our interviews with LAPD detectives. Although some detectives stated that victim recantation was neither a necessary nor a sufficient condition for unfounding, many said they believed that a report could be unfounded only if the complainant recanted her testimony, whereas a few stated that they would always unfound the report if the victim recanted her testimony. For example, one officer stated that "the only way we can unfound is if the victim tells us it did not happen—there is no other way." Other detectives stressed that they would only unfound if the complainant recanted or if her story was utterly impossible. As one officer put it:

> In order to unfound you have to prove that it did not happen and in
> order to do that you have to have a victim who recants her story. If it
> is something that realistically is impossible—she says, "Someone
> flew me to the moon and raped me"—and she continues to maintain
> that it happened, you can unfound. But you must do a thorough
> investigation before you can do that.

Another officer stated categorically that "when the victim says, 'I made a false report,' it gets unfounded." These views regarding the importance of recantation are also reflected in officers' statements about the techniques they use to "get the victim to recant" or to "break her down and admit to what she was really doing." According to one detective, "We present the conflicting evidence to the victim and try to get the victim to admit that it did not occur." Another officer recounted a case in which "we really beat the victim up emotionally because we did not believe her story," and a third stated that the goal with teenagers was to "get them to admit it didn't happen and have them write it down; get them caught in discrepancies and have them tell the story left, right, and center." These comments suggest that at least some LAPD sex detectives believe that recanting is an important, if not a necessary, element of unfounding; they also believe that it is appropriate to use techniques designed to encourage complainants to recant.

It is important to point out that these detectives were in the minority. In fact, many of the officers we interviewed reported that they were skeptical of complainants who recanted, noting that recanting "is often based on fear." Typical of these comments are the following:

> Either it did not happen in the City of Los Angeles or the victim recants the allegation and you actually believe her. I do believe that there are recantations that are lies. For me, it would take the victim clearly indicating that she lied, providing a rational motivation for lying, and we believe her when she says it didn't happen. Recanting does not necessarily mean that we will unfound the case. If we continue to believe that a crime occurred, the case can be cleared as "IC" [investigation continuing].
>
>   Many victims recant because . . . they are tired of dealing with it; they want to go back to normal and they feel responsible for the stress that has emerged. A victim recant can be used but it should be corroborated and followed up by the detective . . . to make sure that the recantation is valid.

When asked how they would clear a case in which the victim recanted but the evidence and case factors suggested that the recantation was motivated by threats or intimidation, most of the officers we interviewed stated that they would present the case to the DA for a prearrest filing decision. Almost without exception, however, these respondents noted that the DA would reject the case. As one officer put it, "I would not unfound if the victim recanted and the evidence suggested that the crime did occur. But the DA would reject it, absolutely." Another detective emphasized that "I believe all of my victims until I can prove that they are not telling the truth. If the victim says that it did not happen, I still present it to the DA and let the DA decide. They will reject it, of course." A third officer stated:

> I will put it in the report that the victim is being uncooperative and that it appears that she is being threatened or pressured. Talk to her

and provide her with referrals to agencies that can help her. But the DA is unlikely to file—you cannot force someone to testify in court and therefore the DA has nothing.

As these comments make clear, when confronted with a complainant who says that the crime did not occur when evidence that suggests it did, LAPD detectives typically do not unfound the case. Rather, they present the case to the LA DA, who rejects it based on the fact that the complainant refuses to cooperate in the investigation and prosecution of the suspect. Our review of these types of cases revealed that the case is then cleared by exceptional means.

Several other findings also merit comment. Using weighted data that took into account the fact that our sample was stratified by LAPD division and, within each division, by the type of case closure, we calculated that the overall rate of false reports for the LAPD in 2008 was 4.5 percent, with about half the cases involving a complainant who recanted. Although this is consistent with estimates of the prevalence of false reports found in recent studies using appropriate methodologies, it is important to point out that our estimate is based on only the unfounded cases we examined. We believe that this rate most likely underestimates the prevalence of false reports among all cases reported to the LAPD in 2008. This is because our interviews with LAPD detectives revealed that some of them were reluctant to categorize a case as "unfounded," even if they believed that it was false or baseless. Some detectives reported that they would sometimes clear the case by exceptional means[7] or keep the case open. Although these detectives were in the minority, their comments suggest that the rate of false reports among rapes reported to the LAPD in 2008 may be somewhat higher than 4.5 percent.

Also of interest is the fact that more than three quarters of the reports classified as false allegations were reports of aggravated rape—the complainant reported that she was forcibly raped and indicated that the rape was perpetrated by a stranger, by multiple assailants, or by a suspect wielding a weapon, or that she suffered collateral injuries. Many of the complainants, especially young teenagers, reported that they were abducted by a man (or men) in a vehicle (often a white van), taken to an unknown location, threatened with physical harm, and sexually assaulted. Most of the complainants who alleged that they were attacked by a stranger provided very vague descriptions of the suspect, stated that they resisted the suspect physically (e.g., by kicking him in the groin or biting him on the face), and that they somehow managed to escape. The fact that the allegations deemed to be false conform so closely to the stereotypical view of forcible rape (or "real rape"; see Estrich, 1987; Kalven and Zeisel, 1966) suggests that complainants believe that their stories will be viewed as more credible if they do not deviate too sharply from society's view of the dynamics of a "real rape." The problem with this is that as a result, the aggravated rape factors are likely to be viewed as red flags by sex detectives and other criminal justice professions. As Lonsway, Archambault, and Lisak (2009: 3) note: "Concerns regarding the legitimacy of a sexual assault report are often triggered by the presence of 'red flags,' based on specific characteristics of the victim, suspect, or assault. Yet many of these 'red flags' are actually based on our cultural stereotypes of what constitutes 'real rape.'" This was confirmed by one of the detectives we interviewed, who described the type of case that would be "red flagged." As this respondent put it, "the stories are pretty wild," noting that they often involve teens who allege that they were raped by multiple men, who manage to escape or who "give outlandish reasons as to why they did not try to escape."

Our findings also suggest that complainants' motivations for filing false rape reports are varied and complex, and that they differ depending on the age of the complainant. Whereas teenagers' false allegations were motivated primarily by a desire to avoid trouble with parents or caregivers or by a need for attention or sympathy, adults' allegations were more typically motivated by a desire for revenge against a partner or by a need to cover up a consensual sexual relationship. Complainants, regardless of age, often had mental health issues, which, while not the primary motivation for filing a false report, overlapped with other motivations, especially attention seeking. These motives also emerged in our interviews with LAPD sexual assault detectives, who were asked what would motivate a complainant to file a false report. Regarding the teenagers who file false allegations, one officer stated, "The one that we get most often is young teenagers who don't make curfew or have done something that they know their parents won't approve of—they ditched school, were using drugs, or had consensual sex . . . they try to place the blame on someone other than themselves." Another detective gave a laundry list of reasons why an adult woman might file a false report: "to get out of trouble, to explain away her actions, to hide consensual sex, to get sympathy, to explain away drug usage or because she will lose her housing or kids if she tests dirty for drugs."

Our study, which is based on data from one of the largest police departments in the United States, improves on prior research on false reports of rape in a number of important ways: we used a definition of a false rape allegation that is consistent with FBI guidelines for clearing cases; we differentiated between false allegations and baseless reports; and we did not assume that recantation was a necessary or a sufficient condition for concluding that a report was a false report. We also did not assume that all of the reports unfounded by the LAPD were false or baseless; rather, we reviewed the detailed case file for each of the unfounded cases and, based on the information in the file, categorized the case as a false allegation, a baseless report, not a false report, or a case that should have been investigated further. We also used the information in the case file to identify complainants' motivations for filing false reports, and we supplemented the data from case files with information gleaned from in-depth interviews with sex detectives. Our study is thus more comprehensive than prior research, and we believe that our findings shed important light on the prevalence and nature of false allegations of sexual assault.

These improvements notwithstanding, our study is not without limitations. Although we were provided with a redacted copy of each case file, we cannot know with any degree of certainty whether the information recorded in the case file was an accurate and unbiased report of what happened and what complainants, witnesses, and suspects said about the alleged incident. In addition, we examined only cases that were unfounded; we did not examine the cases that were cleared by exceptional means, which also may have involved false allegations. This suggests that our estimate of the prevalence of false allegations of rape may underestimate the actual rate.

Conclusion

It is clear from our analysis of sexual assaults unfounded by the LAPD that some girls and women do lie about being sexually assaulted. More than two thirds of the cases that were unfounded by the LAPD in 2008 were false allegations in which complainants deliberately lied about being raped. This clearly is a cause for concern. False allegations of rape feed societal perceptions that many—perhaps even most—rape reports are fabricated and lead to cynicism and frustration among detectives tasked with investigating sexual assaults. They also undermine the credibility of genuine victims and divert scarce resources from the investigation of the crimes committed against them. As Lonsway and her colleagues (Lonsway, Archambault, and Lisak, 2009: 1) concluded, "The issue of false reporting may be one of the most important barriers to successfully investigating and prosecuting sexual assault, especially with cases involving nonstrangers."

Notes

1. Cases not determined to be false reports were coded as "case did not proceed"—that is, the case did not result in a referral for prosecution or disciplinary action because of insufficient evidence or because the victim did not want to cooperate; "case proceeded"—that is, the report resulted in a referral for prosecution or disciplinary action; or "insufficient information to assign a category."

2. We eliminated eight cases that were reported to the LAPD but were unfounded after it was determined that the crime occurred in another jurisdiction.

3. The interviews took place at the division to which the officer was assigned. We took detailed notes but did not record the interviews.

4. For each case closure type in each division, we determined (using LAPD data on all sexual assault cases reported in 2008) the percentage of the stratum (i.e., the percentage of each case closure type in each division) in the population. We then divided the percentage of the stratum in the population by the percentage of the stratum in the sample. Each case in each stratum was multiplied by the proportional weight; groups that had been oversampled had a proportional weight that was less than 1 and groups that had been undersampled had a proportional weight of more than 1.

5. Of course, complainants with mental illnesses should not be treated skeptically solely because of their condition, as research suggests that these individuals may also be at a higher risk of victimization because of their vulnerabilities (Wacker, Parish, and Macy, 2008). In addition, these individuals may be reliant upon their perpetrator for financial support, shelter, or employment and as such may be reluctant to disclose prior victimizations.

6. This is particularly salient because as of January 2010 the LAPD utilizes a noncrime report entitled "Undetermined Sexual Assault." Depending on the training and biases of the supervisors in charge of the patrol officers and detectives who come across these reports, a sexual assault may never wind up as an actual crime report that requires investigation and, ultimately, a case clearance.

7. This would be an inappropriate use of this case clearance type since the *UCR Handbook* states that cases cleared by exceptional means must have an identified suspect and probable cause to make an arrest.

6

The Overuse and Misuse
of Exceptional Clearance

Thirty-five years ago, Susan Brownmiller wrote in *Against Our Will:*
Men, Women and Rape (1975) that the complaints of rape victims often were
met with insensitivity or hostility on the part of police and other criminal
justice officials. Brownmiller noted that, contrary to Lord Hale's assertion
that "rape is an accusation easily to be made," many rape victims did not
report the crime to the police, and those who did soon discovered that, consistent with Lord Hale's homily, it was a crime "hard to be proved."[1]

As we enter the second decade of the twenty-first century, the issue of
police—and prosecutor—handling of sexual assault complaints continues to
evoke controversy and spark debate.[2] Critics charge that police make inappropriate decisions regarding whether rape cases should be accepted for
investigation, misclassify rape and other sex crimes as noncrimes based on
archaic notions of what constitutes "rape," unfound reports at unreasonably
high rates, and fail to adequately investigate the cases they do accept. They
also allege that prosecutors' assumptions regarding "real rapes" and "genuine victims" (Estrich, 1987; LaFree, 1989) lead them to decline to file
charges in cases in which it is clear that a sexual assault occurred but in
which it also is clear that the odds of proving the case to a jury are low. As
Dempsey put it in her testimony at a recent US Senate hearing convened to
investigate the response of the criminal justice system to the crime of rape,
"the chronic failure to report and investigate rape cases is part of a systemic
failure to take rape seriously both within the criminal justice system and
within our communities more generally" (US Senate, 2010).

Missing from these critiques is any discussion of the use (and misuse)
of the exceptional clearance by police. As discussed in Chapter 2, cases can
be cleared—or solved—by the police in two ways: by the arrest of at least
one suspect or by clearing the case exceptionally. Although cases that are
exceptionally cleared do not result in the arrest of the suspect, they are considered solved in the sense that the suspect is known to the police but there
is something beyond the control of law enforcement that precludes the
police from making an arrest (e.g., the victim refuses to cooperate in the
prosecution of the suspect or the suspect has died or cannot be extradited).
If police officers are clearing cases inappropriately—and the rules for doing

so are clearly articulated by the Federal Bureau of Investigation's (FBI's) *Uniform Crime Reporting (UCR) Handbook*—and are either failing to investigate sexual assault cases thoroughly or not making arrests when they have probable cause to do so and the victim is willing to go forward with the case, there is the potential for a miscarriage of justice. Specifically, the misuse of the exceptional clearance raises the possibility that individuals who may in fact be guilty of rape are not arrested, prosecuted, and punished.

Also missing from these critiques is a discussion of the role that the prosecutor plays in clearing cases. Prior research on prosecutorial decision-making in sexual assault cases has focused on the formal decision whether to file charges once an arrest has been made (Frohmann, 1991, 1997; Kerstetter, 1990; Kingsnorth, MacIntosh, and Wentworth, 1999; Spohn and Holleran, 2001). This research assumes—either explicitly or implicitly—that the prosecutor's role in the process begins when the police arrest a suspect and present the case to the screening unit for a charging decision. This ignores the fact that law enforcement officials may present the case to the prosecutor prior to making an arrest and, based on the prosecutor's assessment of the evidence in the case and evaluation of the credibility of the victim, either make an arrest or (inappropriately) clear the case exceptionally. As we demonstrated in earlier chapters of this book, the role of the prosecutor may begin well before an arrest is made and the decisions the prosecutor makes may influence—indeed, determine—how the case is cleared.

In this chapter, we investigate the use of the exceptional clearance in sexual assault cases. We use detailed qualitative and quantitative data on the sample of cases from 2008 to identify the characteristics of cases that are cleared exceptionally and to evaluate the reasons given by police and prosecutors to justify this type of clearance. We begin with a discussion of the circumstances under which cases may be cleared exceptionally. We then examine the characteristics of cases cleared by exceptional means, and evaluate the extent to which these cases meet the four criteria that the FBI requires be met before this clearance type can be used. We end with a discussion of the policy implications of using—and misusing—the exceptional clearance.

Case Clearances:
Cleared by Arrest and by Exceptional Means

According to the *UCR Handbook* (FBI, 2004), offenses are cleared either by arrest or by exceptional means. The handbook states that "an offense is cleared by arrest, or solved for crime reporting purposes, when at least one person is (1) arrested, (2) charged with the commission of the offense, and (3) turned over to the court for prosecution (whether following arrest, court summons, or police notice)" (p. 79). Regarding exceptional clearances, the handbook notes that there may be occasions where law enforcement has conducted an investigation, exhausted all leads, and identified a suspect but is nonetheless unable to clear an offense by arrest. In this situation, the agency can clear the offense by exceptional means, provided that each of the following questions can be answered in the affirmative (pp. 80–81):

- Has the investigation definitely established the identity of the offender?
- Is the exact location of the offender known so that the subject could be taken into custody now?
- Is there enough information to support an arrest, charge, and turning over to the court for prosecution?
- Is there some reason outside law enforcement control that precludes arresting, charging, and prosecuting the offender?

To illustrate the types of cases that might be cleared by exceptional means, the handbook provides a list of examples, many of which involve the death of the offender or an offender who is unable to be arrested because he or she is being prosecuted in another jurisdiction for a different crime or because extradition has been denied. One of the examples provided is when the "victim refuses to cooperate in the prosecution," but there is an added proviso stating that this alone does not justify an exceptional clearance and that the answer to the first three questions must also be yes (p. 81).

In his review of the development of the uniform crime reporting system, Feeney (2000–2001, p. 14) notes that the instructions contained in the early editions of the *UCR Handbook* defined exceptional clearances very narrowly[3] and reflected an expectation that "most clearances would be based on arrests and that the number of exceptional clearances would be limited." He bolsters this by pointing out that since the inception of the UCR the FBI has labeled its tables of clearance data "cleared by arrest." According to Feeney (2000–2001: 18), "There can be little doubt that arrest is the decisive event in the vast majority of instances in determining whether a clearance is to be recorded or not."

Feeney also takes issue with the fact that some jurisdictions have interpreted the term "charged" in the definition of cleared by arrest (i.e., cleared by arrest requires that the suspect be charged with the commission of the offense) to mean charged by the prosecutor. He argues that the term meant (and continues to mean) charged by the police[4] and not charged by the prosecutor. He bases this on the fact that the developers of the UCR system envisioned collecting data not only on offenses known to the police but also on persons charged by the police. According to Feeney (2000–2001: 15), they used this term, rather than "persons arrested," to differentiate between "two types of arrests: those made for the purpose of prosecution and those considered to be 'suspicion' arrests." That is, they wanted to distinguish between persons who were arrested and charged with a crime by the police and persons who were arrested and brought to the station as a result of an officer's suspicions that they were involved in a crime. As he points out (p. 15), "The term 'charged by the police' was their way of denoting the more normal kind of arrest."

Feeney's historical overview of the development of the UCR system, then, suggests that there was an expectation that most crimes (that were cleared) would be cleared by arrest, which would require that a suspect be arrested and charged with a crime by the police, and that exceptional clearances, which were narrowly defined, would be just that—exceptional.

Research on Case Clearances

Because the FBI does not differentiate between cases cleared by arrest and those cleared by exceptional means, most research examining case clearances—either over time or across jurisdictions—has been conducted using the overall case clearance rate (Addington, 2006; Alderden and Lavery, 2007; Lee, 2005; Puckett and Lundman, 2003; Regoeczi, Jarvis, and Riedel, 2008). In fact, with the exception of a study of Chicago homicide data (Riedel and Boulahanis, 2007), a more recent study using National Incident-Based Reporting System (NIBRS) data (Jarvis and Regoeczi, 2009), and one study of sexual assault case clearances (Bouffard, 2000), there are no studies that examine the predictors of different types of case clearances and none that examine clearances using national data.

Jarvis and Regoeczi (2009: 175) argue that there are compelling reasons for separating cases cleared by arrest and cases cleared by exception. First, although both types of cases are considered solved for reporting purposes, cases cleared by exceptional means do not result in the arrest of the suspect. This clearly is an important difference. In addition, the cases that fall into the two categories may vary widely in terms of victim, suspect, and case characteristics; thus, combining them into a single "case cleared" category raises the possibility that the effects of these characteristics may be under- or overstated. Finally, combining the two types of cases can inflate a law enforcement agency's reported case clearance rate.

The validity of these points was confirmed by Riedel and Boulahanis (2007), who used Chicago homicide data from 1988 to 1995 to investigate the similarities and differences in cases cleared by arrest and by exceptional means. More specifically, they examined cases cleared exceptionally because the case was "barred to prosecution," which meant that the Felony Review Unit of the Cook County State's Attorney's Office did not accept the case for prosecution. It is interesting that in an earlier study Boulahanis (1998) reported the results of interviews with police and with a prosecutor in the Felony Review Unit in which he asked them who made the decision to exceptionally clear a case. According to the police, the decision was made by the prosecutor, who decides whether to approve the charges; in contrast, the prosecutor stated that the decision was "controlled solely by the police department." As Boulahanis (1998: 35) noted, because "all cases that are not approved because of a lack of evidence may be resubmitted for review," the decision to investigate further or to clear the case by exceptional means rests solely with the police department.

Riedel and Boulahanis (2007) found that 10.7 percent of homicide cases reported to the Chicago Police Department from 1982 to 1995 were cleared by exceptional means, while 64.6 percent were cleared by arrest. Thus, "including exceptional clearances among arrest clearances can substantially increase the latter total" (p. 156). When the authors examined the likelihood that the case would be exceptionally cleared (i.e., barred to prosecution), they found that cases cleared exceptionally were more likely to be domestic homicides and to have occurred in a private indoor or public outdoor location rather than a vehicle. In addition, cases involving white offenders were less likely than those involving African American offenders to be cleared by exceptional means. Moreover, cases involving male victims and male offenders were less likely than those involving female victims and male offenders to be cleared by exceptional means. Riedel and Boulahanis (2007: 162), who were careful to point out that the results of their study could not be generalized due to the fact that there are "no systematic studies of the phenomena" of exceptional clearances, called for additional research designed to provide data on the frequency of exceptional clearances and circumstances in which they are used.

Bouffard's (2000) study of case closures in sexual assault cases reported to an unnamed law enforcement agency was a more comprehensive analysis than either the Riedel and Boulahanis (2007) or the Jarvis and Regoeczi (2009) studies. This study examined five different types of case closures: unfounded, cleared by arrest, cleared by exceptional means because of victim's lack of cooperation, cleared by exceptional means due to lack of prosecutorial merit, and open. For this particular law enforcement agency, 27.9 percent of the reports were unfounded, 18.1 percent were cleared by arrest, 31.6 percent were cleared by exceptional means, and 22.4 percent were still open at the time of data collection (Bouffard, 2000, Table 1). Bouffard found that the probability that the report would be unfounded was reduced in cases in which the victim had a prior relationship with the suspect and in cases in which the victim agreed to a sexual assault exam; reports of first- and second-degree rape, on the other hand, were more likely than other crimes to be unfounded. Not surprisingly, Bouffard also found that cases in which the victim and the suspect had a prior relationship were more likely to be cleared exceptionally (due to a lack of victim cooperation and due to a decision that the case did not merit prosecution). The author of this study concluded that the variables included in the models "appeared to have different effects on each type of case closure" (Bouffard, 2000: 540).

Considered together, the limited amount of research on case clearances highlights the importance of separately analyzing cases cleared by arrest and by exceptional means. The factors that affect these outcomes are different, and testing only for their effects on the overall case clearance rate is likely to produce misleading results and lead to inaccurate conclusions about the police investigative function.

Clearing Sexual Assault Cases in Los Angeles

The process used by the Los Angeles Police Department (LAPD) and the Los Angeles County Sheriff's Department (LASD) to clear sexual assault cases, which is described in detail in Chapter 2, is similar to the process reported by Riedel and Boulahanis (2007) for homicides handled by the Chicago Police Department: reports of sexual assault are either unfounded, cleared by arrest, cleared by exceptional means, or unsolved and the investigation is continuing. If the detective investigating the crime has identified a suspect and has probable cause to arrest the suspect, the detective will either arrest the individual and then present the case to a deputy district attorney (DDA) from the Victim Impact Program (VIP)[5] of the Los Angeles County DA's Office for a formal filing decision, or delay making an arrest and present the case to a DDA for a prearrest charge evaluation decision. The DDA reviewing the case prior to arrest of the suspect can either accept the case for prosecution, send the case back to the investigating officer for further investigation, send the case to the city attorney for prosecution as a misdemeanor, or decline the case for prosecution. If the evidence in the case meets the DA's standard for filing—proof beyond a reasonable doubt—the suspect will be arrested and the case will be cleared by arrest. If the case is sent back for further investigation or if the evidence is deemed insufficient to justify charging, the investigating officer will either continue the investigation and, once additional evidence is obtained, resubmit the case for a second review by the DA or clear the case by exceptional means.

It is important to note that, historically—although it has been inconsistently practiced—the LAPD's policy has been that a felony crime can be cleared by arrest only if the DA files felony charges in the 48-hour window of time after an arrest. In other words, the LAPD interprets the *UCR Handbook*'s statement that "an offense is cleared by arrest . . . when at least one person is (1) arrested, (2) charged with the commission of the offense, and (3) turned over to the court for prosecution" to require the filing of charges by the prosecutor. Thus, if the suspect is arrested but the DDA reviewing the case declines to file charges—depending on informal norms at the detective's division and the preferences of his or her supervisor—the case will be cleared by exceptional means, and not cleared by arrest. This is contrary to the policy statements in the *UCR Handbook,* which indicate that cases can be cleared by exceptional means if the police have an identified suspect but, for reasons beyond their control, are unable to make an arrest. Conversely—albeit also inconsistently—the LASD accurately interprets the *UCR Handbook*'s criteria to require solely the arrest of the offender and turning him or her over to the court for prosecution, irrespective of the prosecutorial decision to file felony charges.

To summarize, although the responsibility for clearing cases rests with law enforcement officials, the process of clearing cases in Los Angeles involves discretionary decisions by both police or sheriff's detectives and the prosecutor. The DA influences case clearances through the prearrest charge evaluation process, in which cases are reviewed for evidentiary sufficiency before an arrest is made. If the evidence is deemed sufficient, an arrest is made; if not, the case is either investigated further and resubmitted to the DA or cleared exceptionally. As Riedel and Boulahanis (2007: 156) noted regarding a similar process in Chicago, both agencies benefit from this system:

> On the one hand, the Felony Review Unit does not have to include in its conviction percentage the cases that were never prosecuted. On the other hand, cases barred to prosecution are included in exceptional clearances so that the total clearance rate of CPD [Chicago Police Department] appears substantially higher than it actually is.

The Exceptional Clearance of Sexual Assault

Data on cases cleared by the LAPD and the LASD were presented and discussed in Chapter 4. These data documented that from 2005 through 2009 both law enforcement agencies cleared a substantial proportion of cases by exceptional means. Of the 5,031 rapes and attempted rapes reported to the LAPD, 33.5 percent were cleared by exceptional means and 12.2 percent were cleared by arrest. The proportion of cases reported to the LASD that were cleared by exceptional means was even larger: 54.4 percent of the rapes and attempted rapes were cleared exceptionally, compared to 33.9 percent that were cleared by arrest. Thus, cleared by exceptional means is the modal case clearance type for the LASD and accounts for a third of all case outcomes for the LAPD.

Because we did not have access to case files for the 2005–2009 cases, we were not able to provide more detailed descriptive data on these cases. Instead, we use data on sexual assaults reported to the LAPD and the LASD in 2008 to examine the characteristics of cases cleared by exceptional means. There were 125 LAPD cases and 277 LASD cases from 2008 that were cleared by exceptional means. Information on these cases was collected from redacted copies of the complete case files, which were provided to us by each agency. As explained in Chapter 1, these files included the initial report taken by the patrol officer, the follow-up reports written by the detective to whom the case was assigned for investigation, and the charge evaluation worksheets for cases that were presented to the DA for a charging decision (either before or after arrest). The files included the victim's statement, summaries of interviews with witnesses, the suspect's statement (if the suspect was interviewed), the results from forensic evidence collection, and descriptions of evidence that was collected at the scene of the crime.

Table 6.1 presents information on the case or crime characteristics, the victim characteristics, the suspect characteristics, and characteristics of the police investigation for these exceptionally cleared cases. Although a discussion of all of these data is beyond the scope of this chapter, we can paint a picture of the "typical" exceptionally cleared case. The typical case that was cleared by exceptional means was a case in which:

- The most serious charge was rape.
- The suspect subdued the victim using bodily force only.
- The suspect and victim were acquaintances or intimate partners.
- The victim did not engage in any risk-taking behavior (drinking, using drugs, walking alone late at night, accepting a ride from a stranger) at the time of the incident.
- The victim did not have a motive to lie and did not make inconsistent statements during interviews.
- The victim did not report the crime immediately.
- The victim was able to identify the suspect by full name and address.
- The suspect (of those interviewed by police) either claimed that the victim consented or that the incident was fabricated.
- There was no physical evidence to corroborate the victim's allegations.
- There were no witnesses who could corroborate the victim's allegations.

In the sections that follow, we examine the cases cleared by exceptional means by the LAPD and the LASD in 2008. We begin with a discussion of each agency's practice of changing the case clearance from cleared by arrest to cleared by exceptional means if the DA refuses to file felony

Table 6.1 Characteristics of Sex Crimes Cleared by Exceptional Means, LAPD and LASD, 2008

	LAPD (N = 125)		LASD (N = 277)	
	N	%	N	%
Case/Crime Characteristics				
Type of Crime				
Rape	92	73.6	193	70.2
Attempted rape	9	7.2	25	9.1
Sexual battery	24	19.2	22	8.0
Statutory rape/sex crime with a child	—	—	35	12.8
Suspect used bodily force only to subdue victim	101	80.8	229	82.7
Suspect used a weapon	9	7.2	27	9.7
Suspect drugged victim	6	4.9	23	8.6
Relationship between victim and suspect	26	20.8	57	20.8
Strangers				
Nonstrangers	63	50.4	145	52.9
Intimate partners	36	28.8	72	26.3
Victim injured	56	44.8	124	44.8
Victim also physically assaulted	58	46.4	101	36.5
Rape plus stranger or weapon or injury to victim	49	39.2	113	40.8
Rape plus stranger or weapon	18	14.4	57	20.6
Victim Characteristics				
Background Characteristics				
Age (mean)	25.7		28.7	
Race/ethnicity				
Caucasian	42	33.6	65	24.8
Hispanic/Latina	54	43.2	122	46.6
African American	22	17.6	60	22.9
Asian American/other	7	5.6	15	5.7
Credibility Factors				
Criminal record	16	12.8	13	4.7
Gang affiliation mentioned in report	2	1.6	2	0.7
Drinking at time of incident	45	36.0	70	25.5
Drunk at time of incident	39	31.2	46	16.8
Using illegal drugs at time of incident	10	8.0	20	7.3
Passed out (not drugged)	19	15.2	27	9.8
Prior sexual relationship with suspect[a]	37	45.7	63	40.1
Walking alone late at night	8	6.4	8	2.9
Accepted a ride from a stranger	4	3.2	8	2.9
Mental health issues	14	11.2	27	9.8
Sex worker	10	8.0	4	1.5
Inconsistent statements to police	25	20.2	29	10.5
No physical or verbal resistance	33	26.4	72	26.0
Verbal resistance only	20	16.0	55	19.9
Physical resistance only	15	12.0	21	7.6
Verbal and physical resistance	57	45.6	129	46.6
Investigating officer questions credibility	20	16.0	12	4.4

(continues)

Table 6.1 Cont.

	LAPD (N = 125)		LASD (N = 277)	
	N	%	N	%
Cooperation with Law Enforcement				
Reported within one hour	29	23.2	33	11.9
Had a forensic medical exam	63	50.4	99	36.0
Declined forensic medical exam	7	5.6	12	4.3
Identified suspect by full name and address	75	60.0	170	61.4
Cooperative during police investigation	67	54.0	165	60.0
Recanted her allegation	5	4.0	10	3.6
Could not be located	20	16.0	38	13.8
Had a motive to lie	32	25.6	23	8.4
Suspect Characteristics				
Affiliated with a gang	10	8.0	30	10.8
Police interviewed suspect	72	57.6	121	43.7
Defense in statement to police[b]				
Consent	37	51.4	50	42.0
Incident fabricated	29	40.3	53	44.5
Incorrect ID	1	1.4	—	—
Admitted/confessed	5	6.9	16	13.4
Police Investigation/Evidence				
Some type of physical evidence	53	42.4	103	37.2
Mean number of police interviews of victim	1.95		1.79	
Mean number of witnesses	0.60		0.77	
Police interviewed witnesses[c]	43	78.2	92	87.6
Police conducted pretext phone call	12	9.6	13	4.7

Notes: a. Of cases involving nonstrangers and intimate partners.
b. Of the identified suspects who spoke with the police.
c. Of the cases with witnesses where the suspect spoke to the police.

charges. We then attempt to determine whether these cases meet the four criteria that are required for an exceptional clearance.

Evaluating Exceptional Clearances

In order to clear a case by exceptional means, a law enforcement agency must be able to identify the suspect and must know the suspect's exact location so that he or she can be arrested. In addition, there must be enough evidence to support the police officer's decision to arrest and charge the suspect and to turn him or her over to the court for prosecution, as well as something beyond the control of law enforcement that prevents law enforcement from arresting and charging the suspect with a crime. Moreover, each of these four criteria must be met in order to exceptionally clear the case.

The Mutual Exclusivity of Arrest and the Exceptional Clearance

We began this project with an assumption that cases in which the police or sheriff's department makes an arrest would be categorized as cleared by arrest. However, Table 6.2, which presents data on 2008 cases reflecting the criteria for clearing a case by exceptional means, reveals that both agencies clear cases by exceptional means when the suspect is arrested but the prosecutor declines to file charges. There were 40 such cases (32% of all exceptional clearances) in the LAPD sample and 53 (19.9% of all exceptional clearances) in the LASD data. In other words, upon making the arrest, the case is cleared by arrest, but if the DDA reviewing the case declines to file charges, the case clearance is (sometimes) changed from cleared by arrest to cleared by exceptional means.

Analyzing the origins of this dynamic highlights the need for the FBI to clarify and refine aspects of the UCR[6] program. First, as Feeney (2000–2001) noted in his discussion of the development of the Uniform Crime Reporting system, to clear by arrest requires a booking procedure by the police, which leaves the suspect subject to the court's discretion as to prosecution. Although use of the term "charged" has generated some confusion among law enforcement agencies as to whether it is the police or the prosecutor who must file charges, the *UCR Handbook* clearly states that the exceptional clearance is to be used when the suspect's identification and location are known and there is enough evidence to justify the arrest and prosecution of the offender, but for reasons beyond police control they are unable to make an arrest (FBI, 2004: 80–81). Stated simply, if an arrest is made, the case is to be cleared by arrest. Thus, these cases should have remained cleared by arrest.

Table 6.2 Criteria for Exceptional Clearance of Sex Crimes, LAPD and LASD, 2008

	LAPD (N = 125)		LASD (N = 267)[a]	
	N	%	N	%
Suspect identified and can be located	121	96.8	191	71.5
Suspect not arrested, DA said there was insufficient evidence	55	44.0	77	28.8
Suspect not arrested, victim refused to cooperate	26	20.8	61	22.8
Suspect arrested but DA declined to file charges	40	32.0	53	19.9
Suspect not identified or cannot be located	4	3.2	76	28.4

Note: a. There were 10 LASD cases with missing data; therefore, the number of cases is 267 rather than 277.

The use—or misuse—of the exceptional clearance when a suspect is arrested but the DA refuses to file charges is based on an LAPD policy stating that a case can be cleared by arrest only if felony charges are filed; in contrast, the LASD policy is consistent with UCR guidelines but the policy is not always followed by LASD detectives. The fact that the LAPD clears a case by arrest only if felony charges are filed by the DA means that—practically speaking—their arrest practices are based upon a prosecutorial standard of proof beyond a reasonable doubt, rather than the police standard of probable cause.

In the following sections, we discuss the four criteria that must be met to exceptionally clear a case, beginning with an identified suspect and a known location for that suspect.

Criteria Required for Clearing by Exceptional Means

The first two criteria for clearing a case by exceptional means are straightforward and objective. There must be an identified suspect and knowledge of the exact location where the suspect can be found. Therefore, all of the cases that were cleared in this way should, by definition, meet these criteria. As shown in Table 6.2, there were only four cases (3.2%) in the sample of exceptionally cleared cases from the LAPD in which the suspect was either not identified or was identified but his location was not known. In contrast, of the 2008 cases exceptionally cleared by the LASD, 76 (28.4%) were cases in which the suspect was not identified or could not be located, 43 (15.5%) were cases without an identified suspect, and 33 (12.9%) were cases in which an identified suspect could not be located. The fact that more than one fourth of the LASD cases that were cleared by exceptional means did not meet these basic criteria means that they are using this clearance category inappropriately in a substantial number of cases. Applying just the first two criteria articulated by the *UCR Handbook* suggests that these cases (4 LAPD cases and 76 LASD cases) should not have been cleared; they should have remained open until a suspect was identified and his location was established.

The third and fourth criteria required to exceptionally clear a case pertain to the sufficiency of the evidence needed to clear a case this way and the inability of the police to clear the case by making an arrest. The *UCR Handbook* (2004: 80–81) states that to exceptionally clear a case, there must be enough information to support arresting, charging, and turning the suspect over to the court for prosecution, as well as something beyond the control of law enforcement that prevents them from arresting the suspect. In other words, the police have probable cause to make an arrest but are prevented from doing so by something beyond their control—for example, the suspect has died, is being prosecuted for another crime in a different jurisdiction, or cannot be extradited or the victim refuses to cooperate in the prosecution of the suspect.

Determining whether the sexual assault cases cleared by exceptional means by the LAPD and the LASD meet these two criteria is complicated by the fact that there is no objective indicator in the case file of whether the investigating officer had probable cause to make an arrest. We do not know, in other words, whether the officer had sufficient evidence to make an arrest and cleared the case exceptionally when unable to arrest the suspect or whether the officer simply presented a weak case (i.e., a case without probable cause to make an arrest) to a DDA for a prearrest filing decision and cleared the case exceptionally after the attorney reviewing the case decided that the evidence did not meet the office filing standard of proof beyond a reasonable doubt.

Determining whether the cases meet these criteria is also complicated by the fact that the *UCR Handbook* does not precisely define what is meant by "reasons outside the control of law enforcement that prevent arresting, charging, and prosecuting the suspect." The handbook provides a list of possible situations, many of which involve the death of the suspect, that meet this criterion. The 10 examples provided, which the handbook acknowledges are not exhaustive, include refusal of the victim to cooperate in the prosecution of the suspect but do not include a prosecutorial declination to file charges because of insufficient evidence, which is the most common reason given by LAPD and LASD investigating officers for clearing a case by exceptional means. In short, if the agency has an identified suspect and probable cause to make an arrest, the agency should clear the case by arrest as it is within their control to arrest, charge, and turn the suspect over to the DA for prosecution. To do otherwise is not only counter to the FBI's guidelines, but it becomes an avenue through which to prematurely dispose of the nonstranger sexual assault cases, which are the most common type of sexual assault and require specialized investigation to overcome the consent defense.

Although we cannot determine whether the officer investigating the crime had probable cause to make an arrest, we can evaluate the reasons given by the officer for clearing the case by exceptional means, as these were documented in the case files. Of the 121 LAPD exceptionally cleared cases in which the suspect was identified and his location was known, 55 (44%) were cases in which the prosecutor stated that there was insufficient evidence to try the case before a jury and 26 (20.8%) were cases in which the victim did not want to cooperate in the prosecution of the suspect (the remaining 40 cases, or 32%, were cases in which the police did make an arrest but the case was exceptionally cleared when the DA declined to file felony charges). Of the 191 LASD cases, 77 (28.8%) involved a prosecutorial assessment that the evidence was insufficient and 61 (22.8%) involved a reluctant victim (the remaining 53 cases, or 19.9%, were cases in which sheriff's deputies did make an arrest). In other words, the exceptionally cleared cases in both agencies most often involved a prosecutorial assessment of insufficient evidence, followed by the victim declining to cooperate with the prosecution. Although they are not mutually exclusive and can occur simultaneously, we address prosecutorial assessments of evidence first, followed by victim cooperation.

Exceptional clearances based on insufficient evidence. In order to analyze exceptional clearances that occur when a prosecutor declines to file charges, it is important to understand what prosecutors need to file charges in sexual assault cases; that is, how much legally admissible evidence is sufficient to prove the defendant's guilt beyond a reasonable doubt in front of a jury. DDAs interviewed for this project stated that the prearrest charge evaluation process determines whether the evidence amassed by law enforcement at the time of screening justifies prosecution, or whether additional investigation is required before the suspect can be arrested and turned over to them for prosecution. When asked what they needed to file felony charges, prosecutors unanimously stated that office policy requires corroboration of the victim's allegations, especially in "she said/he said" cases in which the suspect and victim are nonstrangers.[7] Corroboration was described as some form of documentation, independent of the victim's word, that "the jury can look at" and that substantiates her claims: evidence of vaginal or anal trauma, eyewitnesses, bodily injuries, ripped clothing or other signs of force at the crime scene, phone records, security camera video, a fresh complaint witness,[8] a pretext[9] phone call, or a 911 call from the victim or a witness. One respondent summed up corroboration as "pieces of evidence that couldn't be explained unless the victim was victimized."

In reference to the avenues for acquiring such evidence, prosecutors remarked on the need to "ask the right questions to get the whole story and look for corroboration in those little points. If the victim said, 'I was afraid and I called my mother,' get the phone records." Prosecutors also spoke of the need to examine the suspect's history—prior relationship partners, friends, acquaintances, and family who can speak to behavioral patterns—and criminal record—including crime reports and arrests, not just convictions. They emphasized the importance of these types of evidence, which could be used to demonstrate the suspect's propensity toward aggressive behavior, sexual or otherwise. Also of importance, they noted, are such things as the suspect's postassault behavior in terms of attempts to contact the victim, activity on social media websites such as Facebook, and, perhaps most important, whether the suspect made any incriminating admissions to the police.

According to both detectives and prosecutors, one of the biggest challenges in obtaining corroborative evidence is delayed reporting of the assault.

The problem with delayed reporting is that any injuries from the assault will likely be healed and witnesses may no longer be available; delayed reporting also drastically decreases[10] the probability of retrieving any biological evidence from either the victim's body (crime scene number 1) or the actual crime location (crime scene number 2). Notably, detectives and prosecutors who reported receiving the most training and expressed the most job satisfaction commented that delayed reporting is the norm and is to be expected in all types of sexual assault cases, regardless of the victim's age. Given the ubiquity of delayed reporting, especially in nonstranger sexual assaults, they emphasized the critical importance of specialized training in interviewing victims and interrogating suspects. For example, a detective in a specialized unit made the following observation:

> The DA's Office needs as much training as we do. I did a presentation about trauma and interviewing and most of those attending were DA's. Their reviews were more enlightening to me than the detectives'. Their eyes were opened in terms of interviewing a traumatic victim. We're so used to interviewing the day it happened. With sexual assault you have to go backwards and do a comprehensive cognitive interview because memory fails with trauma. VIP training is specialized but there are times where you will get a DA who screens these cases and closes the door. They are in the law enforcement family and they stick together and defend their own even when they're wrong, as we do.

Formal policies requiring proof beyond a reasonable doubt and corroboration of the victim's testimony prior to filing can, of course, be loosened, or even circumvented, as a result of informal norms on charging that reflect the discretion accorded to individual prosecutors and the varying supervisory styles at courthouses throughout the county. As one prosecutor stated: "The reality of what happens is different than what policy dictates. Many DAs do not file when they are not easy cases."[11] Along similar lines, another prosecutor stated, "If I thought it was an absolutely righteous case and there was anything to corroborate what the witness said and I was unsure what a jury would do, but I thought I could do it, then I would file." It is also important to consider these issues in relation to the police decision to arrest, along with how a detective's perceptions and handling of a sexual assault report send a message to the prosecutor about what interviewees from all three agencies often referred to as the "righteousness" of a case. For example, a prosecutor stated that "usually when they bring in a case we'll ask, 'Is it a filing or a reject?' They'll often say 'a reject.'" Additionally, a detective who had just come from doing a case "drop-off" at the DA's office prior to being interviewed for this study reported feeling pleasantly surprised that the DA filed charges in the case because she had been sure it would be rejected. The detective attributed the filing to having made the effort to speak to the prosecutor in person rather than just sending the case file over by fax.

Given the frequency of references to it, perhaps the most important underlying factor is how police and prosecutors evaluate the victim's believability and credibility. Most respondents emphasized that their evaluation of the strength of evidence in the case was closely linked to their assessment of the victim's credibility, and some prosecutors stated that they would file charges in a weak case if the victim was a "righteous victim." This is evidenced by the following statement from a prosecutor:

> Do I file things I think will be hard to prove? Yes. If I interview a victim I find incredibly compelling and there's a richness to the detail, a believability and ring of truth to how she describes things, then I will file it, explaining to her that the odds are really low and is she still willing to go forward? I tell her we have problems here and we could very well lose. If I have a go-ahead from the victim then I will go forward. It's all about the victim. She is on trial. All the legislation we have about not revictimizing the victim, but at the end of the day we are putting her on trial; why she wore what she wore, went where she did, and so on. She is being judged.

Although interviewees repeatedly emphasized the serious nature of rape, they focused most often on suspects and their own apprehensions concerning making arrests and filing criminal charges, rather than the consequences of victimization for rape survivors and the subsequent impact on their behavior during a criminal investigation. For example, a prosecutor commented: "We are supposed to interview the victims prearrest to determine credibility and gather other information that would help strengthen our case, although it does not happen every time. Sometimes they arrest the suspect and bring the case to us after the arrest but that is rare." This suggests that law enforcement officials believe that it is important to assess the victim's credibility before taking action against a suspect. The law enforcement officials interviewed for this project also emphasized that rape is unique because, of the two crimes (rape and homicide) deemed to be the most serious, it is the only one in which there is a live victim who makes or breaks the case. Given this reality, then, it is critical that the way in which information is obtained from victims does not create any further complications for what is already a difficult crime to prosecute. For instance, a prosecutor noted:

> The problem with police and prosecutors is that we ask different types of questions so reports based on our interviews may *appear*

to be inconsistent but in reality it is an artifact of questioning. Everything is discoverable so any interviews with the victim prior to trial [go to] the defense. . . . For example: the victim tells the detective, "He touched me." The detective writes, "Victim said suspect penetrated me with his finger." Those are two different charges. I have to ask for clarification and now this becomes two different statements (the officer interpreting it as penetration and me clarifying it) and it makes the victim look like a liar, which undermines her credibility. (Emphasis added)

In summary, filing decisions in sexual assault cases are based on prosecutorial assessments of the sufficiency of the evidence, which vary depending on the depth and quality of the detective's investigation, the prosecutor's perceptions of victim credibility, and the available corroboration. Upon being presented with a case, if a prosecutor decides that sufficient evidence exists and the police have not already arrested the suspect (and cleared the case by arrest), he or she will issue a warrant and the police will arrest the suspect and clear the case by arrest; from there, the prosecutor takes over. Conversely, if the prosecutor decides that the evidence as it currently stands is insufficient, he or she will either outright reject the case or reject it for further investigation. It is at this point that some detectives clear the case exceptionally, although other detectives stated that the case should be kept open and investigated further.

The importance of this juncture in an investigation cannot be underestimated, given that the police retain the authority to gather more evidence and present the case again (Riedel and Boulahanis, 2007), whereas prosecutors cannot work with a case that never comes before them, and will be less inclined to take on a case that, on paper, is unclear, inconsistent, and raises doubts about the victim's credibility. By the time a victim is interviewed by the DA's office she has already been interviewed at least twice by the police, by a patrol officer and by a detective. In other words, rapport—good or bad—is already established. Nevertheless, the power of the police notwithstanding, the findings from this study indicate that prosecutors are equally—if not more—powerful players in this process, especially given the informalities of their interdependent relationship with law enforcement and the subsequent impact on the extent to which the police investigate allegations of sexual assault.

Exceptional clearances based on lack of victim cooperation. A situation in which the victim refuses to cooperate in the prosecution of the suspect is listed as an example of a case that might be cleared by exceptional means, provided that the other three criteria are met. All the LAPD and LASD cases that were exceptionally cleared because the victim refused to cooperate were cases with identified suspects whose locations were known.

Further analysis of these cases (for both agencies combined) revealed that two thirds of them were "simple rapes" (Estrich, 1987), which did not involve strangers, weapons, or visible injuries to the victim. In terms of relationship, 62.1 percent of the cases involved nonstrangers and 26.4 percent involved intimate partners. In almost all the cases (95.4%) the victim did not report the crime within one hour; in fact, in about 70 percent of the cases the victim did not report the crime within 24 hours and in 21.8 percent of the cases the victim waited one month or longer to report the crime. It is interesting that the police did not interview the suspect in 70.1 percent of these cases. Perhaps these victims decided that they did not want to cooperate in the prosecution of the case because they did not view themselves as "genuine victims" (LaFree, 1989); they were not attacked by strangers wielding guns or knives, and perhaps as a result, they waited at least one day before reporting the crime to the police.

Given the salience of victim cooperation to the success of a case, we asked sexual assault survivors about the decision to report to police and their experiences with the criminal justice system. One woman who was raped in her home by a stranger while her boyfriend was tied up and forced to watch offered the following:

> I wish their communication was better. I saw the rapist's face twice but when police asked me about the sketch they kept asking me more questions, which I couldn't answer. I needed them to stop pressing me but they kept asking questions about the incident. The police had no clue how to talk to me, especially as the rape lasted five hours. I felt interrogated. They could have been more sensitive to the trauma. It's all about the approach by the police.

The following reflections come from a woman whose experience was emblematic of the classic she said/he said scenario:

> I was raped two years ago at a New Year's Eve party so I knew everyone there, including my rapist. I was pretty drunk and this guy who I'd known since I was five asked me to follow him to another room where he pushed me on the bed and I passed out. There were injuries to my arms, face, and I was incredibly sore. I'd never passed out before. A friend found me passed out on the bed and the rapist ran out. I reported the following day at night. There were several hours in-between. I never remembered being raped. I remember trying to fight him off and my next memory is of my friends holding my hair and I'm vomiting. I woke up the next morning thinking I had not been raped but there was a pain in my vagina and then I realized what happened. I talked to my mother and she noticed I wasn't wearing

tights or underwear. I spent the whole day deciding whether to report or not. I decided to tell my father who wouldn't be able to stand it if there was no justice, so he called the police, who came to my house. Three police cars showed up with their lights flashing. I was harshly interrogated by a male officer. The female officer present never said anything. The police officer was incredibly rude and harsh; well, not rude, harsh. Their main focus was that I was drunk and how drunk was I but they never considered if I was too drunk to consent. . . . I gave a statement and again they fixated on how much I had drank and moved towards blaming me because the rapist was someone I knew. The plan was to have me call him and to tape his call. It was a really stressful exercise. The rapist spoke with a lawyer and came in voluntarily to speak with the police. At that point they believed him because I was drinking a lot and they made the assumption it was consensual.

After a thoughtful pause she added:

One of the things that still bothers me is during the initial interrogation I was asked if I'd blacked out before and I said no and later in the investigation the facts were mingled and I was misquoted several times. They [the police] asked if I'd ever got physically ill from drinking and I told them yes, a dozen or so times when I was in college. Meanwhile my rapist was never arrested and charges [by the DA's office] were rejected because in the report it said that I'd been known to black out, but this was inaccurate and not what I'd told them. I asked them to bring out the tape from the initial interrogation when I was told there was no tape and it wasn't recorded. My friends were at the party and could pinpoint people who were present at the party. I gave their contact info to police. And I kept asking if my rape kit had been processed. I was told there was no point in processing the rape kit once the rapist stated that sex had occurred.

When asked what she would do if someone disclosed a sexual assault to her and wanted advice about whether to report and cooperate with the prosecution, she stated:

I would not report but if I knew who it was I would take revenge. I don't believe that reporting acquaintance rape does anything for the victim. I would express what happened to me but I would share my experience and that taking care of it yourself may give you results because my experience was so negative. I have lost a lot of friends over this. I haven't seen my rapist but I've seen his friends. Evidence from my case was going to be presented to another DA but I was frustrated and decided to just not think about it anymore so I gave up on prosecuting. The DA's office was looking for a slam-dunk and my case wasn't a slam-dunk.

The preceding reflections provide context to the decision not to coop- erate with the prosecution as it relates to a victim's experience with the police, which sets the tone for subsequent interaction with the DA's office. Many of the victims, including those who were assaulted by strangers, reported not being believed and stated that their credibility was challenged by the police. For instance, consider the reflections from a woman who was kidnapped at gunpoint by a stranger during winter break at college. After being held hostage for almost 24 hours, she went to a local hospital in fear of being pregnant or having caught a sexually transmitted disease, which triggered a call to the police from the hospital staff:

> They asked me if I wanted a woman police officer; I didn't care. A police officer is a police officer. I had never had any contact with the police. I didn't know they might treat you differently. Immediately they told me I was lying and on drugs. Straight up! "You're on drugs." My eyes were bloodshot because I was so stressed and traumatized. [They kept saying] "You're lying, you're lying! Stand up, close your eyes, and count to 30. Can you count to 30?" I got to 30. Apparently they talked to my friends, because they were two guys. They said: "You put her up to this. You told her to do this for fun. You are all on drugs. Here is how it is: stop telling me this fairytale. Tell me the truth or you will personally go to prison for lying to a police officer. And I will send you to an all-women prison so women could rape you." I was stunned. Why was I defending myself? The victim shouldn't have to. The officer said most women would rather die than be raped. Then he told me at least three or four times to say I was lying and this won't go on further. He said we can drop this and forget all about it. For a moment I thought that maybe I should say that I was lying so I wouldn't have to deal with this anymore.

These statements indicate that despite the existence of rape law reform and victim advocacy, adult female sexual assault victims—whether assaulted by strangers or nonstrangers—continue to be met with scrutiny and distrust by both the criminal justice system and society at large (as represented by juries). Illustrating the salience of this specific to nonstranger sexual assault, a prosecutor commented: "General society still has an archaic perception that if a woman voluntarily goes with a man to have a drink and she is intoxicated—although no one wants to articulate it—there is still an idea that she is loose. I'm not sure if it is the job of the police or the district attorneys to change that, but it needs to happen." Similarly, Temkin (2010: 715) noted that false beliefs about rape are "many and various," but some of the "most damaging" include the following: true rape is rape by a stranger; true rape takes place outdoors and involves physical violence against a victim who does all she can to resist; a woman can always prevent rape by fighting off her assailant; a woman can always withhold consent to sex now matter how drunk she is; women have only themselves to blame for rape because of their clothes, drinking habits, previous sexual relationships, and risky behavior; consent to sex can be assumed because of dress or certain types of behavior, such as flirting or kissing; and genuine victims report rape immediately, display strong emotions when recounting the events in question, and always give a thoroughly consistent account.

The persistence of rape myths provides a context for understanding attrition of sexual assault cases in the criminal justice system because if police action is based on erroneous stereotypes about what rape is and what a "real" victim should do, victims whose cases fail to meet these criteria will not be given the respect, time, and investigative resources they deserve. The same logic applies to prosecutors. If erroneous stereotypes and misconceptions (see Frohmann, 1991; Gruber, 2009) cloud prosecutors' perceptions of "real rape," their course of action when presented with acquaintance rape—which, according to this study, is the prototypical type of rape seen in Los Angeles City and County—will inevitably fall short of the rights guaranteed by Marsy's Law[12] to crime victims under the California Constitution.

Conclusion: The Misuse of the Exceptional Clearance

The purpose of this analysis was to investigate law enforcement's use (and misuse) of the exceptional clearance in sexual assault cases. A key finding is that both the LAPD and the LASD clear a substantial number of cases by exceptional means. In fact, cases cleared by exceptional means accounted for more than half of all case clearances for the LASD and for a third of all case clearances for the LAPD. This clearly is inconsistent with Feeney's (2000–2001: 18) assertion that UCR guidelines (as articulated in early *UCR Handbooks*) reflect an expectation that "most clearances would be based on arrests and that the number of exceptional clearances would be limited." For these two law enforcement agencies, exceptional clearances of sexual assault reports are common, not exceptional.

An important implication of this is that UCR data on "cases cleared by arrest" are misleading. Combining exceptional clearances with cases cleared by arrest resulted in 2005–2009 arrest rates for rape and attempted rape of 88.7 percent for the LASD and 45.7 percent for the LAPD, but the "true" arrest rates (i.e., the percentage of cases that were cleared by the arrest of a suspect) were only 34.7 percent (LASD) and 12.2 percent (LAPD). Combining the two types of case clearances, in other words, substantially inflates the rates of "cases cleared by arrest" for each agency.

Our review of the pathways through which LAPD and LASD sexual assault detectives clear cases by arrest or exceptional means, in conjunction with the role that the LA County DA's Office plays in this process by screening cases prior to arrest, revealed that the exceptional clearance is being used too frequently—and in some cases, inappropriately—in sexual assault cases. Although many detectives and prosecutors conduct themselves professionally and with integrity, myths and stereotypes about adult female[13] rape victims and what constitutes "real" rape continue to influence police and prosecutorial efforts in these cases. We discuss the implications of these findings for policy and practice in Chapter 8.

Notes

1. In 1734, Lord Chief Justice Matthew Hale wrote that concerning rape, "it must be remembered . . . that it is an accusation easily to be made and hard to be proved, and harder to be defended by the party accused, tho never so innocent" ([1736] 1971).

2. For example, in May 2010, the New York Police Department publicly apologized to a rape victim whose case was inappropriately downgraded from a felony sexual assault to a misdemeanor, and in June 2010 the Baltimore Police Department came under fire after it was revealed that their unfounding rate—30 percent—was the highest in the nation. These, and other, exposés of the treatment of rape victims led to a Senate Hearing in September 2010 on "Rape in the United States: The Chronic Failure to Report and Investigate Rape Cases" (US Senate, 2010).

3. In the 1929 handbook, they were limited to (1) suicide of the offender, (2) double murder, (3) deathbed confession, and (4) confession by an offender already in custody.

4. For clarification, we spoke with the FBI section chief who oversees the UCR program. He clarified that, according to the FBI, "charged" means a police booking procedure that results in the suspect being turned over to the courts for prosecution, not the filing of charges by a prosecutorial agency (R. Casey, personal communication, January 14, 2011).

5. According to the Victim Impact Program's informational pamphlet, "victims and law enforcement officers reap tangible benefits from a vertical prosecutor who seeks to put victims at ease and provide more effective prosecution of highly sensitive cases" (http://da.co.la.ca.us/pdf/vip.pdf).

6. The need for revisions to the UCR program specific to the significant positive impact it would have on the investigative efforts of local police and sheriffs' departments in sexual assault cases was an important focus of discussion during the September 2010 Senate hearing. See Tracy (2010: 7–10) for an overview of the

efforts to facilitate change at the federal level, along with Berkowitz (2010: 9-10) and Dempsey (2010: 5-9).

7. It is interesting that all prosecutors interviewed for this study agreed that stranger cases are extremely rare; their prototypical cases involve either adult acquaintances or children molested by family members or other known authority figures or acquaintances. The major difference between adult and child cases, many noted, is that jurors (and society in general) inherently trust child victims yet are inherently distrusting of teenage and adult female victims.

8. Someone the victim discloses to or interacts with after the assault who can speak to her behavior, appearance, or some other issue that is consistent with the allegations.

9. Pretext phone calls involve the police recording the victim calling the suspect to discuss what transpired with the goal of obtaining incriminating statements. Detectives and prosecutors repeatedly emphasized the importance of doing a pretext phone call in nonstranger cases.

10. Sexual assault nurse examiners now conduct forensic evidence collection up to 96 hours after an assault, whereas standard practice previously was only up to 72 hours postassault (G. Abarbanel, personal communication, November 9, 2010).

11. Echoing this sentiment, another prosecutor stated: "There is a wide range of DDA interpretation as to what sufficient evidence will result in a conviction. I will say this because it is anonymous, that there are people who are attracted to sex crimes because you can get high sentences and they reject ones that are not a slam-dunk."

12. California Constitution, Article 1, § 28. The first of the Sixteen Rights is "To be treated with fairness and respect for his or her privacy and dignity, and to be free from intimidation, harassment, and abuse throughout the criminal or juvenile justice process."

13. Several prosecutors noted anecdotally that male rape victims are not received with the same distrust and skepticism as female rape victims, and the few cases they were aware of involving male victims were fully prosecuted.

7

Intimate Partner Sexual Assault

> You have to be open to everything that comes your way and not be judgmental about the victim's life. I have handled several spousal cases, and some of them involved truly violent men. To tell the truth, some of the guys [detectives] are kind of cynical about those kinds of cases.
>
> —LAPD detective

What follows is a description of the circumstances surrounding an intimate partner sexual assault that was reported to the Los Angeles County Sheriff's Department (LASD) in 2008. The 20-year-old victim and 21-year-old suspect had been dating five years and had two children in common. The suspect did not have a criminal history. The couple had previously lived together but at the time resided in separate locations. On the day of the incident, the suspect met the victim at her residence to retrieve his vehicle and an argument ensued because the suspect believed the victim was cheating on him. The suspect grabbed the victim by her hair and yelled at her to go upstairs so they would not argue in front of their children. Once upstairs he grabbed the victim by her face and pushed her onto the bed. When she told the suspect to stop, he stated he was going to impregnate her so she could never leave him. The suspect then removed the victim's clothing, which the victim allowed because she feared he would beat her; he subdued her using bodily force only, and he vaginally raped her.

The victim and suspect's daughter called 911 when she heard the victim screaming because the victim had previously instructed her children to call the police if they ever heard a commotion. The LASD arrived immediately and arrested the suspect on-site for rape. When interviewed, the suspect admitted to physically assaulting the victim three times previously but stated in this particular incident that all he did was push the victim and that the sexual contact was consensual. He conceded the victim: (1) was crying during the incident; (2) told him to stop; and (3) removed his penis from her vagina twice and told him she did not want to have sex; but he denied raping the victim. When the LASD interviewed the witnesses (the suspect and victim's two children), they corroborated the victim's story; they told the officers they heard the victim screaming at the suspect to get off her. As

191

they took the suspect to jail, the law enforcement officers issued the victim an emergency protective order. Within forty-eight hours, the District Attorney's (DA's) Office had filed one count of spousal rape against the suspect.

This case demonstrates some of the unique characteristics of intimate partner sexual assault. Sometimes there is co-occurring physical violence, and the related chaos can translate to more immediate reporting, in the form of a 911 call, than we found to be the case in other suspect-victim relationships. Similarly, there may be witnesses, such as children, other family members, or neighbors. In this particular scenario, law enforcement arrived while the sexual assault was in progress, but that is not always the case. Our review of case files suggests that when there are no witnesses and it is not visibly obvious that a sexual assault occurred, the likelihood of victim self-disclosure is influenced by the extent to which rapport is established with the investigating officer.

The purpose of this chapter is to explore the context of intimate partner sexual assault; specifically, to identify the characteristics of victims, suspects, and cases, and to examine the correlates of case outcomes. We focus on the influence of both legal and extralegal case factors (e.g. evidence, victim credibility) on law enforcement and prosecutorial decisionmaking. Given the limited amount of research that highlights the convergence of intimate partner abuse and sexual assault, we also contextualize intimate partner sexual assault by analyzing its situational characteristics and consequences. The present analyses are based on a subsample of 161 sexual assault complaints involving intimate partners drawn from our larger sample of sexual assaults that came to the attention of the LAPD and LASD in 2008. We define *intimate partners* as a victim and suspect who are age 18 or older and married, cohabiting, dating, divorced, or legally separated. In addition, cases were categorized as involving intimate partners if the victim reported having a child with the suspect.

Contextualizing Intimate Partner Sexual Assault

Case Characteristics and Outcomes

Table 7.1 presents the descriptive statistics for case characteristics. Over three quarters of cases of intimate partner sexual assault were rape (78.8%, n = 126)—this includes vaginal penetration, oral copulation, sodomy, and penetration with a foreign object, followed by attempted rape (16.9%, n = 27), sexual battery (2.5%, n = 4) and unlawful sex (1.9%, n = 3). The most common relationship found in this sample is current dating partners (27.3%, n = 44) followed by former dating couples (24.2%, n = 39) and married couples (19.9%, n = 32). In regard to evidence, the majority of cases did not

Table 7.1 Case Characteristics of Intimate Partner Sexual Assault Reported to LAPD and LASD, 2008

	(N = 161)	
	N	%
Type of Sexual Assault		
Rape	126	78.8
Attempted rape	27	16.9
Sexual battery	4	2.5
Unlawful sex/statutory rape	3	1.9
Suspect-Victim Relationship		
Cohabitating	2	1.2
Father of victim's children	20	12.4
Legally separated	11	6.8.
Married	32	19.9
Domestic partner	10	6.2
Former dating	39	24.2
Dating	44	27.3
Divorced	3	1.9
Evidence		
No witnesses	107	66.5
At least one witness	54	33.5
Witness corroborated victim's story	14	31.1
Witness corroborated suspect's story	3	10.7
Forensic exam conducted	78	48.4
Any type of physical evidence found	67	41.6

involve witnesses (66.5%, n =107). However, 41.6 percent (n = 67) of investigations resulted in the collection of some type of physical evidence—clothing, bedding, skin sample, saliva, blood, or semen. In almost half (48.4%, n = 78) of the cases, the victim underwent a forensic medical exam.

As indicated by Table 7.2, half of the of intimate partner sexual assault cases (50.9%, n = 82) were cleared exceptionally,[1] and the second most frequent case clearance was by arrest (32.9%, n = 53). There were only 15 cases in which the investigation was continuing and only 11 that were unfounded.

Victim Characteristics

Table 7.3 presents the descriptive statistics for victim characteristics. The mean age of victims in this sample is 31.2 years. More than half of the victims are Latina/Hispanic (58.2%, n = 92), representing the most frequent race or ethnicity. The second most frequent race or ethnicity is Caucasian (17.7%, n = 28), followed by African American (15.8%, n = 25), and then Asian American (8.2%, n = 13).

Table 7.2 Case Outcomes of Intimate Partner Sexual Assault Reported to LAPD and LASD, 2008

	(N = 161)	
	N	%
Cleared by arrest	53	32.9
Cleared exceptionally	82	50.9
Investigation continuing	15	9.3
Report unfounded	11	6.8

Table 7.3 Victim Characteristics of Intimate Partner Sexual Assault Reported to LAPD and LASD, 2008

	(N = 161)	
	N	%
Age (mean)	31.2	
Race/Ethnicity		
Caucasian	28	17.7
Latina/Hispanic	92	58.2
African American	25	15.8
Asian American	13	8.2
Credibility Factors		
Criminal record	7	4.3
Gang affiliation	1	0.6
Drinking	18	11.3
Drunk	9	5.6
Using illegal drugs	2	1.2
Passed out (not drugged)	2	1.2
Mental health issues	8	5.0
Injured during assault	94	58.4
Inconsistent statements	16	10.0
No resistance	28	17.4
Verbal resistance only	28	17.4
Physical resistance only	7	4.3
Verbal and physical resistance	98	60.9
Cooperation with Law Enforcement		
Reported within one hour	40	24.8
Identified suspect by name/address	154	95.7
Recanted her allegations	19	11.9
Moved residences after the assault	14	8.8
Did not want suspect arrested	27	16.9

Two broad categories make up relevant victim characteristics: credibility factors and cooperation with law enforcement. Very few of these victims had criminal records, were affiliated with gangs, or had mental health issues; moreover, very few were engaged in any type of risky behavior at the time of the incident. More than half (58.4%, n = 94) of the victims in this sample suffered some type of collateral injury (e.g., bruises, scrapes, bites) during the incident, and the overwhelming majority (82.6%, n = 133) of victims resisted in some manner. Victims most often resisted both physically and verbally (60.9%, n = 98), followed by verbal resistance only (17.4%, n = 28), and physical resistance only (4.3%, n = 7). Finally, a noteworthy victim cooperation variable includes promptness of reporting. Only one quarter (24.8%, n = 40) of victims reported the incident to law enforcement within one hour. On the other hand, only 19 (11.9%) recanted and only 27 (16.9%) indicated that they did not want the suspect arrested.

Suspect Characteristics

Table 7.4 presents the descriptive statistics for suspect characteristics. The mean age of suspects in this sample is 33.6 years. More than half of the suspects in this sample are Latina/Hispanic (56.0%, n = 89), representing the most frequent race or ethnicity. The second most frequent race or ethnicity

Table 7.4 Suspect Characteristics of Intimate Partner Sexual Assault Reported to LAPD and LASD, 2008

	(N = 161)	
	N	%
Age (mean)	33.6	
Race/Ethnicity		
Caucasian	34	21.4
Latino/Hispanic	89	56.0
African American	28	17.6
Asian American	4	2.5
Other	4	2.5
Credibility Factors		
Gang affiliation	9	5.6
Drugged victim	4	2.5
Previously sexually assaulted victim	44	30.3
Previously physically assaulted victim	73	47.4
Inconsistent statements to police	9	5.6
Incident Factors		
Method of force		
Bodily force	142	88.2
Gun	7	4.3
Knife	4	2.5
None	4	2.5
Other	4	2.5
Defense to police		
Consent	45	51.7
Incident fabricated	23	26.4
Confessed	19	21.8
Arrested	87	54.7

is Caucasian (21.4%, n = 34), followed by African American (17.6%, n = 28), Asian American (2.5%, n = 4), and other races and ethnicities (2.5%, n = 4).

Two broad categories make up relevant suspect characteristics: credibility factors and incident factors. Suspect credibility variables of note include past assaults. In almost half (47.4%, n = 73) of the cases, the suspect had previously physically assaulted the victim, and in nearly a third (30.3%, n = 44) of the cases, the suspect had previously sexually assaulted the victim. The most common method of force found in this sample is bodily force (88.2%, n = 142), followed by gun use (4.3%, n = 7). Finally, the majority (51.7%, n = 45) of suspects who were interviewed by the police claimed that the sexual contact was consensual, followed by reporting that the victim had fabricated the report (26.4%, n = 23). Only 19 (21.8%) of the suspects in this sample confessed to the police.

It is interesting to note the suspects' behavior pre- and postassault. The most common way the suspect approached the victim prior to the assault was through a demand for sex (57.5%, n = 88). For example, one suspect told the victim, "You're going to have sex whether you like it or not." The second most common suspect approach was stalking (22.2%, n = 34), followed by attempting reconciliation (9.8%, n = 15). The most common postassault behavior of suspects was fleeing the scene (33.9%, n = 43), followed by acting normal (17.3, n = 22), and then by going to sleep (12.6%, n = 16).

Relationship Characteristics and Patterns of Sexual Assault

The majority of couples in this sample do not have children and only 5 percent (n = 8) had restraining orders in place at the time of the incident. However, it should be noted that in 33.7 percent (n = 54) of the cases, a restraining order resulted from the incident.

When looking at the factors that surrounded the incidents, two characteristics must be noted: patterns of sexual assault and precipitating incidents. The majority of the incidents in this sample can be classified as force only (69.6%, n = 112), meaning that the suspect compelled his partner to have sex by using only the amount of force needed to complete the assault (Finkelhor and Yllo, 1985). In contrast, 28 percent (n = 45) of the intimate partner sexual assaults can be classified as battering rape. Battering rape involves a pattern of behavior where forced sex is combined with battering (Finkelhor and Yllo, 1985). Only four of the incidents can be classified as involving sadistic or obsessive sexual assaults. This type of assault involves a pattern of behavior characterized by sexual aggression that is coupled with perverse interests (Finkelhor and Yllo, 1985). Obsessive rapes have been found to involve biting, burning, genital mutilation, bondage (Finkelhor and Yllo, 1985; Groth, 1979), and the use of pornography (Bergen, 1996). To illustrate, in one case the victim moved to a hotel and registered under a fake name to escape the suspect. It took two weeks for the suspect to find her, at which point he forced his way into her room and physically and sexually assaulted her while pouring hot wax over her body. As the victim cried and pled for the suspect to stop, he stated: "Tell me what you have been doing behind my back. You have embarrassed me in front of my friends! What if I pour hot wax all over your body? No one will want that pretty face of yours." The victim eventually escaped the hotel room without any clothing or belongings by jumping to an adjacent balcony.

The most common precipitating incident in this sample was a conflict over sex (40.6%, n = 65). For example, in one case the suspect attacked the victim after she refused to have sex with him throughout the day. The victim refused because she was still sore from her recent cesarean section surgery. The suspect became angry and vaginally raped the victim. The suspect questions the victim's fidelity in 18.6 percent of cases, representing the second most common precipitating incident. An example involves a suspect and victim who had been dating nine years when the suspect terminated the relationship. They had been broken up for 10 months when the victim returned home to find the suspect in front of her residence demanding to know if she was in a new relationship. When the victim refused to provide details, the suspect pulled her hair, choked her with one hand, and threw her phone on the floor with the other, and stated: "If you have a boyfriend I will do something to him. This is just the beginning."

Threats

Given the frequency with which they emerged, we created a typology of threats while coding the case files based on the tactics used by the suspect to gain compliance from the victim. The categories include: threats to kill the victim or the victim's family; threats to harm the victim or the victim's family; threats of noninjurious harm or authority (for example, threatening to have the victim deported); misogynist tactics; and implications of future harm. Misogynistic tactics involve: (1) the suspect calling the victim derogatory names; (2) telling her that she "wanted" the assault to occur; or (3) telling her the assault was somehow her fault. The most common type of threats involved death (43.1%, n = 25), followed by bodily harm (20.7%, n = 12), and misogynistic tactics (19.0%, n = 11). Given the suspect-victim relationship, the prominence of death threats provides context to the finding that bodily force was the primary means to subdue victims.

The following sections turn to the findings from the quantitative analyses of the decision to arrest and to file charges against suspects in intimate partner sexual assaults, followed by findings from interviews with detectives, prosecutors, and victims to identify emergent issues at the intersection of sexual assault and domestic violence (DV).

Correlates of Outcomes of
Intimate Partner Sexual Assault Cases

Given the paucity of research investigating the processing of intimate partner sexual assault cases, we selected independent variables that prior
research has identified as relevant to case processing in sexual assault or
intimate partner abuse. We also avoided variables that had substantial
amounts of missing data. Variables can be grouped into three categories:
relationship characteristics; indicators of case seriousness; and strength of
evidence. Our models include a number of variables that measure relationship characteristics. The first is whether the suspect had previously sexually
or physically assaulted the victim. We also included a variable that measured whether the victim and suspect had children. Last, we included a composite variable of factors that measure the "common" or "traditional" notions of domestic violence. This variable is coded 1 if an accusation of
infidelity, conflict over money, or conflict over children was present in the
case. The rationale is that cases with at least one domestic violence motive
reflect traditional notions of domestic violence and, as a result, are taken
more seriously by the criminal justice system.

We controlled for several variables that measure the evidentiary factors
in the case. The first is whether the victim had a forensic medical exam. We
also included a composite measure of evidence that is coded 1 if any of the
following types of evidence were collected from the victim or the scene of
the incident: clothing, semen, skin, fingerprints, blood, hair, or bedding. We
included variables that measure whether the suspect was interviewed by the
police, and if the victim cooperated with the investigation. We also included
a dichotomous indicator of whether there were witnesses to the incident.
Last, we included whether the victim made a prompt report, which we define as a report within one hour of the incident.

Our models also include a number of variables that measure case seriousness. We included a variable that measures whether the victim suffered
some type of collateral injury, for example, bruises, cuts, or choke marks.
We also measure whether the victim verbally or physically resisted. Last,
and consistent with Finkelhor and Yllo's (1985) discussion of battering
rape, we include whether the suspect physically assaulted the victim at the
time of the incident.

The Decision to Arrest

The results of our analysis of the decision to arrest are presented in Table
7.5. As these data indicate, relationship characteristics of the victim and
suspect do not predict arrest decisions; rather, these decisions are based on
the indicators of case seriousness and on evidentiary factors. Specifically,
the police were almost four times more likely to arrest the suspect if he

Table 7.5 Police Decision to Arrest in Intimate Partner Sexual Assault: Logistic Regression Analysis

	B	S.E	Exp(B)
Agency	−.424	.471	.654
Relationship Characteristics			
Suspect previously sexually assaulted the victim	.253	.504	1.288
Suspect previously physically assaulted the victim	.372	.483	1.451
The suspect and victim have children	.245	.491	1.278
At least one domestic violence motive was documented	−.234	.494	.791
Indicators of Case Seriousness			
Victim was injured at time of assault	.422	.510	1.525
Victim resisted (verbally, physically, or both)	−.301	.217	.740
Suspect physically assaulted victim at time of incident	**1.362***	.613	3.906
Evidentiary Factors			
Victim had a forensic examination	.224	.624	1.250
Some physical evidence was collected	.870	.577	2.388
Suspect was interviewed by police	**1.259***	.457	3.520
Victim cooperated with investigation	**1.104***	.492	3.015
There was at least one witness to the incident	.034	.511	1.034
Victim reported within one hour	**1.188***	.587	3.282
Constant	−2.627	.861	.072

Note: * P < .05

physically assaulted the victim at the time of the incident. Evidentiary factors that made arrest at least three times more likely were if the suspect was interviewed by the police, if the victim cooperated with the investigation, and if the victim reported within one hour.

The Decision to File Charges

Most of the intimate partner sexual assault cases in our sample were referred to the DA for filing consideration (either before or after the arrest of the suspect). Out of 161 total cases, 112 (89.6%) were referred to the DA or the city attorney. However, only 35 (31.2%) of the 112 cases resulted in the filing of charges against the suspect. The results of our analysis of the decision to file charges are presented in Table 7.6. As these data indicate, prosecution decisions are based primarily on the relationship characteristics of the involved parties and the evidentiary factors in the case. In contrast to law enforcement's decision to arrest, indicators of case seriousness were not statistically significant predictors of prosecutors' filing decisions.

Consistent with the decision to arrest yet more pronounced, the likelihood of charging was affected by the victim's willingness to cooperate with the investigation. In fact, prosecutors were 20 times more likely to file charges if the victim was willing to cooperate in the investigation and prosecution of the case. Due to the salience of victim cooperation in the prosecutor's decision to file charges, we analyzed case files to ascertain the

Table 7.6 District Attorney's Decision to Charge in Intimate Partner Sexual Assault: Logistic Regression Analysis

	B	S.E	Exp(B)
Agency	.546	.669	1.726
Relationship Characteristics			
Suspect previously sexually assaulted the victim	−.914	.737	.401
Suspect previously physically assaulted the victim	**1.439***	.656	4.216
The suspect and victim have children	.211	.639	1.234
At least one domestic violence motive was documented	**2.162***	.946	8.687
Indicators of Case Seriousness			
Victim was injured at time of assault	1.427	.799	4.167
Victim resisted (verbally, physically, or both)	.023	.265	1.024
Suspect physically assaulted victim at time of incident	−.763	.821	.466
Evidentiary Factors			
Victim had a forensic examination	−.888	.839	.412
Some physical evidence was collected	.943	.780	2.567
Suspect was interviewed by police	−.343	.644	.710
Victim cooperated with investigation	**3.035***	1.127	20.797
There was at least one witness to the incident	−.021	.648	.979
Victim reported within one hour	.872	.716	2.391
Constant	−6.707	1.830	.001

Note: * P < .05

circumstances that surround victims' refusal to cooperate. Victims most often reported refusing to prosecute because they were not interested in continuing with the criminal justice process (42.2%, n = 19), followed by the victim blaming herself for the assault or making excuses for the suspect's behavior (26.7%, n = 12). Finally, two relationship variables influenced the decision to file charges: whether the suspect had previously physically assaulted the victim, and if the suspect and victim's relationship involved prior domestic violence factors (e.g., conflict over children, conflict over money, accusations of infidelity). The district attorney was 8.7 times more likely to file charges if at least one domestic violence factor was present in the victim and suspect's relationship.

Considered together, our findings reveal the factors that influence law enforcement and prosecutorial decisionmaking in intimate partner sexual assault are both overlapping and distinct. Not surprisingly, victim cooperation was a statistically significant predictor of official action for both; however, law enforcement's decision to arrest centered primarily on evidentiary factors specific to the present, such as the immediacy of reporting, the suspect's use of physical violence during the incident, and whether the suspect was interviewed. Prosecutors' decisions, by contrast, more heavily centered on the past (prior physical assaults of the victim, domestic violence motives documented in the case file) and the future (whether the victim was willing to cooperate as the case moved forward).

The following section examines detectives', prosecutors', and victims' perspectives on intimate partner sexual assault. Collectively they demonstrate the unique dynamics specific to these cases and underline the need for ongoing scholarly focus on this type of violence to counter the continued tendency for it to remain invisible (Basile, 2002; Berman, 2004; Russell, 1990; Tellis, 2010; Yllo, 1999).

Detectives, Prosecutors, and Victims' Reflections About Intimate Partner Assault

Law Enforcement

We turn to the qualitative data[2] to analyze how detectives and prosecutors interviewed during the study described case processing of intimate partner sexual assault relative to other victim-offender relationships, followed by a review of findings from a focus group with survivors of intimate partner sexual assault. To begin, we found that both acquaintance and intimate partner sexual assault were characterized by detectives and prosecutors as falling under the "he said/she said" category, but we had to make a point of probing specifically about cases involving intimate partners, as they were seldom the first type of example that an interviewee would reference. It is interesting that interviewees described intimate partner sexual assault cases as the ones that are both least and most likely to be prosecuted. For instance, an LAPD detective stated: "Spousal rapes are rarely filed unless there is a confession. It's the whole thing of they are not going to put the victim through it if they don't believe in the end they'll convince twelve people this happened. Always the same explanation is given to the victim." Another noted that "domestic ones are difficult because they aren't reported in a timely manner and they get reported collaterally with something else. Almost as an aside they say, "He raped me too." You would think they would come in and say that initially." Along similar lines, an LASD detective commented that "it is not uncommon for them [the suspect and victim] to get back together and it totally muddles your case. The victim becomes uncooperative and in essence become a defense witness. If that happens then it won't be filed, and if it has been filed it will either be dismissed or a jury will find the defendant not guilty." Emphasizing the value of DNA evidence in an intimate partner case as primarily helpful to prosecute other crimes, an LAPD detective stated:

> I do not see a lot of those. I see the physical violence but not the rape cases. It is not that they aren't handled, it is that people feel it is too difficult and it becomes a he said/she said. In spousal cases DNA is

great because they likely have raped someone else. Many detectives have the tendency to make them [intimate partner sexual assault cases] a lower priority.

Other LAPD and LASD detectives emphasized that sexual assaults involving intimate partners are not inherently insurmountable, but the challenge is getting them reported on the front end. According to an LAPD detective:

> Spousal rape [a spousal] is absolutely the hardest but we seldom ever get those. Those are difficult, even if you have injury, because he argues she likes it rough. [It] takes the difficulty from acquaintance rape one step further. However, we are successful with spousals in getting a domestic filing and not a sex crime. There are techniques for investigating acquaintance or spousal rapes to get statements from him without him knowing, but the issues we face are first getting the report.

Taking the first step of making a report dovetails with the issue of perception and whether a victim defines what transpired as sexual assault (Bergen, 1996; Fisher and Cullen, 2000). But this also extends to the criminal justice professionals tasked with responding to these types of cases. Another detective noted that an intimate partner suspect-victim relationship "makes it more difficult to try and prove that instance was forced, but nonetheless it has to do with circumstances. What led to that day [or] incident? Past domestic incidents will have an impact, and a lot of times talking to friends and family of both helps you get a better picture of what type of relationship they have." The detective went on to say:

> I have had a spousal rape case filed. You can get filings, but they are hard. Again it comes down to perception. It's easier to get filing when it's mixed with domestic violence. It adds evidence to the case. Often victims will back off after things settle down, but we have had successful filings. It is a little harder, especially when there are children involved. It makes it harder for the woman to continue with the case—they may recant because they're trying to protect their family.

Detectives stated it is sometimes easier to prosecute if the suspect and victim are no longer living together. "If he forces her when coming over for the kids, for example," noted an LAPD detective, adding, "She [the victim] doesn't have the problem of trying to leave; she already has. I've seen these successfully prosecuted." While emphasizing the challenges of an out-of-custody suspect, an LASD detective concurred, stating, "Those are particularly difficult, especially when there is an ex-husband and during the investigation he . . . continued to harass and bother her." The detective went on to say these cases are "not particularly difficult to get filed if we can show other evidence of harassment, violence, and abuse."

A prominent theme that underlined discussion of the feasibility of prosecution in these types of cases is the presence of evidence. Some detectives emphasized that, given the co-occurrence of other forms of abuse in this suspect-victim relationship, these cases tend to yield more injuries, paper trails, and witnesses than similarly situated "he said/she said" sexual assaults. For instance, a detective recalled:

> I've handled spousal rapes and I've had success with a couple of them. They are obviously very difficult to prove. In cases where I was successful there were prior marriages and a history of DV which was helpful. By interviewing ex-wives I was able to uncover a history of physical and sexual abuse that was identical to what the current victim was describing. If you can develop a pattern of conduct, like with any case, that is certainly helpful.

Considered together, detectives' statements provide context to the statistically significant evidentiary factors and indicators of case seriousness in our quantitative analyses of arrest and charging decisions in these types of cases. Before turning to prosecutors, it is important to address another notable distinction among interviewees' responses, given its consistency throughout all of the interview topics: LAPD and LASD detectives evidenced one of two approaches toward sexual assault victims and cases, "innocent until proven guilty" or "guilty until proven innocent." The best possible example of the former attitude specific to this type of case comes from an LAPD detective, who began by stating that intimate partner sexual assault is the most frustrating sexual assault to investigate because of the lack of prosecution by the DA's Office:

> There seems to be a sense of, if you have had numerous sexual encounters with somebody then you should be expected to have sex with them whether you want to or not. Unless there is other evidence of violence such as physical injuries or visible evidence of force those cases are not going to get filed. Isn't rape the most violent of all physical assaults? If a woman acquiesces because children are in the next room and she doesn't want to wake them, we as [a] community look and say we are not going to prosecute it. I understand the lack

of substantial evidence to take to the courtroom, but let's take a stand on these 50/50 situations and let the jury decide rather than letting the DA decide and focusing instead on conviction rates. There are far more cases with women in spousal rape situations where they should be filed. Again, you have to look at motivations. They might say rape when wanting custody [while] going through a divorce. The DA's office hangs their hat on [the fact that] there could be a motive to lie, but again, for a lower-income woman with three or four kids to have the courage to come to us and make a spousal rape report, I think it's phenomenal they make it through the doorway in the police station to begin with.

As the preceding statement demonstrates, the "innocent until proven guilty" approach emphasizes the complexity of sex crimes, that by and large victims are cooperative, false reports are rare, and the police and prosecutors set a tone to which victims respond. Detectives from both departments who fit this profile stated that sexual assault is treated as a "second-class" crime by department leadership and that nothing will change for the better until that attitude improves. Conversely, detectives who evidenced a "guilty until proven innocent" approach emphasized that "real" rape involves strangers, and cases in which alcohol and illegal drugs are involved are what one detective described as "self-victimization," meaning that victims must be held accountable for where they go and how much they drink. These detectives expressed anything from refusal to a strong reluctance to make an arrest in a "he said/she said" case, and they reiterated that victim credibility is ruined if there are any inconsistencies in statements, whereas their colleagues emphasized that the manner in which patrol, detectives, and DAs gather information can generate the very inconsistencies that, ultimately, DAs can capitalize on. An emblematic response from a detective who uses this framework and who was asked about intimate partner sexual assault follows:

> We see about three to four yearly but I haven't seen a credible one in a long time. Again it's the victim's point of view, if she felt compelled to have sex with this guy every night for the last six years. Why haven't you done something about it or reported it? I haven't seen anything worth filing [criminal charges for] in a long time.

In conclusion, these approaches toward sexual assault cases and victims require further study because they highlight the individual-level factors that, in conjunction with agency- and victim-related factors, can impact whether sexual assaults are thoroughly investigated. The next section examines findings from interviews with prosecutors and concludes with findings from a focus group with survivors of intimate partner sexual assault.

Deputy District Attorneys

The LA County DA's Office has both a Family Violence Unit and a Sex Crimes Unit. Generally speaking, intimate partner sexual assault cases are handled by the Family Violence unit, based on the relationship length between the suspect and victim and whether other domestic violence factors are present, but other relevant factors include staffing considerations and supervisor discretion. Further, many deputy district attorneys (DDAs) stated that there is a lot of overlap and transfer between both units, which results in many prosecutors having experience in both areas. When we asked the DDAs interviewed for this project to explain how the suspect-victim relationship impacts charging decisions, some stated that they had little to no experience with intimate partner cases because they are a rarity. One attorney stated: "I have no experience with spousal rapes. It has come through a few times but it's very rare. I don't think it's reported. We don't get them very often." Another representative response came from this DDA, who stated:

> I've never tried a spousal rape case. I know they are harder to get filed. I don't see many get filed. I think it is because for a lot of the women it is more a threat of violence in the future and constant emotional battering down and not so much injury. No corroboration and no one witnesses, and it is left to his word against hers.

Other DDAs who also lacked experience prosecuting intimate partner sexual assault pondered both the consequences for victims and potential juror perceptions. For instance, one stated:

> I have never had to do a spousal rape, but I have done boyfriend/ girlfriend. In these cases the victim has feelings for this person with whom she has been intimate. They are difficult cases because [the victims] still have an emotional attachment to the perpetrator but at the same time have been violated.

Another commented, "My guess is that in a spousal rape case the jury would not convict unless the victim has a black eye or a broken arm and the duct tape and rope were found."

Other DDAs responded based on experience with sexual assaults involving intimates, and called attention to the idea that this form of sexual assault contrasts with jurors'—and, by proxy, society's—perception of sexual assault. As one attorney noted:

> Time is the only way to make change in society. Thirty years ago there were jury instructions stating that a rape charge is easily made by the victim. Justice Arabian refused to give that instruction and he

is now on the California Supreme Court. Not many jurors publicly state it, but they will say they needed more [to convict than just the victim's word].

A prominent theme to emerge was how problematic it is to disentangle consent in a relationship that previously involved consensual sex, as is most often the case with intimate partners. "If they previously had a relationship and were broken up for a while," a prosecutor stated, "those are easier. If during a consensual sexual act the victim says 'stop' and the suspect continues, that is considered rape. Legally it makes sense but it is a different reality to prove." Echoing this sentiment, another prosecutor stated: "There are a lot [of suspects and victims] who are boyfriend/girlfriend and have been dating a while. It is much more difficult to prove and the testimony is they had consensual sex the day before. Even if [we have] DNA it doesn't help."

As these statements demonstrate, interviewees spoke to the challenges of overcoming the consent defense, and they varied in their assessments of the prosecutorial utility of DNA evidence in nonstranger cases. One attorney stated at first that intimate partner cases were so much harder

> because you have to convince the jury she didn't want it because they're married, but I'm finding . . . if he's in custody and they call from jail, they will always call and threaten her. I had sixty phone calls from one suspect to a victim; twenty-eight received calls. All it takes is a fax to request the records, but you need time to listen to the phone calls. You pick time frames: maybe right around the time of arrest, right around the time of arraignment, prelim, and particular court dates, because that's when you get "please do not," or he threatens; or you get them calling mom or someone else. That's something we're starting to do.

Similarly, an attorney reflected on the difficulties for victims when a lack of evidence undermines the ability to prosecute, and elaborated:

> I had one woman storm out of an interview when I told her that her case would not be filed. . . . I understand the frustration. You take a victim who has been abused over and over again but has not officially documented any of that abuse and now is reporting a sexual assault. Because the prior abuse is not documented anywhere, we can't get any corroboration for any of the prior acts. This is complicated if the victim waited six months to report this crime. No matter what the officer did, we can't get any forensic evidence because we can't do a SART [Sexual Assault Response Team] exam. So victims are frustrated.

Another interviewee described an intimate partner case that was tried in court on a transcript because the victim failed to appear after the preliminary hearing. The attorney stated:

> These types of cases are very hard for jurors because she has consented, for example, sixteen times previously. What's the history of their relationship? Does the defendant have a reasonable belief that the victim consented? . . . Most spousal rapes are not reported and victims are much more quick to report physical assault.

Prosecutors varied in their emphasis on the likelihood of a conviction as the primary basis for filing decisions. As was the case with law enforcement, we noticed two opposing attitudes among prosecutors on the approach toward sexual assault cases and victims, which we characterized as those who "look for corroboration" versus those who "look for reasons to reject." Prosecutors who look for corroboration focused on evidence proving the legal elements of the crime and were more willing to take a chance on a jury. For instance, one prosecutor described corroboration as

> physical injuries, an admission by the suspect, or other pieces of evidence that corroborate the victim's story that couldn't be explained unless the victim was victimized. . . . I had [a case] where a girlfriend broke up with her boyfriend and he came to her house, banged on the door, and took her in his car to his house and raped her. She escaped and when the police found her it was rainy and she had no keys, no shoes, and no phone. It corroborates she was kidnapped. My corroboration was the cops in that case. You need to ask the right questions to get that corroboration, to get the whole story, and look for the corroboration in those little points. If victim says, "I was afraid and called my mom," get the phone records.

Another example comes from a prosecutor who referenced the challenge of demonstrating victim credibility in intimate partner cases:

> Right now I have two. . . . Both are cases involving sodomy and conservative Hispanic women who don't believe in anal intercourse. The suspect-victim relationship influences the case. Whenever you have an intimate relationship, you have to look for the potential motive to lie. If you assess all of those issues in the profile interview and still find the victim credible, you can find a way to present it to the jury and it is still righteous.

While concerned about a victim's motive to lie, this prosecutor reiterated that if the victim is believable and the legal elements are met, then the case is fileable.

Conversely, prosecutors who "look for reasons to reject" stated that they only file charges in cases most likely to secure a conviction. They also uncritically referenced gender bias in jurors more often when they held this perspective rather than the "look for corroboration" perspective. For example, to illustrate the point that intimate partner sexual assault and physical abuse are "incredibly correlated," a head deputy explained:

> She's only acquiescing because he just beat her. They have a track record of having sex once a week, and then he rapes her after he beats her. I believe there are many women in communities in our country who think women are chattel. In Southern California we have hundreds of domestic violence cases involving newcomers and Hispanics. Date rape is usually a onetime thing, but a wife will say in spousal rape, "Well, he wanted sex so I let him do it," but maybe this time he punches her. She says, "I didn't want the kids to get upset so I didn't say anything." She says she didn't want to do it, and thinks, "I am a person with innate self worth and dignity," because of acquiescing so many times. It's like a Jerry Springer [confrontational TV show]. Why don't they get divorced? We win [trials] with bad injuries and if we get a confession from that guy. Those [intimate partner cases] are most difficult because you have a track record: she's up on the stand and the guy is saying, "Ask her about the time she asked me to tie her up."

Other interviewees offered examples of prior unsuccessful attempts at prosecuting intimate partner sexual assault, which appeared to decrease their likelihood of trying these types of cases in the future. For example, an attorney stated:

> If they had an intimate relationship and there is no physical evidence it is likely to get rejected. Under rape shield laws prior consensual sex comes in, which is enough reasonable doubt not to convict. If it's an acquaintance rape with no prior sexual relationship those are better; it depends how long they have known each other. Men can become aggressive at any time, but when a victim testifies and they have known each other a while they will grill her on his lack of prior violence in terms of prior sexual contact with the defendant, and now she's saying something forceful happened. For example, I had a case involving a CEO and his secretary who began dating and then broke up. He had given her money; she had disclosed before. They had prior rough sex. I never got past a prelim[inary hearing] on that case.

This prosecutor demonstrates how one may develop a more cautious approach over time depending on experiences with cases, supervisors, and the overall work environment. It is important to note that working sex crimes and domestic violence and the nature of the contact with the suspects and victims will inevitably have an impact on criminal justice personnel, which must be addressed on an ongoing basis via training, continuing education, and supervision. The final portion of this chapter focuses on the perspectives of a sample of survivors of intimate partner sexual assault who agreed to speak about their experiences in hopes that the criminal justice system will improve its response to sexual assault and domestic violence.

Intimate Partner Sexual Assault Survivors

> I had been with him for three years [when I was first raped]. I remember when I walked into the hospital they were asking questions. They asked if I was raped and did he force you to have sex and I said yes. And I said most of the time he did force me to have sex but at the end he told me it was always my fault and that was how I wanted it. He was always confusing and always put the blame on me. It's been six weeks since it[3] happened but I'm still scared and it hurts because I'm pregnant.
>
> —A survivor

As we analyzed sexual assault reports and interviewed detectives and prosecutors, the importance of hearing from victims[4] directly became clear, given the frequency with which victim cooperation was cited as a contributing factor in attrition in sexual assault cases. To ensure anonymity and confidentiality, we did not collect any sociodemographic information about the women. However, they were a diverse and multilingual group in terms of age, ethnic background, religion, and current relationship status (single, married, engaged, and in a relationship). Semistructured questions focused on the decision to report and their cooperation with the criminal justice process, but given the emotionality and personal connection to the topic, the flow of conversation followed the tone set by participants.

With the exception of one woman, whose doctor contacted law enforcement, none of the women in the focus groups reported being raped by their partners to the police. When asked about the decision to report (or not), responses ranged from not knowing that it was a crime to feeling that it would be a waste of time. Some women attributed a reluctance to report to embarrassment, fear of being judged, and a lack of knowledge. Another stated, "I did not know that you have the right to say anything." Another characterized her decision to not report being raped by her husband as coming from the fact that she had been sexually abused her whole life: "Nobody ever listened to me at juvenile hall when I told them that this sexual assault happened in my home. Nobody paid attention then so why would they pay attention now?"

Another added: "In some cases it's more dangerous to tell than not to tell. It jeopardizes our kids and ourselves because these men are all violent." Nodding in agreement, another stated: "So much of the abuse becomes normalized. You hear it so much that it becomes normal." Tearing as she spoke, another woman said: "You talk yourself into liking it so that you don't hate yourself so much. You learn to not feel dirty." Elaborating on this theme, another woman disclosed: "I could hardly talk for days after forced oral sex, but I could not admit that he was being domestically abusive. Verbal abuse was what hurt me more because at least I was praised for sex. The verbal was worse because of the horrible things he said." Others talked about the myriad ways that their relationship with the suspect impacted their responses to the abuse and violence. For instance, one woman stated:

> When you have children you don't want to tear the family apart. There is a weight on the mother to keep the family together so you must be subjected to the way he chooses to treat you. Keeping this from the kids you need so much strength to deal with the emotional, sexual, and mental abuse. I never reported to the authorities. Never reported.

Another woman described a two-year abusive relationship and echoed the difficulty of reporting. She stated she froze any time law enforcement arrived at her house:

> Law enforcement never removed him until the last arrest. At the time I never called the police and I acted like nothing happened. He would [usually] call the police because I was screaming or crying after he would sexually assault me. He would call the police and pretend he was taking care of me and the police would come and believe his story. Looking back I don't know why I never reported. The final arrest I called his father who was a cab driver and I told him there was something wrong with his son. I asked his father to come and get him because he would always manipulate the police. He always called me a cunt, a whore, demanding food, care, and attention, and I went into an automatic mode and function. A girlfriend who was a colleague often saw me looking like a stone. I asked my girlfriend to drive one time because I was wearing a hood and she saw that I was bruised.

Other women emphasized that reporting to law enforcement does more harm than good. For instance, one woman stated: "I had one friend who did everything but these guys are never prosecuted. Nothing happens even though you've done everything you can." She went on to say:

The guy would break in so she took those steps but there were no consequences for violating restraining orders. When I did go to the police station nobody asked questions about what happened. They never asked anything and never once did they say, "Ma'am let us help you." They'd say, "There's nothing we can do." [The suspect] neglected to pick up the child and the police were no help. I asked for help because of his child endangerment but the cops would never help.

Others chimed in one after the other. "The police are no help," stated one woman. "Social services [agencies] are more helpful," she added. Another noted, "The police just want to know how he hit you." After a nod of agreement another offered: "Are you scared? If not, the police don't tend to come." Concurring, a woman said: "Police reports are a waste of time. He could do nothing that would get him in trouble." Then a woman who had been quiet until this point commented rather adamantly: "No matter how violent he is, the court wanted you to work it out. They would encourage that even with women who were scared. Even petrified women were encouraged to work it out, so why trust the criminal court system?"

Another aspect of the decision to not report that was common to women's responses was that silence allowed them to maintain a sense of denial. Consider this woman's disclosure: "I knew he was raping me. Part of me knew it was happening and part of me didn't want to know. Only one person kinda knew and it was hard to talk about and admit. I can hardly talk about it in group [in the present day]." Her fellow group members nodded again in agreement, and another added: "After four years I still haven't told my parents [about the abuse], especially about the rape. Nobody knew I was being raped. I isolated myself from my family for ten years. It was how I protected myself from my family and protected my children." As an affirmation that this was a common coping strategy, another woman stated, "I never told anyone until I got to the rape center."

Two women disclosed having gone to the suspect's mother for help but to no avail. The first said: "I told his mother because everyone else would say, 'Why are you staying?' Nobody understood the fear, the anxiety, and being trapped. He'd spent all my money. I was trapped physically. My mother said she was scared of what he would do because he's sick." The other stated: "I told his mother we were fighting over sex and she said this was my responsibility. It was the feedback, though I never believed it."

One of the women reflected on the importance of reporting after having some time and space from the abuse. She stated: "I recommend reporting even though the police say there's nothing that can be done. It is frustrating but it puts it on his record and creates a history so it helps this way. Leaving a record of disclosure can make a big difference." Participants nodded in agreement that while their prior interactions with law enforcement were not necessarily favorable, they would recommend reporting intimate partner abuse in all of its forms to law enforcement to establish a paper trail and increase the likelihood of successful prosecution. It is important to note that while none of the women directly reported to law enforcement that they were sexually assaulted by their partner, they had numerous interactions with law enforcement throughout the course of their abusive relationships both in their homes in response to calls for help and at police stations during child custody exchanges. A woman described her request for help at a police station as follows:

> A female officer looked at me like I had 17 heads. Another police person just stared and was cold when I asked for help. I was visibly bruised but there was no understanding. The male officer was more help than the female. My friend spoke up and said, "Why couldn't you have done what the male officer said?" [Officers at one station] had me sitting in the public area until I started screaming on the floor. Then they moved me to another room.

Another woman described a combination of being both helped and disrespected by law enforcement when she reported. "There was not enough probing," she said. "They just asked a few questions. One police officer was mean. He was abrupt so I refused to talk. But the other guy came over and sat with me for hours and let me cry. The other police officer was mean."

One woman's experience is notable due to her outspoken appreciation of the treatment she received from the LAPD. Her partner had a criminal record and was being pursued by law enforcement on other matters in addition to his violence against her. She encapsulated her story:

> I dated him for five years. I never thought of anything he did as sexual assault. I didn't realize that I was sexually assaulted until the police came to my house and asked questions. If you say, "Did he rape you?" you're not going to necessarily get the full response. The officer, who was male, asked me, "Did he force you to have sex?" And I said yes, all of the time. But I never thought of that as sexual assault. I never used the word rape because I was in a relationship so therefore I never considered it rape, although it would be painful, until the big, strong gentleman [the police officer] reminded me that it was rape. He had a way of asking questions, which helped me.

In summary, the survivors of intimate partner sexual assault interviewed for this study described fear and denial as the main reasons they did not report being sexually assaulted by their partner to law enforcement. Nevertheless, it is important to underline that they all stated that they had had numerous contacts with law enforcement during the course of their abusive relationships. Notwithstanding the difficulties associated with disclosing intimate partner abuse, collectively they encouraged all victims to report to the police in hopes that the suspect will establish a record, which will lead to a formal sanction such as an arrest and prosecution. There was consensus that survivors would likely be forthcoming and cooperative if the criminal justice representative tasked with their case is professional, empathic, and does not communicate by word or action that they are wasting his or her time.

Before turning to participants' recommendations for improving the criminal justice system's response to sexual assault, we provide some insight into victim decisionmaking by presenting the story of Mary,[5] who was raped by her husband both during and after their marriage, as a case study. Her case is notable due to a third party making the report, which is built-in corroboration, and the fact that the police made an immediate arrest. Here is her story:

> I was married at 15 and my husband was 32. He raped me and it was very rough. I had no information about sex. I was from [another country]. I was told I was out of control. I was married for 10 years but never felt right with him. I was raped for 7 years every night. I talked to his family but was told that this was my job; his family said there was something wrong with me. I was disgusted. I could not look at my father. I felt dirty, nasty, and like a very horrible person. After 10 years of being with him there was a lot of sexual assault going on. I felt that marriage was a nasty thing and after I got divorced I still got raped and never reported it to the police. During this whole time . . . he would threaten that he would take my boys. And I was not allowed to have friends and I had no family here. I didn't know what rape was. I was scared of him because he threatened to kill me. He kept reminding me that if he would kill me nobody would notice that I was gone. When I finally called the police the officers came to my house and they talked to him. They basically told him to calm down and he told them that I was on my period and I went crazy. The police never came to help me. I divorced him and he still came to my apartment and raped me as if nothing ever happened. He raped me in front of our children. They were in the next room. After he raped me he would say now you're my wife again. I was accused of asking for the rape because I wasn't wearing long clothes. My doctor finally called the police. The police asked me to call him and let him talk about raping me [a pretext phone call]. I didn't want to send him to

jail because of my sons. I was afraid he would take this out on the boys. The DA would not file the rape case because she said my ex-husband had a cultural defense. He was arrested but they let him go within three hours. The DA said the rapist has to believe he's raping in order for the DA to prosecute. When the DA decided not to prosecute it was a great disappointment. Everyone thought I'd made up the whole situation even though they had the evidence and I was cooperative. I sat with the DA and told them everything but the police and judges say they cannot do anything. The DA encouraged me to move on. My boys are six and five. They do not want to see their father. He is abusing his new wife and doing this in front of the children, which upsets them.

Of the 10 victims of intimate partner sexual assault interviewed during this study, only Mary's case became known to police because her doctor reported it. The police immediately arrested her ex-husband, the suspect, but a DDA declined to file charges because, according to the prosecutor, the suspect could use a cultural defense; that is, he had to realize he was sexually assaulting the woman in order to be prosecuted. The prosecutor went on to say that the best thing the victim could do is to "move on." The suspect has since remarried and the victim's two sons—who do not like having contact with their father—state that he is currently abusing their stepmother. Overall, focus group participants reported being cooperative with the criminal justice process despite the fact that cooperation was not necessarily reciprocated by law enforcement or prosecutors, and all stated that they would advise victims to report to the police so that suspects will be sanctioned and accrue a criminal history. It is also important to emphasize that deference to the knowledge of the detective and prosecutor was a consistent theme in these women's stories; in other words, they responded to the tone set by the criminal justice officials they encountered. In closing, they offered some advice to the criminal justice system officials who work these types of cases. Their suggestions center primarily on better treatment of victims by the police and prosecutors, being clearly made aware of their rights from the beginning, and better interviewing and report-writing skills. For example, one woman stated: "I was not told about the right to have an advocate. I requested my mother be there and was told I could not by law enforcement." Another stated the issue with law enforcement is

They don't let us get the information out. They just question and after a while I'm thinking what they might be thinking and I felt they were trying to turn the situation around. I think if they approached in a more compassionate way, like being a good listener, it would be better. In my situation the most compassionate person I dealt with was a nurse, so there was something in her training that was conducive to getting more information.

Numerous comments of a similar nature followed. "The more the police pressure you the more there would be a benefit of a therapist to slow the process down," noted one woman. She added: "Victims do not need to feel the pressure. The police would yield much more if they would slow down the pressure." Another woman described frustration with the reporting process itself. "I had to tell my story four times," she said. "It felt like I was talking to a wall the first time, second time, and the third time." Another chimed in that the hardest part was "no breaks during statements; all of this waiting around and then no breaks during the statements." Calling attention to the nonverbal, she stated: "They always gave the impression they wanted to get this over quickly so I never felt I could think events through. I felt like my story was continually being attacked and that they were always poking holes." Highlighting the importance and impact of the dynamic between victims and dtectives, another woman stated:

> The detectives have no idea how their questions affect you. It is scary when someone gives you advice. You listen to them like a doctor. I didn't know what to do. We want to cooperate. Well, you're the detective, what do you say?

Finally, one woman suggested that senior law enforcement officials should "reprimand the officers who don't take their job seriously. That would be the biggest thing." In closing, it is important to underline that participants' comments focus primarily on their interactions with law enforcement in response to physical abuse in their relationships because, with the exception of Mary (and in her case, the doctor made the report), none of them contacted law enforcement when they were sexually assaulted by their partner. The next section concludes the chapter with a review of our findings to inform future scholarly inquiry about the situational characteristics and criminal justice response to intimate partner sexual assault.

Conclusion: Policing and Prosecuting Intimate Partner Sexual Assault

Our quantitative analyses found that law enforcement's decision to arrest in cases of intimate partner sexual assault was primarily driven by evidentiary considerations (e.g., victim cooperation, promptness of reporting, if they interviewed the suspect) and indicators of case seriousness such as a co-occurring physical assault. This suggests an investigation that includes a suspect interview and yields evidence from a prompt report will result in a proactive law enforcement response. Next we found that prosecutors' charging decisions in intimate partner sexual assault cases were primarily driven by factors related to the future and the past. Specifically, prosecutors were 20 times as likely to file charges—the strongest predictor—if the victim was willing to cooperate in the investigation and prosecution of the case, and if the suspect and victim's relationship history included prior physical assaults and other factors associated with "traditional" domestic violence such as a conflict over sex or money or accusations of infidelity. These findings demonstrate the importance of reporting physical and sexual assault to law enforcement to ensure formal documentation exists—regardless of the relationship between the suspect and victim—because it increases the likelihood of both police and prosecutorial action.

Our qualitative data, which we generated through interviews with detectives, DAs, and survivors of intimate partner sexual assault, provide insight about the interactions between victims, detectives, and prosecutors, and the factors that impact their respective decisionmaking at the individual level. We found that some detectives approached sexual assault victims with an assumption that they were "innocent until proven guilty," and their prosecutor counterparts were those who "look for corroboration" of sexual assault allegations. Conversely, there were also detectives who approached sexual assault victims with the assumption that they were "guilty until proven innocent," and their prosecutor counterparts were those who "look for reasons to reject" sexual assault cases, especially those involving nonstrangers and delayed reporting. Consistent with the quantitative findings, "innocent until proven guilty" detectives and prosecutors who "look for corroboration" emphasized that these cases are prosecutable provided the detectives and prosecutors gather evidence and develop a good rapport with the victim. "Guilty until proven innocent" detectives, by contrast, demonstrated a lack of understanding about the dynamics behind delayed reporting and emphasized that they seldom, if ever, see an intimate partner[6] case worth filing. Finally, whereas prosecutors who look for corroboration emphasized the ability to take cases that meet the legal elements[7] of the crime to trial, prosecutors who look for reasons to reject focused primarily on the ability to secure a conviction as the basis for filing decisions and reiterated the difficulty of proving a lack of consent.

Our focus group with 10 survivors of intimate partner sexual assault provided them a voice to discuss their view of the dynamics that emerge during interactions between victims and law enforcement, in addition to the factors that often incline women not to report. With few exceptions, the women reported that denial, fear, and a feeling that reporting would only cause further harm prevented them from taking action. Each woman had a personal example of a situation in which an officer was either patient and respectful, or dismissive and rude. It is important that the extent to which a woman's experience was either positive or negative had an impact on her likelihood of further self-disclosure and cooperation with law enforcement.

The findings of our mixed methods analysis of processing of intimate partner sexual assault cases in Los Angeles have important implications for future research and for practice. The first is in the realm of evidentiary concerns. The detective cited earlier who noted the value of DNA evidence in spousal cases for its potential to solve other crimes spoke to a larger theme that emerged throughout our interviews. Detectives and prosecutors were inconsistent in their assessment of the value of testing rape kits for DNA evidence in nonstranger cases, particularly cases involving intimates. While the LAPD and LASD's current practices are to test every kit, stranger cases are prioritized, followed by acquaintances, and then intimates. Current policies notwithstanding, some detectives and prosecutors told us that testing every kit is critical because even if the suspect argues consent, the location of saliva and DNA can assist with interrogations, locking a suspect into a story, and potentially identifying him as a suspect in other unsolved cases. Others disagreed, stating that testing every nonstranger kit is unnecessary and solely a political gesture to appease advocates because DNA is irrelevant once the suspect argues consent. Given that our findings highlight the salience of evidence for effective prosecution of these cases, it is important for future researchers, policymakers, and senior criminal justice officials to develop evidence-based guidelines for case-carrying detectives and prosecutors that delineate how DNA evidence will be used to prosecute nonstranger sexual assault.

A second issue, which we address in further depth in the following chapter, is the importance of ongoing training and its potential impact on victim satisfaction. A common theme that emerged during interviews with detectives and prosecutors was the notion that one should only work sex crimes and domestic violence cases by choice, given their complexity and intensity. Findings from our focus group with survivors of intimate partner sexual assault affirmed the need for an empathic and appropriately trained first responder, given the particularly vulnerable position that this type of victim faces at the intersection of sexual assault and intimate partner abuse. For instance, should her case be investigated by a Major Assault Crimes (MAC) or Sex Crimes detective at LAPD? Should the case be referred to the Family Violence Unit or the Victim Impact Program Unit at the LA County DA's Office? Should she receive supportive services at a domestic violence shelter or a rape treatment center? Future research should examine the best responses to cases of intimate partner sexual assault and victims, given the criminal justice system and social service agencies' continued tendency to respond to domestic violence and sexual assault as mutually exclusive issues.

Notes

1. The inappropriate use of the exceptional clearance is discussed at length in Chapters 2, 4, and 6.

2. Chapter 2 describes the interviewee sample from each agency.

3. Her husband stabbed her while they were in a car and she jumped out of the moving vehicle to escape.

4. We are very grateful to Gail Pincus and the Domestic Abuse Center for partnering with us to ensure that victims had an opportunity to share their experiences with regard to the decision to report to law enforcement, and their overall impressions of the criminal justice system. In consultation with extant literature and the victim advocates and clinical experts at the respective agencies, we ascertained that spousal or intimate partner rape victims are less likely to share honestly in a group with other rape victims given stereotypes that spousal rape is not "real" rape, and thus they are less likely than other victims to report to the police. Thus, we conducted a focus group solely with spousal or intimate partner rape victims (n = 10) to validate their experience and increase the likelihood of forthright self-disclosure about the situational context of their victimization and the decision to report.

5. We use a pseudonym to protect her confidentiality.

6. Rather, they focus on cases involving nonstrangers more generally. "Guilty until proven innocent" detectives' overall emphasis was on stranger rape as the only "real" rape that is worth investigating.

7. It is important to note that the LA County DA's Office website states: "We will file criminal charges whenever there is *legally sufficient evidence* of a family violence crime and hope that all victims cooperate with our efforts. However, because our client, the People of the State of California, has an interest in protecting the safety of family violence victims and holding perpetrators accountable for their crimes, the District Attorney's Office will proceed with family violence prosecutions with or without the victim's cooperation" (emphasis added). Retrieved August 23, 2012, from http://da.lacounty.gov/familyviolence/.

8

Taking Sexual Assault Seriously

When it comes to rape people say to be wary of strange men. But it's not the stranger who comes inside the house. It's known suspects and victims who met at a club or bar, or friends, or maybe they dated. Usually they are drunk or inebriated or unconscious. The jury may say, "You may have said no, but your actions said yes." The law is clear that even one word of no means no, but jurors want signs of actual force because they want signs, but it's the victim saying no that makes it rape.

—VIP Deputy District Attorney (DDA)

[The problem lies with] divisions getting nonstranger cases where [the suspect's] ID is known and the detective takes the case to the DA and gets a reject. No one tested the rape kit and the suspect argues consent. There is a big push to push all of these cases through and then they reappear at Robbery Homicide Division as a cold case. And nothing happens to spousal rapes ever.

—LAPD detective

This study employed a mixed methods approach to examine sexual assault case processing decisions and outcomes for cases that were reported from 2005 to 2009 and were investigated and prosecuted by the Los Angeles Police Department (LAPD), the Los Angeles County Sheriff's Department (LASD), and the Los Angeles (LA) County District Attorney's (DA's) office. We analyzed trends from 2005 through 2009 in the three case closures utilized by law enforcement per the Federal Bureau of Investigation's (FBI's) Uniform Crime Reporting (UCR) program: cleared by arrest; cleared exceptionally; and unfounded (relative to cases that remained open); and we examined outcomes for cases that resulted in an arrest. We also analyzed a combined total of 944 case files from 2008 to gain in-depth understanding of the victim, suspect, and case characteristics specific to the sexual assaults that were known to law enforcement in one of the largest and most diverse counties in the United States.

To provide a more comprehensive assessment of the investigative and prosecutorial context, we interviewed 106 detectives and prosecutors to examine how they work together to prosecute sexual assault; specifically,

219

their decisionmaking strategies on receiving a sexual assault report, ranging from how they assess victim credibility and build rapport with victims, to when detectives close a case and what inclines a prosecutor to file or decline charges. Finally, we spoke with 17 women who were sexually assaulted by strangers, acquaintances, and intimates about their experiences with the criminal justice system and how the system can improve service provision to future victims.

Summary of Key Findings and Conclusions

Case Attrition and the Overlapping Roles of Police and Prosecutors

Consistent with prior research, the primary conclusion of this study is that there is substantial attrition in sexual assault cases reported to the LAPD and the LASD. Stated another way, very few sexual assault reports lead to the arrest, prosecution, and conviction of a suspect. Based on the data for 2005 through 2009 and considering only the cases that met the UCR definition of "forcible rape" and that involved victims over the age of 12, there were 5,031 sexual assaults reported to the LAPD and 2,269 sexual assaults reported to the LASD. The percentage of cases that were cleared by the arrest of an adult suspect was 11.7 percent for the LAPD and 27.1 percent for the LASD.[1] Only 9.7 percent of the 5,031 cases reported to the LAPD and 17.8 percent of the 2,269 cases reported to the LASD resulted in the filing of charges against the suspect, and only 7.8 percent of the LAPD cases and only 14.0 percent of the LASD cases resulted in a conviction. Among cases reported to the LAPD, in other words, only 1 in 9 was cleared by arrest, fewer than 1 in 10 resulted in the filing of charges, and only 1 in 13 resulted in a conviction. For the LASD, about 1 in 4 reports was cleared by arrest, 1 in 6 resulted in the filing of charges, and 1 in 7 resulted in a conviction.

The overlapping roles of police and prosecutors. As these data illustrate, the locus of case attrition is the decision to arrest or not; the majority of reports of sexual assault do not result in the arrest of a suspect. However, it is important to point out that the decision whether to arrest the suspect, although formally within the control of law enforcement, reflects decisions made by both detectives and DAs. Detectives for both law enforcement agencies will either arrest the suspect and present the case to the DA for a filing decision or present the case to the DA for a filing decision before making an arrest. In the latter situation, if the DA reviewing the case determines that the evidence does not meet the standard of proof beyond a reasonable doubt, the detective investigating the case will not make an arrest but rather will clear the case by exceptional means (which is an inappropriate use of this type of case clearance). As we discuss in more detail later, presenting the case to the DA prior to arrest subjects sexual assault cases to a higher standard of proof than is required by law to make an arrest.

An important consequence of prearrest charge evaluations is the failure to arrest in "problematic" cases (e.g., he said/she said cases or cases involving victims who were engaged in risk-taking behavior such as drinking or using illegal drugs) in which the identity of the suspect is known and there is probable cause to make an arrest, but the detective investigating the case believes that it would be difficult—although not impossible—to prove the suspect's guilt at trial. Some of these are cases in which the victim is unwilling to cooperate in the investigation and prosecution of the suspect. However, interviews with detectives for the two law enforcement agencies revealed that often the cases that are presented to the DA before an arrest is made are cases that have not been thoroughly investigated by law enforcement, which are presented to the district attorney in anticipation of a "reject."

The conclusion that the prearrest charge evaluation process is being used by law enforcement to dispose of problematic cases is supported by the findings of the quantitative analysis of the prosecutor's decision to file charges or not. In cases presented for filing consideration prior to an arrest, charge rejection was significantly more likely if the victim engaged in risky behavior; charge rejection was significantly less likely if the victim physically and verbally resisted the suspect, if the victim made a prompt report, if the suspect used some type of weapon during the commission of the crime, if the victim was willing to cooperate with law enforcement as the case moved forward, and if there was evidence or witnesses that could corroborate the victim's allegations. The results for the analysis of the decision to reject charges following arrest were very different. In fact, only three variables—whether the victim had a motive to lie, whether the suspect used a weapon during the commission of the crime, and whether the victim was willing to cooperate—had a statistically significant effect on the postarrest charging decision. This suggests that cases in which the victim engaged in risky behavior at the time of the incident are likely to be screened out before law enforcement makes an arrest, as are cases in which the victim did not verbally or physically resist the suspect or failed to make a prompt report, cases in which there is a lack of physical evidence to corroborate the victim's story, and cases without any witnesses who can attest to the victim's allegations.

The conclusion also is supported by the qualitative data obtained from interviews with detectives for the two law enforcement agencies and with

DDAs. We asked respondents to comment on the prearrest charge evaluation. A number of DAs confirmed that the charge evaluation process influences (indeed, determines) whether the suspect will be arrested. One stated, "So, if they know we won't file then they don't arrest." Another similarly said, "If we reject at the prefiling interview, they usually won't make an arrest because we won't be filing the case." Detectives from both law enforcement agencies agreed with this. Although a minority stated that they made probable cause arrests based on a thorough investigation regardless of their assessments of the likelihood that charges would be filed, the majority said that weak or problematic cases are resolved by "taking them to the DA's office to let them decide." As one LAPD detective put it, "Sometimes if we're unsure we have what we call drop-offs, in which we present paperwork to their office and they'll tell us what to do." Another said, "If I've investigated a case and I think all things being equal the suspect should not have an arrest jacket put on him and I know that case will be rejected anyway, I am going to take it to the DA's office and get it rejected." Detectives then close these cases under the mistaken impression that if they do not make an arrest and a prosecutor declines to file charges based on insufficient evidence to prove the case beyond a reasonable doubt at trial, they can count the case as solved per the FBI's Uniform Crime Report criteria to clear by exceptional means.

The conflating of probable cause and proof beyond a reasonable doubt. The net effect of the prearrest screening process is that law enforcement's arrest standard in some sexual assault cases has been transformed from probable cause to proof beyond a reasonable doubt to convict at a jury trial. This amounts to more scrutiny of rape victims than is required—and indeed, this level of scrutiny has been rejected—by California case law. For example, in 1986, six years after the removal of the resistance requirement in rape cases (1980 Cal. Penal Code § 261[2]), the California Supreme Court[2] stated:

> In so amending section 261, subdivision (2), the Legislature has demonstrated an unwillingness to dictate a prescribed response to sexual assault. . . . The elimination of the resistance requirement is also consistent with the modern trend of removing evidentiary obstacles unique to the prosecution of sexual assault cases. By removing resistance as a prerequisite to a rape conviction, the Legislature has brought the law of rape into conformity with other crimes such as robbery, kidnapping and assault, which require force, fear, and nonconsent to convict. In these crimes, the law does not expect falsity from the complainant who alleges their commission and thus demand resistance as a corroboration and predicate to conviction. . . . The amendment of section 261, subdivision (2), acknowledges that *previous expectational disparities, which singled out the credibility of rape complaints as suspect, have no place in a modern system of jurisprudence.* (Emphasis added)

Two years later[3] and again in 1992[4] the California Supreme Court affirmed the following precedent: "In California, conviction of a sex crime, including rape, may be sustained upon the uncorroborated testimony of the prosecutrix."

Legal scholars have documented the false assumptions that underlie prompt complaint requirements, corroboration requirements, and cautionary instructions to juries (among other things such as psychiatric exams and lie detector tests for victims), which have characterized the experience of female rape victims in the criminal justice system (Anderson, 2004; Temkin, 2010; see LeGrand, 1973 for current parallels to the 1970s). Prompt complaint requirements assume that "real" victims report immediately, an assumption that conflicts with national data and the findings from this study, both of which provide consistent evidence to the contrary (Anderson, 2004: 11; Fisher and Cullen, 2000; Tjaden and Thoennes, 2006). Corroboration requirements assume that "real" victims would have corroboration such as injuries and torn clothing, and that failure to produce it means that the victim was not really raped (Anderson, 2004: 12). This, too, is counter to the findings from extant research (Bachman, 2000; Tjaden and Thoennes, 2006) and the present study, both of which indicate that nonstranger sexual assault—often precisely because of the victim-suspect relationship—typically involves bodily force or verbal threats without the presence of weapons or serious bodily injury.

Finally, cautionary instructions to juries assume that jurors are inherently biased in favor of rape victims (Anderson, 2004:12), which is counter to the findings from extant research about juries (Kalven and Zeisel, 1966) and prosecutorial discretion in rape cases (e.g., Frohmann, 1997; Spohn, Beichner, and Davis-Frenzel, 2001). Moreover, criminal justice officials interviewed for this study attributed the difficulty inherent in prosecuting sexual assault in part to jurors' biases against female rape victims.

The Misuse of the Exceptional Clearance in FBI Uniform Crime Reporting

As discussed in detail in Chapter 6, a key finding of this study is that each law enforcement agency's case clearance data are compromised by the misuse of the exceptional clearance. The high rates of exceptional clearances for the LAPD and the LASD result from the misuse of this case clearance type in three interrelated situations. The first is when cases that result in the arrest of a suspect (and that are initially categorized as cleared by arrest) are cleared by exceptional means when the DA declines to file charges. This is based on an LAPD policy to clear by arrest only when the prosecutor files felony charges and reflects a need for training for the LASD, whose policy is consistent with UCR prescriptions to clear by arrest if a suspect is arrested. A second example of the incorrect use of the exceptional clearance is when the suspect is not identified or his location is not known;

this is more problematic for the LASD (28.4% of its exceptionally cleared cases did not meet these two criteria) than for the LAPD (only 3.2% of its exceptional cleared cases failed to meet these criteria). Because an identified suspect and knowledge of the suspect's location are required in order to clear a case by exceptional means, these cases should not have been cleared but rather should have remained open until a suspect was identified.

The third situation in which cases may be cleared incorrectly by exceptional means is where probable cause to arrest the suspect exists but the detective chooses instead to present the case to the DA's Office for a pre-arrest charge evaluation and the charges are rejected based on insufficient evidence. This situation is problematic in that it does not involve something beyond the control of law enforcement that prevents the arrest of the suspect. There is probable cause to make an arrest but the case is cleared exceptionally because a prosecutor determined that the evidence is insufficient to prove the case beyond a reasonable doubt to a jury. In this situation, the case should not have been exceptionally cleared as it is within the control of the police to arrest and charge the suspect and turn him or her over to the court for prosecution.

A superficial reading of this is to see it merely as a failure to conform to UCR guidelines. However, in and of itself that failure is salient because if these issues are present in the LAPD and LASD, it is likely that other law enforcement agencies clear cases similarly. Ultimately, prearrest charge evaluations and the misuse of the exceptional clearance raise the question of the value of an arrest; is the difference between the probable cause arrest standard for law enforcement and the proof beyond a reasonable doubt to convict in a trial standard for prosecutors purely a theoretical distinction? Further research should examine the extent to which prearrest charge evaluations occur in sexual assault cases (and other crimes) in other jurisdictions and the degree to which charge declinations in cases evaluated prior to arrest lead to exceptional clearance of the case.

Implications for researchers. Our findings regarding the misuse of the exceptional clearance and the overlapping roles played by police and prosecutors in arrest decisions have important implications for researchers. Like prior researchers, we began our project on police and prosecutorial decisionmaking in sexual assault cases with an assumption that law enforcement's decision to arrest and the DA's decision to file charges were separate decisions that reflected different standards of proof and different decision rules. We recognized that prosecutors' filing decisions would be based in part on the adequacy of the investigation conducted by law enforcement and on the willingness of the victim to cooperate as the case moved forward, which, in turn, would be affected by the handling of the case by the investigating officer (I/O). We also recognized that the I/O's decision to arrest might reflect, to some extent, his or her beliefs about the likelihood of successful prosecution. However, we did not expect to find that the decision to arrest the suspect would in many cases be determined by the DA's evaluation of the case or that a substantial proportion of cases would be rejected for prosecution prior to the arrest of the suspect. We also did not expect to find that DAs' filing decisions would affect the way that law enforcement cleared cases for UCR reporting purposes.

The concept of "cleared by arrest" plays a key role in research on police and prosecutorial decisionmaking. Policing researchers often operationalize the decision to arrest based on whether the crime was cleared by the arrest of a suspect (Galvin and Polk, 1983; Horney and Spohn, 1996; LaFree, 1980) and researchers examining prosecutorial charging decisions typically examine data on cases that were cleared by arrest and were presented by law enforcement for a formal charging decision (Feldman-Summers and Lindner, 1976; Field and Bienen, 1980; Kingsnorth, MacIntosh and Wentworth, 1999; LaFree, 1980, 1981; Spohn, Beichner, and Davis-Frenzel, 2001; Spohn and Holleran, 2001; Spohn and Spears, 1996: Wooldredge and Thistlethwaite, 2004). Galvin and Polk (1983), for example, used data from the California Bureau of Criminal Statistics to examine case attrition rates, finding that the proportion of reported offenses that were cleared by arrest ranged from 15 percent for burglary to 69 percent for homicide. Similarly, in its classic study of the deterioration of felony arrests in New York City, the Vera Institute of Justice (1981) documented that about 25 percent of all felony arrests made in 1971 resulted in the dismissal of charges; the authors were careful to point out, however, that the data on which their study was based included only incidents that were cleared by arrest (p. 4).

Researchers who define arresting and charging decisions based on whether the case was cleared by arrest assume that all cases that result in the arrest of a suspect are cases that are cleared by arrest and that the only cases on which prosecutors make charging decisions are cases in which a suspect was arrested. As we have shown, these assumptions are not necessarily valid. At least in this jurisdiction (Los Angeles) and for this type of crime (sexual assault), a substantial proportion of cases in which a suspect was arrested were not cleared by arrest; this occurred when the DA reviewing the case following the arrest of the suspect rejected the case for prosecution and the detective investigating the crime changed the type of case clearance from cleared by arrest to cleared by exceptional means. Moreover, a significant number of cases were evaluated—and rejected for prosecution—by the DA prior to the arrest of the suspect. Defining the decision to arrest as cases that were formally cleared by arrest and operationalizing the charging decision as cases that were evaluated following arrest is misleading, as doing so undercounts both types of decisions.

The Decision to Unfound the Report

Another important conclusion of this study is that unfounding sexual assault reports occurs infrequently[5] and that most of the reports that were unfounded by the LAPD were false or baseless. About three fourths of the unfounded cases involved false or baseless allegations; the remaining cases were either clearly not false reports or were ambiguous cases that the research team concluded should have been investigated further before being cleared. Most of the false reports involved allegations of aggravated rape, and in about half of the cases the victim underwent a forensic medical exam and eventually recanted the allegations. Complainants' motivations for filing false reports, which fell into five overlapping categories, included a desire to avoid trouble or a need for an alibi for consensual sex with someone other than a current partner, a desire to retaliate against a current or former partner, a need for attention or sympathy, and guilt or remorse as a result of consensual sexual activity. Many complainants also had mental health issues that made it difficult for them to separate fact from fantasy.

These results suggest that the LAPD is appropriately clearing cases as unfounded most, but not all, of the time. Generally, the I/Os followed UCR guidelines and unfounded cases only after an investigation led them to conclude that the allegations were false or baseless; they typically did not use the unfounding decision to clear—or dispose of—problematic cases. Nonetheless, there were 10 cases with compelling evidence that a crime did occur, including physical evidence from the forensic medical exam or witness statements that corroborated the complainant's allegations, injuries to the complainant that were consistent with her account of the assault, or evidence recovered from the scene of the crime. In most of these cases, a number of which involved complainants and suspects who were intimate partners or acquaintances, the complainant recanted but it was clear that her recantation was motivated by fear of the suspect, pressure from the suspect or his family and friends, or a lack of interest in pursuing the case. It appears that the victim's recantation or lack of interest in prosecuting the suspect led the I/O to conclude that the allegations, while not false, were not provable and that the case therefore should be unfounded.

Coupled with the fact that there were an additional eight cases that the researchers believed should have been investigated further, our findings suggest a need for additional training on the decision rules for unfounding sexual assaults. Patrol officers and sex crime detectives need specialized training to understand the complexities of sex crimes and the interview skills that are conducive to disclosure. Further evidence of this need for training comes from our interviews with LAPD detectives. Although some detectives stated that victim recantation was neither a necessary nor a sufficient condition for unfounding, many said that they believed that a report could be unfounded only if the complainant recanted her testimony and a few stated that they would always unfound the report if the victim recanted her testimony. Finally, some stated that rather than unfound a case they prefer to take it to the DA, regardless of what the victim's statements and the evidence indicate.

The Prevalence of, and Response to, Nonstranger Sexual Assault

The findings from this study indicate that sexual assault by a stranger is the least frequently occurring form of sexual assault in Los Angeles City and County in terms of cases reported to, investigated by, and prosecuted by the LAPD, LASD, and LA County DA's Office. However, both law enforcement officials and prosecutors spoke of public safety—specifically around the need to arrest—as more pressing and serious in cases involving strangers, and detectives more frequently used the term "righteous victim" when describing the victim of a sexual assault by a stranger.

Officials interviewed also agreed that cases involving nonstrangers had unique evidentiary challenges and, as a result, were the most difficult to successfully prosecute. However, as detectives with an "innocent until proven guilty" approach to victims (as compared to those with a "guilty until proven innocent" approach) and prosecutors who "look for corroboration" (compared to those who "look for reasons to reject") emphasized, prosecuting nonstranger sexual assault requires a nonjudgmental attitude along with specialized training and expertise in relevant penal codes and evidence collection strategies to counter the challenges inherent in delayed reporting and the consent defense. Important skills include thorough documentation of statements, creating timelines, understanding social media, trauma interviewing, and interrogation. Although our interviews revealed that there are detectives and prosecutors who passionately pursue justice in these types of cases and—given their interdependent roles—communicate during a case in service of a thorough investigation, they also revealed that cases involving nonstrangers are often viewed with suspicion from the outset and, as a result, are less likely than those cases involving an identified suspect who is a stranger to the victim to proceed through the criminal justice system. Interviews revealed that many detectives evaluated probable cause to arrest differently depending on whether the case involved strangers versus nonstrangers, and, with few exceptions, all detective and prosecutor interviewees stated that prearrest evaluation of nonstranger sexual assault is common. Detectives who stated that they "take the case to the DA for a reject," which is consistent with the "guilty until proven innocent" approach to victims that is most prominent in relation to nonstranger rape, contribute to a work environment that tolerates the underinvestigation of these types of cases.

The Impact of the FBI on Law Enforcement

Prior to 2012, the *UCR Handbook* (FBI, 2004) defined forcible rape as "the carnal knowledge of a female forcibly and against her will. Attempts or assaults to commit rape by force or threat of force are also included; however, statutory rape (without force) and other sex offenses are excluded."[6] The fact that rape was defined as "carnal knowledge" meant that acts that did not involve penile-vaginal penetration—including sexual penetration with an object, oral copulation, and sodomy—were included, not as Part I offenses, but as "other sex offenses" in Part II of the "crimes known to the police." Also not included were reports of sexual penetration with an object, oral copulation, and sodomy that were the "secondary crimes" that accompanied reports of Part I crimes such as robbery, burglary, and aggravated assault. Despite the fact that most experts would categorize sexual penetration with an object, oral copulation, and sodomy as crimes that fall within the definition of rape and sexual assault, the antiquated definition used by the FBI for Uniform Crime Reporting purposes prior to 2012 meant that these serious sex offenses were combined with the less serious sexual batteries (i.e., fondling or touching with sexual connotation) as Part II "other sex offenses."

The implications of excluding these crimes from the definition of forcible rape were documented in Chapter 4. From 2005 to 2009, the LAPD received 5,031 reports of rape and attempted rape; they received 1,061 reports of oral copulation, penetration with an object, and sodomy. If these "other sex offenses" were included in the forcible rape category, the number of reports of forcible rape received by the LAPD during this five-year time period would increase by 21 percent (from 5,031 to 6,092). The figures for the LASD are similar. From 2005 to 2009, the LASD received 2,269 reports of rape and attempted rape; they received 630 reports of oral copulation, penetration with an object, and sodomy. Including these "other sex offenses" in the forcible rape category would have increased the number of reports of forcible rape received by the LASD by more than 27 percent (from 2,269 to 2,899). Stated another way, 17.4 percent of the reports received by the LAPD and 21.7 percent of the reports received by the LASD during these five years were reports of penetration with a foreign object, oral copulation, and sodomy.

The national prominence of the UCR program and its impact on local law enforcement cannot be underestimated. According to the FBI website, in 2009 there were 17,985 city, county, university and college, state, tribal, and federal agencies that participated in the UCR program. Together they represented 96.3 percent of the US population.[7] Part I crimes are deemed the most serious, and police chiefs and sheriffs are held accountable for Part I numbers in their jurisdictions. Moreover, as law enforcement is increasingly evidence-based and numbers-driven in its administration of justice, Part I numbers drive law enforcement executives' resource allocation. As was evident in the findings from Los Angeles City and County, measuring rape using the pre-2012 UCR definition misleads the public about the reality of sexual assault within their communities and undercounts the numbers of sexual assault cases that detectives, as a practical reality, are investigating. The expanded definition of sexual assault that was adopted in 2012 should provide a more accurate picture of the prevalence of sexual assault.

While the expansion of the definition of rape is an important evidenced-based policy change, the findings from this study raise a less frequently discussed issue: FBI clearance data is compromised because the single percentage presented to the public about crime in Los Angeles (or any other jurisdiction) combines cases cleared by arrest and cases cleared by exception. Doing so provides a misleading picture of the extent to which sexual assaults are actually "solved" given that detectives: (1) clear cases exceptionally more often than they clear cases by arrest; (2) clear cases exceptionally after making an arrest when the DA declines to file charges; and (3) clear cases exceptionally following a prearrest charge evaluation when probable cause may exist but they abstain from making an arrest when the prosecutor declines to file charges. Just as defining forcible rape narrowly provides inaccurate estimates of the prevalence of this crime, combining cases that are cleared by arrest with those cleared by exceptional means both encourages the overuse (indeed, misuse) of the exceptional clearance and overestimates the extent to which these crimes are solved.

In the next section, we present policy recommendations for law enforcement, for prosecutors, and for the FBI's UCR program. These recommendations are designed to enhance the reliability and validity of data on sexual assault case outcomes, reduce case attrition, hold those who commit crimes accountable, and improve the treatment of victims who report their crimes to law enforcement agencies.

Policy Recommendations

Policy Recommendations for Law Enforcement

- Regardless of victim age or relationship to the suspect, a professional law enforcement response to sexual assault requires specialized units that are important to department leadership and that are staffed with detectives and supervisors who want to work these types of cases.[8]
- There should be ongoing, specialized training that focuses on interviewing victims, interrogating suspects, and the penal code. Because

nonstranger sexual assault is the most frequent type of case seen by law enforcement, training should specifically address investigation of this type of case. In addition, training should emphasize that delayed reporting is the norm in sexual assault cases. Both patrol officers and detectives require specialized sexual assault training because a poorly written report, inability to build rapport with victims to gather information, and failing to ask appropriate questions often create inconsistencies in victims' testimony that damage their credibility and contribute to case attrition.

- To be effective, law enforcement must engage the victim as an ally in the investigation. A pretext phone call is much more likely to be successful if the victim and detective are "partners" in the process, but there must be additional investigative strategies to rely on other than the pretext call. The Internet, including social networking websites, and cell phone messages were repeatedly cited as salient sources of potential evidence in nonstranger cases.

- Training on case clearances should emphasize that (1) the exceptional clearance should be used only if the case meets all four UCR criteria for using this type of case clearance; (2) cases that result in an arrest cannot by definition be cleared exceptionally and cases rejected by the prosecutor prior to the arrest of the suspect because the evidence does not meet a filing standard of proof beyond a reasonable doubt cannot be cleared by exceptional means; (3) cases in which the police know who and where the suspect is and in which probable cause to arrest exists but the victim refuses to cooperate can legitimately be cleared by exceptional means if the victim's lack of cooperation means that the police cannot make an arrest; and (4) assuming a thorough investigation, in cases in which probable cause exists (and in which the victim is willing to cooperate), the police generally should make an arrest and clear the case by arrest.

- Training on case clearances also should stress that if probable cause to arrest does not exist or if the prosecutor rejects the case for further investigation as a result of a prearrest charge evaluation, the case should be left open and investigated further. These cases should not be cleared by exceptional means, as they do not meet the UCR criterion that there must be "enough information to support an arrest, charge, and turning over to the court for prosecution." The case cannot be solved—that is, cleared—if probable cause to make an arrest does not exist.

- Law enforcement agencies should develop a manual specific to investigating sex crimes that codifies policies and lays out expectations of detectives.

Policy Recommendations for Prosecutors

- Prosecutors should file charges in more sexual assault cases that meet the legal elements of the crime and in which the victim is willing to cooperate. To clarify, we are recommending that in cases in which the victim is cooperative, prosecutors should more often use a legal sufficiency standard, as opposed to a trial sufficiency standard. We are not recommending that prosecutors file charges using a probable cause standard.
- If there is a prearrest charge evaluation, the prosecutor's office should ensure that the case has been thoroughly investigated. If not, the case should be returned to law enforcement for further investigation.
- If a prefiling interview with the victim is required, the prosecutor's office should establish a formal process in conjunction with law enforcement for the interview with the victim so that one interview occurs with representatives from both law enforcement and the prosecutor's office present. This will reduce the trauma for victims and make it less likely that inconsistencies in the words victims use to describe the assault to law enforcement officials and prosecutors will result in the rejection of charges.
- Given the salience of victim consistency and credibility to sexual assault prosecution, it is important to train prosecutors about effective techniques for interviewing traumatized rape victims.
- Our interview data suggested that both law enforcement and prosecutors had varying degrees of clarity as to the value of DNA evidence in nonstranger sexual assault cases in which the suspect utilizes a consent defense. To address this, training should incorporate examples of sufficient evidence to prosecute in cases where the suspect uses a consent defense and clarify department expectations as to how DNA evidence is most effectively used to prosecute nonstranger sexual assault.
- Prosecutors should provide detailed reasons for charge rejection and should provide victims with a copy of the form that explains why charges have been rejected. For quality assurance and continuing education purposes, the most frequently rejected cases could be analyzed to inform training protocols for investigations, evidence collection, and successful prosecution.

Policy Recommendations for the FBI's UCR Program

- Revise the *UCR Handbook* to clarify any law enforcement misunderstanding to the effect that the DA plays a role in case clearances, and to clarify that clearances are based on the police evidentiary standard of probable cause to make an arrest.

- Specifically, clarify that "arrested and charged" in the definition of "cleared by arrest" means a booking procedure by the police, and that a case that results in an arrest cannot be cleared exceptionally since one of the criteria for an exceptional clearance is that there is something beyond the control of law enforcement that prevents them from making an arrest.

- Present the percentage of cases cleared by arrest and cleared exceptionally separately rather than combined, as is the current practice. This contributes to an organizational reluctance to address the misuse of the exceptional clearance by detectives because police leadership are aware that ultimately the FBI presents only one statistic to the public, which is misleading as to how cases are being "solved," especially if the exceptional clearance is being misused, as is the case in Los Angeles.

- Given that rape inherently involves force, it is redundant to label it "forcible rape." Consider renaming the crime "rape" or "sexual assault" to be consistent with established criminological and epidemiological terminology.

Conclusion:
Sexual Assault in Los Angeles City and County

The results of this study demonstrate that sexual assaults reported to the LAPD and the LASD have a high rate of case attrition. Very few cases, especially those that involve nonstrangers, result in the arrest and conviction of the suspect. The high rate of attrition in these cases reflects a collaborative gatekeeping process involving both law enforcement agencies and the DA's Office. The low arrest rate reflects law enforcement's inability to conclusively identify a suspect in all cases involving strangers; more important, it reflects their unwillingness to make an arrest in cases involving nonstrangers absent a DA's assessment that there is proof beyond a reasonable doubt and that the case has a high probability of conviction at trial. This unwillingness to arrest is also based on the incorrect assumption that cases in which the district attorney refuses to file charges can be "solved," or cleared for UCR purposes, through the use of the exceptional clearance. The low overall conviction rate reflects a prearrest and postarrest charge evaluation process in which only cases that meet the standard of proof beyond a reasonable doubt are filed, as well as the requirements that the victim be interviewed prior to filing and that her allegations be corroborated. The result of this highly discretionary decision making process is that

it is primarily the atypical, "slam-dunk cases" that result in the arrest, prosecution, and conviction of the suspect. The more typical cases, in which the
victim and the suspect are nonstrangers and there is probable cause (but not
proof beyond a reasonable doubt) that a crime was committed and the suspect is the person who committed the crime are screened out early in the
process and do not result in the suspect's arrest. The result is that, as was
the case in the era preceding rape law reform, only the crimes perceived as
"real rapes" (Estrich, 1987) with "genuine victims" (LaFree, 1989) are
taken seriously by the criminal justice system.

Notes

1. As we note in Chapter 4, the arrest rate for each agency—and particularly
for the LAPD—would be higher if cases that resulted in an arrest but were (inappropriately) cleared by exceptional means after the DA refused to file charges were
included. Although we could not identify these cases in the 2005–2009 data, our
analysis of the 2008 data revealed that the percentage of cases in which a suspect
was arrested (regardless of whether the case was ultimately cleared by arrest or
cleared by exceptional means) was 32.9 percent for the LAPD and 46.7 percent for
the LASD.

2. *People v. Barnes* (1986) 42 Cal.3d 284.

3. *People v. Poggi,* 753 P.2d 1082, 1095 (Cal. 1988).

4. *People v. Gammage,* 2 Cal. 4th 693, 702, 828 (Cal. 1992).

5. It is important to point out that our conclusions regarding unfounding are
based on data provided by the LAPD. There were too few cases unfounded by the
LASD to include in the analysis. It also is important to note that each law enforcement agency uses a "noncrime report" to document allegations that may or may not
be recategorized as a crime report. Allegations that are handled via a noncrime
report and that are subsequently determined to be false do not need to be unfounded.
Therefore, the data provided to us by the LAPD and the LASD almost certainly
understate the number of reports that were false allegations.

6. In 2012 the definition of forcible rape was changed to "penetration, no matter how slight, of the vagina or anus with any body part or object, or oral penetration by a sex organ of another person, without the consent of the victim." This
broadened definition includes oral copulation, sodomy, penetration with an object,
assaults of male victims, and assaults of female victims by female offenders. U.S.
Department of Justice, Attorney General Eric Holder Announces Revisions to the
Uniform Crime Report's Definition of Rape. January 6, 2012. Available online at
http://www.fbi.gov/news/pressrel/press-releases/attorney-general-eric-holder-
announces-revisions-to-the-uniform-crime-reports-definition-of-rape.

7. Online at http://www2.fbi.gov/ucr/cius2009/about/crime_summary.html

8. In response to the findings and recommendations of this study, the Los
Angeles County Sheriff's Department implemented a policy requiring all sexual
assaults, regardless of the age of the victim, to be handled by the Department's Special Victims Unit. This change went into effect in September 2012.

Bibliography

Addington, L. A. (2006). Using national incident-based reporting system murder data to evaluate clearance predictors. *Homicide Studies, 10,* 140–152.

Addington, L. A., and C. Rennison. (2008). Rape co-occurrence: Do additional crimes affect victim reporting and police clearance of rape? *Journal of Quantitative Criminology, 24,* 205–226.

Alderden, M. A., and T. A. Lavery. (2007). Predicting homicide clearances in Chicago: Investigating disparities in predictors across different types of homicide. *Homicide Studies, 11,* 115–132.

Alderden, M. A., and S. E. Ullman. (2012a). Creating a more complete and current picture: Examining police and prosecutor decision-making when processing sexual assault cases. *Violence Against Women, 18,* 525–551.

Alderden, M. A., and S. E. Ullman. (2012b). Gender difference or indifference? Detective decision making in sexual assault cases. *Journal of Interpersonal Violence, 27,* 3–22.

Anderson, M. J. (2004). The legacy of the prompt complaint requirement, corroboration requirement, and cautionary instructions on campus sexual assault. *Boston University Law Review, 84,* 945, 1–87.

Bachman, R. (1998). Factors related to rape reporting and arrest: New evidence from the NCVS. *Criminal Justice and Behavior, 25,* 1, 8–29.

Bachman, R. (2000). A comparison of annual incidence rates and contextual characteristics of intimate-partner violence against women from the National Crime Victimization Survey (NCVS) and the National Violence Against Women Survey (NVAWS). *Violence Against Women, 6(8),* 839–867.

Bachman, R., and R. Paternoster. (1993). A contemporary look at the effects of rape law reform: How far have we really come? *Journal of Criminal Law and Criminology, 84,* 554–574.

Basile, K. (2002). Attitudes toward wife rape: Effects of social background and victim status. *Violence and Victims, 17,* 341–354.

Battelle Memorial Institute Law and Justice Study Center. (1977). *Forcible rape: A national survey of the response by prosecutors.* National Institute on Law Enforcement and Criminal Justice. Washington, DC: US Government Printing Office.

Baumer, E., R. Felson, and S. Messner. (2003). Changes in police notification for rape, 1973–2000. *Criminology, 41,* 841–872.

Beichner, D., and C. Spohn. (2005). Prosecutorial charging decisions in sexual assault cases: Examining the impact of a specialized prosecution unit. *Criminal Justice Police Review, 16,* 461–498.

Belknap, J. (2010). Rape: Too hard to report and too easy to discredit victims. *Violence Against Women, 16,* 1335–1344.

Bergen, R. (1996). *Wife rape.* Thousand Oaks, CA: Sage.

Berger, R. J., W. L. Neuman, and P. Searles. (1994). The impact of rape law reform: An aggregate analysis of police reports and arrests. *Criminal Justice Review, 19,* 1–23.

Berger, R. J., P. Searles, and W. L. Neuman. (1988) The dimensions of rape reform legislation. *Law and Society Review, 22,* 329–358.

Berman, J. (2004). Domestic sexual assault: A new opportunity for court response. *Juvenile Court Journal,* Summer, 23–34.

Black, D. (1976). *The behavior of law.* New York: Academic Press.

Blumstein, A., and J. Wallman. (Eds.). (2000). *The crime drop in America.* New York: Cambridge University Press.

Bouffard, J. A. (2000). Predicting type of sexual assault case closure from victim, suspect, and case characteristics. *Journal of Criminal Justice, 28,* 527–542.

Boulahanis, J. G. (1998). *Arrest clearances and exceptional clearances: An analysis of Chicago homicides, 1982–1994.* Master's thesis, Southern Illinois University, Carbondale.

Brownmiller, S. (1975). *Against our will: Men, women, and rape.* New York: Ballantine.

Bryden, D., and S. Lengnick. (1997). Rape in the criminal justice system. *Journal of Criminal Law and Criminology, 87,* 1385–1429.

Campbell, R. (1998). The community response to rape: Victim's experiences with the legal, medical, and mental health. *American Journal of Community Psychology, 25,* 355–379.

Campbell, R. (2008). *Multidisciplinary responses to sexual violence crimes: A review of the impact of SANEs and SARTs on criminal prosecution.* Paper presented at the National Institute of Justice Sexual Violence Research Workshop, Washington, DC.

Campbell, R., D. Patterson, and L. F. Lichty. (2005). The effectiveness of sexual assault nurse examiner (SANE) program: A review of psychological, medical, legal, and community outcomes. *Trauma, Violence and Abuse: A Review Journal, 6,* 313–329.

Campbell, R., S. M. Wasco, C. E. Ahrens, T. Self, and H. E. Barnes. (2001). Preventing the "second rape": Rape survivors' experiences with community service providers. *Journal of Interpersonal Violence, 16,* 1239–1259.

Caringella-MacDonald, S. (1984). Sexual assault prosecution: An examination of model rape legislation in Michigan. *Women and Politics 4,* 65–82.

Charmaz, K. (2006*). Constructing grounded theory: A practical guide through data analysis.* Thousand Oaks, CA: Sage.

Clarke, A. (2005). *Situational analysis: Grounded theory after the postmodern turn.* Thousand Oaks, CA: Sage.

Clay-Warner, J., and C. Burt. (2005). Rape reporting after reforms: Have times really changed? *Violence Against Women, 11,* 150–176.

Cornell, D. (1998). Helping victims of rape: A program called SANE. *New Jersey Medicine 2,* 45–48.

Crandall, C., and D. Helitzer. (2003). Impact evaluation of a Sexual Assault Nurse Examiner (SANE) program. National Institute of Justice Document No. 203276; Award Number 98-WT-VX-0027.

Daly, K., and B. Bouhours. (2010). Rape and attrition in the legal process: A comparative analysis of five countries. *Crime and Justice: A Review of Research 39:* 565–650.

Davis, K. C. (1969). *Discretionary justice: A preliminary inquiry.* Baton Rouge, LA: Louisiana State University Press.

Du Mont, J., K. Miller, and T. Myhr. (2003). The role of "real rape" and "real victim" stereotypes in the police reporting practices of sexually assaulted women. *Violence Against Women, 9*, 466–486.

Du Mont, J., and T. L. Myhr. (2000). So few convictions: The role of client-related characteristics in the legal processing of sexual assaults. *Violence Against Women, 6*, 1109–1136

Estrich, S. (1987). *Real rape.* Cambridge, MA: Harvard University Press.

Feder, L. (1998). Police handling of domestic and nondomestic assault cases: Is there a case for discrimination? *Crime and Delinquency, 44*, 3353–3349.

Federal Bureau of Investigation (FBI). 2004. *Uniform Crime Reporting Handbook.* Washington, DC: US Government Printing Office.

Federal Bureau of Investigation. 2006. *Crime in the United States 2006.* Available online at http://www.fbi.gov/ucr/cius2006/data/table_27.html

Federal Bureau of Investigation. 2009. *Crime in the United States, 2009.* Washington, DC: US Government Printing Office.

Feeney, F. (2000–2001). Police clearances: A poor way to measure the impact of Miranda on the police. *Rutgers Law Journal, 32*, 1–114.

Feldman-Summers, S., and K. Lindner. (1976). Perceptions of victims and defendants in criminal assault cases. *Criminal Justice and Behavior, 3*, 135–150.

Field, H., and L. Bienen. (1980). *Jurors and rape: A study in psychology and law.* Lexington, MA: Lexington Books.

Finkelhor, D., and K. Yllo. (1985). *License to rape: Sexual abuse of wives.* New York: Free Press.

Fisher, B., and F. Cullen. (2000). Measuring the sexual victimization of women: Evolution, current controversies, and future research. In *Criminal justice 2000: Measurement and analysis of crime and justice.* US Department of Justice, Office of Justice Programs.

Fisher, B., L. Daigle, and F. Cullen. (2000). *Unsafe in the ivory tower: The sexual victimization of college women.* Thousand Oaks, CA: Sage.

Frazier, P. A., and B. Haney. (1996). Sexual assault cases in the legal system: Police, prosecutor and victim perspectives. *Law and Human Behavior, 20*, 607–628.

Frohmann, L. (1991). Discrediting victims' allegations of sexual assault: Prosecutorial accounts of case rejections. *Social Problems, 38*, 213–226.

Frohmann, L. (1997). Convictability and discordant locales: Reproducing race, class, and gender ideologies in prosecutorial decisionmaking. *Law and Society Review, 31*, 531–555.

Galvin, J., and K. Polk. (1983). NCCD research review: Attrition in case processing: Is rape unique? *Journal of Research in Crime and Delinquency 20*, 126–154.

Glaser, B., and A. Strauss. (1967). *The discovery of grounded theory: Strategies for qualitative research.* New York: Aldine De Gruyere.

Groth, N. A. (1979). *Men Who Rape.* New York: Plenum.

Gruber, A. (2009). Rape, feminism and the war on crime. *Washington Law Review, 84*, 581–660.

Hale, Sir Matthew. *Historia placitorum coronae. The history of the pleas of the crown.* Edited by Sollom Emlyn. 2 vols. London, 1736. Reprint. Classical English Law Texts. London: Professional Books, 1971.

Harris, J. and S. Grace. (1999). A question of evidence? Investigating and prosecuting rape in the 1990s. Home Office Research Study 196. London: Home Office.

Henning, K., and L. Feder. (2005). Criminal prosecution of domestic violence offenses: An investigation of factors predictive of court outcomes. *Criminal Justice and Behavior, 32*, 612–642.

Hindelang, M. J., and M. Gottfredson. (1976). The victim's decision not to invoke the criminal justice process. In W. F. McDonald (Ed.), *Criminal Justice and the Victim.* Beverly Hills, CA: Sage.

Holleran, D., D. Beichner, and C. Spohn. (2008). Modeling the charging agreement between the police and prosecutors in sexual assault. *Crime Delinquency OnlineFirst,* April 10, 2008; doi:10.1177/0011128707308977.

Holmstron, L. L., and A. W. Burgess. (1978). *The victim of rape: Institutional reactions.* New Brunswick, NJ: Transaction Publishers.

Horney, J., and C. Spohn. (1996). The influence of blame and believability factors on the processing of simple versus aggravated rape cases. *Criminology, 34,* 135–162.

International Association of Chiefs of Police (IACP). (2005). *Investigating sexual assaults: Concepts and issues paper.* Alexandria, VA: Author.

Irving, T. (2008). Decoding black women: Policing practices and rape prosecution on the streets of Philadelphia. *NWSA Journal, 20,* 100–120.

Jacoby, J. E. (1980). *The American prosecutor: The search for identity.* Lexington, MA: Lexington Books.

Jarvis, J. P., and W. C. Regoeczi. (2009). Homicide clearances: An analysis of arrest versus exceptional outcomes. *Homicide Studies, 13,* 174–188.

Johnson, D. R. (1995). Prior false allegations of rape: Falsus in uno, falsus in omnibus? *Yale Journal of Law and Feminism, 7,* 243–276.

Jordan, J. (2004). Beyond belief? Police, rape and women's credibility. *Criminal Justice, 4,* 29–59.

Kalven, H., and H. Zeisel. (1966). *The American jury.* Boston: Little Brown.

Kanin, E. J. (1994). False rape allegations. *Archives of Sexual Behavior, 23,* 81–91.

Kelly, L. (2010). The (in)credible words of women: False allegations in European rape research. *Violence Against Women, 16,* 1345–1355.

Kelly, L., J. Lovett, and L. Regan. (2005). *A gap or chasm? Attrition in reported rape cases.* Home Office Research Study 293. London: Home Office Research, Development and Statistics Directorate.

Kennedy, R. (1997). *Race, crime, and the law.* New York: Random House.

Kerstetter, W. A. (1990). Gateway to justice: Police and prosecutorial response to sexual assaults against women. *Journal of Criminal Law and Criminology, 81,* 267–313.

Kerstetter, W. A., and B. Van Winkle. (1990). Who decides? A study of the complainant's decision to prosecute in rape cases. *Criminal Justice and Behavior, 17,* 268–283.

Kingsnorth, R., J. Lopez, J. Wentworth, and D. Cummings. (1998). Adult sexual assault: The role of racial/ethnic composition in prosecuting and sentencing. *Journal of Criminal Justice, 26,* 5, 359–371.

Kingsnorth, R., R. MacIntosh, and J. Wentworth. (1999). Sexual assault: The role of prior relationship and victim characteristics in case processing. *Justice Quarterly, 16,* 2, 275–302.

Kinney, L., E. Bruns, P. Bradley, J. Dantzler, and M. Weist. (2007). Sexual assault training of law enforcement officers: Results of a statewide survey. *Women and Criminal Justice, 18,* 81–100.

Konradi, A. (2007). *Taking the stand: Rape survivors and the prosecution of rapists.* New York: Praeger.

LaFree, G. (1980). The effect of sexual stratification by race on official reactions to rape. *American Sociological Review 43,* 843–854.

LaFree, G. (1981). Official reactions to social problems: Police decisions in sexual assault cases. *Social Problems, 28,* 582–594.

LaFree, G. (1989). *Rape and criminal justice: The social construction of sexual assault.* Belmont, CA: Wadsworth.

Lally, W., and A. DeMaris. (2012). Gender and relational-distance effects in arrest for domestic violence. *Crime and Delinquency, 58,* 103–123.

Law Enforcement Assistance Administration. (1977). *Forcible rape: A national survey of the response by police* (Vol. 1). Washington, DC: US Government Printing Office.

Lee, C. (2005). The value of life in death: Multiple regression and event history analyses of homicide clearance in Los Angeles County. *Journal of Criminal Justice, 33,* 527–534.

LeGrand, C. E. (1973, May). Rape and rape laws: Sexism in society and the law. *Southern California Law Review, 61,* 3, 919–941.

Liao, T. F. 1994. *Interpreting probability models: Logit, probit, and other generalized models.* Thousand Oaks, CA: Sage.

Lievore, D. (2004). Victim credibility in adult sexual assault cases. *Trends and Issues in Crime and Criminal Justice, 288,* 2–6.

Lisak, D., L. Gardinier, S. C. Nicksa, and A. M. Cote. (2010). False allegations of sexual assault: An analysis of ten years of reported cases. *Violence Against Women, 16,* 1318–1334.

Lizotte, A. J. (1985). The uniqueness of rape: Reporting assaultive violence to the police. *Crime and Delinquency, 31,* 169–190.

Loh, W. D. (1980). The impact of common law and reform rape statutes on prosecution: An empirical study. *Washington Law Review, 55,* 543–562.

Lonsway, K. A. (2010). Trying to move the elephant in the living room: Responding to the challenge of false rape reports. *Violence Against Women, 16,* 1356–1371.

Lonsway, K. A., J. Archambault, and D. Lisak (2009). False reports: Moving beyond the issue to successfully investigate and prosecute nonstranger sexual assault. *The Voice* (American Prosecutors Research Institute), *3,* 1–11.

Mahoney, P. (1999). High rape chronicity and low rates of help-seeking among wife rape survivors in a nonclinical sample. *Violence Against Women, 5,* 993–1016.

Maier, S. L. (2008). "I have heard horrible stories": Rape victim advocates' perceptions of revictimization of rape victims by the police and medical system. *Violence Against Women, 14,* 786–808.

Martin, P. Y. (2006). *Rape work: Victims, gender and emotions in organization and community context.* New York: Routledge.

Martin, P. Y., and R. M. Powell. (1994). Accounting for the "second assault": Legal organizations' framing of rape victims. *Law and Social Inquiry, 19,* 853–890.

Marsh, J. C., A. Geist, and N. Caplan (1982). *Rape and the limits of law reform.* Boston: Auburn House.

McCahill, T., L. Meyer, and A. Fischman. (1979). *The aftermath of rape.* Lexington, MA: Lexington Books.

McDowell, C. P., and N. S. Hibler. (1987). False allegations. In R.R. Hazelwood and A.W. Burgess (eds.), *Practical aspects of rape investigation: A multidisciplinary approach.* New York: Elsevier.

Orenstein, A. (2007). Special issues raised by rape trials. *Fordham Law Review, 76,* 1585–1608.

Page, A. (2008). Gateway to reform? Policy implications of police officers' attitudes toward rape. *American Journal of Criminal Justice, 33,* 44–58.

Puckett, J. L., and R. J. Lundman. (2003). Factors affecting homicide clearances: Multivariate analysis of a more complete conceptual framework. *Journal of Research in Crime and Delinquency, 40,* 171–193.

Raphael, J. (2008). Book review: "Until proven innocent: Political correctness and the shameful injustices of the Duke lacrosse rape case." *Violence Against Women, 14,* 370–375.

Regoeczi, W. C., J. Jarvis, and M. Reidel. (2008). Clearing murders: Is it about time? *Journal of Research in Crime and Delinquency, 45,* 135–161.

Riedel, M., and J. G. Boulahanis. (2007). Homicides exceptionally cleared and cleared by arrest. *Homicide Studies, 11,* 151–164.

Reskin, B., and C. Visher. (1986). The impacts of evidence and extralegal factors in jurors' decisions. *Law and Society Review, 20,* 423–438.

Robinson, A. L., and M. S. Chandek. (2000). The domestic violence arrest decision: Examining demographic, attitudinal, and situational variables. *Crime and Delinquency, 46,* 18–37.

Rose, V. M., and S. C. Randall. (1982). The impact of investigator perceptions of victim legitimacy on the processing of rape/sexual assault cases. *Symbolic Interaction, 5,* 23–26.

Rumney, P. N. S. (2006). False allegations of rape. *Cambridge Law Journal, 65,* 128–158.

Russell, D. E. H. (1990). *Rape in marriage.* Bloomington: Indiana University Press.

Sable, M. R., F. Danis, D. L. Mauzy, and S. K. Gallagher. (2006). Barriers to reporting sexual assault for women and men: Perspectives of college students. *Journal of American College Health, 55,* 157–162.

Sack, E. J. (2010). Is domestic violence a crime? Intimate partner rape as allegory. *St. John's Journal of Legal Commentary, 24,* 535–566.

Schuller, R. A., and A. Stewart. (2000). Police responses to sexual assault complaints: The role of perpetrator/complainant intoxication. *Law and Human Behavior, 24,* 535–551.

Soulliere, D. M. (2005). Pathways to attrition: A qualitative component analysis of justifications for police designations of sexual assault complaints. *The Qualitative Report, 10,* 416–438.

Spears, J., and C. Spohn. (1997). The effect of evidence factors and victim characteristics on prosecutors' charging decisions in sexual assault cases. *Justice Quarterly, 14,* 501–524.

Spohn, C. (1994). Black-on-black and black-on-white crime: A comparison of sexual assault case outcomes. In P. Ray Kedia (Ed.), *Black-on-black crime: Facing facts—Challenging fictions.* Briston, IN: Wyndham Hall Press.

Spohn, C., D. Beichner, and E. Davis-Frenzel. (2001). Prosecutorial explanations for sexual assault case rejection: Guarding the gateway to justice. *Social Problems, 48,* 206–235.

Spohn, C., and D. Holleran. (2001). Prosecuting sexual assault: Comparison charging decisions in sexual assault cases involving strangers, acquaintances, and intimate partners. *Justice Quarterly, 18,* 651–689.

Spohn, C., and J. Horney. (1991). "The law's the law, but fair is fair": Criminal justice officials' assessments of the rape shield laws. *Criminology, 29,* 301–325.

Spohn, C., and J. Horney. (1992). *Rape law reform: A grassroots revolution and its impact.* New York: Plenum Press.

Spohn, C., N. Rodriguez, and M. Koss. (2008, November). *The "victim declined to prosecute": Accounting for lack of cooperation in sexual assault cases.* Paper presented at the annual meeting of the American Society of Criminology, St. Louis, Missouri.

Spohn, C., and J. Spears. (1996). The effect of offender and victim characteristics on sexual assault case processing decisions. *Justice Quarterly, 13,* 649–679.

Spohn, C., and K. Tellis. (2010, November). *Police decision making in sexual assault cases: An analysis of crimes reported to the Los Angeles Police Department in 2008.* Paper presented at the annual meeting of the American Society of Criminology, San Francisco, California.

Stanko, E. (1988). The impact of victim assessment on prosecutors' screening decisions: The case of the New York county district attorney's office. *Law and Society Review, 16,* 225–240.

Taylor, J. (1987). Rape and women's credibility: Problems of recantations and false accusations echoed in the case of Cathleen Crowell Webb and Gary Dotson. *Harvard Women's Law Journal, 10,* 59–115.

Tellis, K. (2010). *Rape as a part of domestic violence: A qualitative analysis of case narratives and official reports.* El Paso, TX: LFB Scholarly Publishing LLC.

Tellis, K. M., and C. Spohn. (2008). The sexual stratification hypothesis revisited: Testing assumptions about simple versus aggravated rape. *Journal of Criminal Justice, 36,* 252–261.

Temkin, J. (2010). Challenging rape myths in the courtroom. *New Criminal Law Review, 13,* 710–734.

Theilade, P., and J. L. Thomsen. (1986). False allegations of rape. *Police Surgeon, 30,* 17–22.

Tjaden, P., and N. Thoennes. (2006). *Extent, nature, and consequences of rape victimization: Findings from the National Violence Against Women Survey.* Washington, DC: US Department of Justice, National Institute of Justice.

US Bureau of Justice Statistics (USBJS). (2002). *Rape and sexual assault: Reporting to police and medical attention, 1992–2000.* Washington, DC: USBJS.

US Bureau of Justice Statistics. (2007). *Criminal victimization, 2006.* Washington, DC: USBJS.

US Bureau of Justice Statistics. (2008). *Felony defendants in large urban counties.* Washington, DC: USBJS.

US Senate. (2010). *Rape in the United States: The chronic failure to report and investigate rape cases.* Committee on the Judiciary, Subcommittee on Crime and Drugs, US Senate, 111th Congress. Testimony from Carol Tracy and Michelle Madden Dempsey.

Vera Institute of Justice. (1981). *Felony arrests: Their prosecution and disposition in New York City's courts.* New York: Longman.

Wacker, J. L., S. L. Parish, and R. J. Macy. 2008. Sexual assault and women with cognitive disabilities. *Journal of Disability Policy Studies, 19,* 86–94.

Walker, S. (2005). *The new world of police accountability.* Thousand Oaks, CA: Sage.

Whately, A. (1996).Victim characteristics influencing attributions of responsibility to rape victims: A meta-analysis. *Aggression and Violent Behavior, 1,* 81–95.

Wooldredge, J., and A. Thistlethwaite. 2004. Bilevel disparities in court dispositions for intimate assault. *Criminology 42,* 417–456.

Yllo, K. (1999). Wife rape: A social problem for the 21st century. *Violence Against Women, 5,* 1059–1063.

Index

About the Book

Cassia Spohn and Katharine Tellis assess the criminal justice system's response to sexual assault, exploring the complex dynamics that shape the actions of police and prosecutors.

The authors draw on unparalleled access to Los Angeles detectives, prosecutors, and case files to make sense of the factors that affect the outcomes of sexual assault claims. Following cases from victim report, to police investigation, to the decision to charge—or not to charge—they provide new insights into why shockingly few sexual assault claims lead to an eventual criminal conviction.

Cassia Spohn is professor of criminology and criminal justice at Arizona State University. **Katharine Tellis** is assistant professor of criminal justice and criminalistics at California State University, Los Angeles.